C000257222

'This book explicitly maps those defending the Israeli apartheid and examining how the British government in the oppression of Palestinians. It the literature and whilst it focuses explains that Israeli regime and supporters' strategies are a direct response to over a century of Palestinian resistance. This book thus not only makes an important academic contribution but also a political one to a struggle that is ultimately for freedom and justice.'

Yara Harawi, author of *The Stone House*

'*Friends of Israel* is a meticulous study of the organisations seeking to reverse widening support for the Palestinian cause in Britain. On a topic that is fraught with exaggeration, distortion, and propaganda, Aked proceeds with precision and nuance, giving us a much-needed, authoritative analysis. Grounded in anti-racism, *Friends of Israel* paints a complex picture of Zionism in Britain, giving readers the tools to oppose both anti-Semitism and Israeli apartheid.'

Arun Kundnani, author of *The Muslims Are Coming!*

'At last, a thoughtful, meticulously researched study of the well-organised disinformation campaign against Palestinian rights and BDS and for supporting Apartheid Israel in Britain. In a work comprising the multiplicity of aspects of the Israel Lobby work in the British public and political spheres, Hil Aked offers the means for deconstructing Zionist myths, innate in British discourse since the Balfour Declaration, if not before. A must for anyone interested in understanding and countering this oppressive influence.'

Haim Bresheeth-Zabner, author of *An Army like No Other*

'In this compelling analysis and history of Britain's sordid relationship with Israel, we come to understand the individuals and organisations committed to endless occupation and violence against Palestinians, along with those courageous enough to imagine a humane alternative.'

An   *Laboratory*

'Not only the definitive study of political influence, state propaganda and lobbying by British actors on behalf of "Brand Israel", but also a passionate defence of the universal application of anti-racist principles. Hil Aked has grasped the indivisibility of the fight against Israeli Apartheid and the fight against anti-Semitism. A lucid and thoroughly courageous intervention that will stand the test of time.'

Liz Fekete, Director, Institute of Race Relations, author of *Europe's Fault Lines*

'No one who reads Hil Aked's meticulously researched book can be left in any doubt about how Israel's friends operate to subvert British popular perceptions and the British political process in favour of Zionism. An essential and timely expose of an important and hitherto neglected subject.'

Ghada Karmi, author of *Return*

'Those who support Palestine in Britain know too well that they are targeted by a well-oiled and ruthless campaign. This is the first book that examines closely and meticulously this campaign of suppression and silencing. Now more than ever before, it is important to learn how Israeli propaganda and pro-Israel lobbyists in Britain operate. Hil Aked's brilliant book is a must-read.'

Ilan Pappe, author of *Ten Myths about Israel*

'This book is as urgent as it is a long-awaited critique of the Zionist movement and all those in government and civil society who support and defend Israeli apartheid, or work to dismiss and vilify solidarity with Palestinians. Hil Aked's is a brave intervention in addressing a topic considered taboo in part due to a concerted effort by pro-Israel advocates to resist, and make dangerous, critical scrutiny. This book deserves to be widely read and will be treasured by all those who support the Palestinian struggle for liberation.'

Nadine El-Nany, author of *(B)ordering Britain*

Friends of Israel

*The Backlash against
Palestine Solidarity*

Hil Aked

VERSO
London • New York

In solidarity with Palestinians everywhere struggling for freedom, justice and equality;
and for my family, and chosen family, with love.

First published by Verso 2023
© Hil Aked 2023

1 3 5 7 9 10 8 6 4 2

Verso
UK: 6 Meard Street, London W1F 0EG
US: 388 Atlantic Avenue, Brooklyn, NY 11217
versobooks.com

Verso is the imprint of New Left Books

ISBN-13: 978-1-78663-765-9
ISBN-13: 978-1-78663-767-3 (US EBK)
ISBN-13: 978-1-78663-766-6 (UK EBK)

British Library Cataloguing in Publication Data
A catalogue record for this book is available from the British Library

Library of Congress Cataloging-in-Publication Data

Names: Aked, Hil, author.
Title: Friends of Israel : the backlash against Palestine solidarity / Hil
  Aked.
Description: First Edition Paperback. | London ; New York : Verso, 2023. |
  Includes bibliographical references and index.
Identifiers: LCCN 2022056878 (print) | LCCN 2022056879 (ebook) | ISBN
  9781786637659 (Paperback) | ISBN 9781786637673 (ebk)
Subjects: LCSH: Zionism – Great Britain – Public opinion. | Propaganda,
  Zionist – Great Britain. | Propaganda, Israeli – Great Britain. | Boycott,
  divestment, and sanctions movement – Great Britain. | Economic
  sanctions – Israel. | Great Britain – Public opinion.
Classification: LCC DS149.5.G4 A34 2023 (print) | LCC DS149.5.G4 (ebook)
  | DDC 320.540956940941 – dc23/eng/20230105
LC record available at https://lccn.loc.gov/2022056878
LC ebook record available at https://lccn.loc.gov/2022056879

Typeset in Sabon by Biblichor Ltd
Printed and bound by CPI Group (UK) Ltd, Croydon, CR0 4YY

Contents

List of Tables
and Figures

Tables

Figures

Preface

This book departs from the premise that Palestinians are struggling for freedom, justice and equality against the oppressive violence of a state practising settler colonialism, ethnic cleansing and apartheid. For many decades, Palestinians have been saying that Israel's regime constitutes apartheid, defined by the Rome Statute of the International Criminal Court as 'inhuman acts . . . committed in the context of an institutionalised regime of systematic oppression and domination by one racial group over any other racial group'.[1] Between 2020 and 2022, Israeli human rights groups Yesh Din and B'Tselem, followed by leading international NGOs Human Rights Watch and Amnesty International, reached the same conclusion.[2]

I wrote this book because I believe that all actors – civil society organisations as well as governments – working to shore up support for Israeli apartheid, or to marginalise and repress solidarity with Palestinians, ought to be held publicly accountable and should not be immune to criticism. Their actions cause harm, albeit indirectly. To try to illustrate this harm, each chapter of this book opens with anecdotes juxtaposing the activities and narratives of the 'Israel lobby' or 'Zionist movement' (terminology I define and explain in what follows) with the reality, as lived by Palestinians. The book focuses on pro-Israel actors, so it inevitably decentres Palestinians to a certain extent. However, it situates the Israeli government and Zionist movement's strategies as responses to a century of Palestinian resistance.

Israel's government is only able to sustain its apartheid system due to the impunity it is granted on the international stage. In particular, Britain's role in and responsibility for Palestinians' oppression has historically been, and remains, pivotal. Yet to examine and critique pro-Israel organisations is not to argue that their activities are the only, or even the main, reason for Britain's alliance with Israeli apartheid. On the contrary, as we will see, the Zionist movement – and the state of Israel itself – were supported in the early years due to their perceived utility to the British Empire. In a sense, this dynamic of dependency remains, though today more so in Israel's relationship to US empire. The book does show, however, that the Israel lobby today plays a supporting role in maintaining Israeli apartheid, alongside the British, US and, of course, Israeli governments.

In particular, the Zionist movement is a key mover in an intensifying campaign of repression against the Palestine solidarity movement, with the support of both the Israeli and British governments. This book therefore argues that the British Zionist movement not only exists but can and does, in some contexts, wield considerable power – especially in coordination with state actors. It contributes to the oppression of Palestinians both through helping to maintain British government complicity and, often more visibly, through working to repress Palestine solidarity initiatives. This is demonstrated with detailed empirical evidence. Rather than fetishising or exaggerating the Zionist movement's power, however, the book highlights its limitations and the potential for resistance. Specifically, it shows that the global Boycott, Divestment and Sanctions (BDS) movement – initiated by Palestinians in 2005 – has been effective enough to provoke a massive counter-campaign led by the Israeli government and yet, despite this repressive backlash, continues to grow across the world. In what follows, I highlight the strong parallels between the Israeli government's counter-campaign and the propaganda campaign waged in previous decades by the South African apartheid regime, which similarly sought to counteract a global boycott campaign emanating from civil society.

My interest in studying this topic as a researcher grew out of time spent doing solidarity activism in the occupied West Bank, a period which had a profound effect on me. I witnessed the pervasive injustice and brutality of Israeli apartheid alongside the dignity, humanity and steadfastness (*sumud*) of Palestinians' daily resistance. Engaging in solidarity activism in Britain subsequently, it was impossible to ignore the Zionist movement: its most far-right elements would show up to stage aggressive counterprotests at demonstrations, waving Israeli flags and hurling racist abuse at Palestinians, Arabs and Muslims. I am proud to support the BDS movement and firmly believe that decolonisation in Israel/Palestine will mean not only liberation for Palestinians but also peace, through justice, for Israelis. I wrote this book – the first of its kind focusing on the Zionist movement in Britain – not out of a belligerent glee in controversy or a desire to sensationalise or provoke, but in the hope that subjecting Israel's support networks here to critical scrutiny could make a contribution, however small, to undermining settler colonialism in Palestine.

I also believe this book is necessary on a second count: fighting anti-Semitism. Currently, in Britain there is a cultivated and pernicious ignorance about Israel's oppression of Palestinians, about our long-standing complicity, and about the activities of the Zionist movement. In the absence of informed and rigorous discussion, anti-Semitic conspiracy theories can gain traction. A clear, seriously researched and robustly anti-racist analysis can, however, demystify pro-Israel networks and in the process rebuff such ideas, carving out space for a healthier discussion. The book seeks, therefore, to be an anti-racist intervention in this taboo topic.

Simultaneously, what follows serves as a corrective to misguided narratives which position support for Israel as a problem of 'foreign influence' undermining British democracy. Instead, I situate Israel's support networks as a long-standing *part* of the British establishment and foreground the harm done to Palestinians. Inevitably, the book is also a case study in British politics and Britain's grossly unequal power relations, highlighting the need for more transparency and democratisation. But principally, my concern is with British actors' complicity in the systematic denial of Palestinian rights.

What is at stake in Palestinians' struggle for freedom transcends Israel/Palestine itself. Indeed, Palestinian liberation is intertwined with other liberation movements around the world. The situation in Palestine is historically rooted in imperialism, ongoing settler colonialism and state racism; Israel is a carceral society in which prisons, policing, borders, militarism and other forms of state violence combine to devalue and destroy the lives of a racialised people; it is a quintessential case of the denial of refugee rights and of unequal access to housing, water and land. When the organised Zionist movement defends Israel, it implicitly makes the case that such inequities should be tolerated not just in Palestine, but everywhere. To oppose these arguments is not only to support Palestinian liberation and contribute to efforts to create alternatives to a status quo characterised by seemingly endless violence and suffering; it is also, more broadly, to argue against a world defined by borders, walls and racial injustice.

Abbreviations

AIPAC – American Israel Public Affairs Committee

ABC – Anti-Boycott Co-ordinating Committee

Aman – Israeli Military Intelligence (Hebrew acronym for Agaf ha-Modi'in)

APPG – All Party Parliamentary Group

BDS – Boycott, Divestment and Sanctions

BICOM – Britain Israel Communications and Research Centre

BIPAC – British-Israel Public Affairs Committee

BIRAX – Britain Israel Research and Academic Exchange Partnership

CAABU – Council for the Advancement of Arab–British Understanding

CFI – Conservative Friends of Israel

CAMERA – Committee for Accuracy in Middle East Reporting in America

DCMS – Department for Culture, Media and Sport

EUMC – European Union Monitoring Centre (now Fundamental Rights Agency)

IHRA – International Holocaust Remembrance Alliance

IDF – Israel Defense Forces

LFI – Labour Friends of Israel

LMEC – Labour Middle East Council

NGO – non-governmental organisation

NIS – New Israeli Shekel

NUS – National Union of Students

PACBI – Palestinian Campaign for the Academic and Cultural Boycott of Israel

SOAS – School of Oriental and African Studies, University of London
UCU – University and College Union
UJIA – United Jewish Israel Appeal
UJS – Union of Jewish Students
UKLFI – UK Lawyers for Israel
WZO – World Zionist Organization
ZF – Zionist Federation of Great Britain and Ireland

Introduction

This book, the first on the contemporary British Zionist movement, answers three basic but critical questions. Firstly, focusing on the most influential organisations and individuals, it asks: who are the key actors defending Israeli apartheid in Britain? Secondly, it explores their strategies and tactics in different arenas of society. Finally, it seeks to assess how powerful they really are – and, in doing so, to highlight possibilities for the pro-Palestine movement. I do not attempt to construct a fallacious argument that absent the influence of the Zionist movement, the British government would somehow be supportive of Palestinian rights. Instead, I focus on the way the Zionist movement has been *forced* to mobilise in response to a resurgent Palestine solidarity movement. In particular, since its launch in 2005, the growth of the Boycott, Divestment and Sanctions (BDS) campaign – which puts pressure on Israel to comply with international law – has prompted a backlash which throws into sharp relief the existence of the Zionist movement and the power it can wield in some contexts.

Though the story of the counter-campaign against BDS is, in large part, one of solidarity between repressive right-wing nation-states such as Israel, Britain and the US, pro-Israel groups play an important supporting role in this drama. Indeed, one of this book's central contentions is that the civil society–led nature of the BDS movement has heightened the importance of Zionist organisations in civil society from the perspective of the Israeli government. In shedding light on the conscious strategising, strenuous organising, and significant achievements of Israel's various 'friends' in Britain, the book examines five different arenas: Parliament, civil society and the cultural sphere, local government and the legal sphere, universities, and the media. While levels of influence and tactics vary in each realm, several common themes recur, including top-down modes of intervention, censorship, 'lawfare', the concept of 'delegitimisation' and the discourse of 'new anti-Semitism' (both of which seek to stigmatise criticism of Israeli apartheid), the manufacturing of civil society, and informal cooperation with state actors across state–private networks. This cooperation, the book shows, is central to the Israeli government's counter-BDS strategy. As well as providing global context, the account is also historically informed and points to important precedents – in particular apartheid-era South Africa's efforts to defeat a global boycott campaign with similar tactics. Emphasising British complicity in Palestinian oppression, the chapters that follow trace the evolution of the British Zionist movement from its work to counter the Arab League boycott in previous decades through to its anti-BDS activism today. First, however, the racial politics of Israel/Palestine, particularly as it pertains to the terminology we use when discussing the 'Israel lobby', must be addressed.

Taboo and terminology

As Palestinian American scholar Edward Said and others have noted, the topic of the 'Israel lobby' is significantly taboo.[1] This is in part the result of a deliberate effort by pro-Israel actors themselves to resist – and indeed stigmatise – critical scrutiny. But the existence of very real racist fantasies about 'Jewish power' must also be acknowledged. In combination, these two factors have helped to create a situation in which virtually any critique of the Zionist movement is liable to be interpreted, or disingenuously represented, as anti-Semitic. This serves to deter almost all scholarly examinations of Zionism in Britain and the topic has come to be regarded as largely off limits. This situation, of course, suits the Israel lobby and necessitates a direct response.

The 2006 *Report of the All-Party Parliamentary Inquiry into Antisemitism* states: 'No-one would seek to deny that there is well-organised support for Israel in Britain, but in some quarters this becomes inflated to the point where discourse about the "lobby" resembles discourse about a world Jewish conspiracy.'[2]

Indeed, it would be hard to explicitly deny the existence of the Zionist movement in Britain. Despite a degree of opacity, it is not a secret: it is a visible network of organisations with offices and websites, staffed by employees with business cards and LinkedIn profiles. But is it possible to write about this admittedly 'well-organised support for Israel' without overstating its power and, critically, without 'ethnicising' the issue? Is it possible to write an anti-racist book about the pro-Israel lobby? I hope to show that it is.

Words are powerful, and language matters. This book uses the phrases 'Israel lobby' and 'Zionist movement / lobby', as well as 'pro-Israel movement / lobby' and, occasionally, 'Israel-advocacy movement'. In using the words 'Israel' and 'Zionist' as interchangeable prefixes before the terms 'lobby' and 'movement', I take as a given journalist and political commentator Peter Beinart's words that 'Zionism is what Israel does'.[3] Nonetheless, the term 'Zionism' is relevant and useful because it pinpoints the ideology underpinning the state of Israel's apartheid practices. It also invites us to bear in mind the spectrum of political persuasions, from liberal Zionism to revisionist Zionism, contained therein.

'Israel lobby' should not be interpreted as 'code' for 'Jewish lobby', a phrase this book never uses. It is vital to distinguish between Judaism, an ethno-religious and cultural identity, and Zionism – understood here as an ethno-nationalist political ideology and movement defined by a commitment to an inherently exclusionary Jewish state. The fact that in some quarters, Judaism and Zionism are deliberately equated is not a reason to accept the blurring of this critically important conceptual distinction. Using the terminology of a 'Jewish lobby' to speak about pro-Israel activism is empirically inaccurate, as well as politically irresponsible and harmful. The Israel lobby is very far from incorporating all Jewish people and is, moreover, far from exclusively Jewish. The contemporary power of Christian Zionism deserves special mention in this regard,[4] and indeed, some of the most important supporters of Israel discussed in this book – including Arthur Balfour, Orde Wingate, Terence Prittie, Luke Akehurst, Nigel Goodrich, Sajid

Javid, Michael Gove, Priti Patel and Joan Ryan – are non-Jewish Zionists. More importantly, the idea that a 'Jewish lobby' is behind support for Israel is an anti-Semitic trope which erroneously 'reduces political activity to ethnicity' and reinforces the idea that there is only one 'Jewish political position'[5] when in reality, in the words of scholar and activist Joel Kovel, 'there is no one way of being Jewish'.[6]

This, then, is definitively not a book about a 'Jewish lobby'. Rather, it is a book about the Israel lobby: a group of organisations and individuals defined not by their ethno-religious identity but by their *political activities* in support of a specific nation-state (Israel), and the nationalist ideology (Zionism) underpinning that state's apartheid practices towards Palestinians. Since Israel defines itself as a 'Jewish state' and is the embodiment of a Jewish nationalist movement, many of the people who feature in this book are indeed Jewish, but their activities are never represented as a function of their ethno-religious identity. Instead, what brings them into the purview of this study is their ideological commitment to, and *organised political activity in support of*, Israeli apartheid and some brand of political Zionism. Likewise, it should be made crystal clear that all organisations scrutinised in this book – even those which are Jewish communal organisations rather than explicitly Zionist bodies – are included because of strong empirical evidence of pro-Israel activism. As chapter 3 explains, the leadership of several Jewish communal organisations (such as the Board of Deputies and the Jewish Leadership Council) choose to present Zionist advocacy as an inherent part of their work and state explicitly that they 'lobby for Israel' – but this work should not be presumed to represent the will of wider British Jewish communities.

While 'lobby' is an appropriate word to describe forms of influence which involve the cultivation of direct, persuasive relationships with policymakers,[7] Israel's various friends actually engage in a much-broader array of activities. They also fundraise, educate, donate, produce knowledge from within academia and think-tanks, work to change legislation, run PR campaigns, campaign digitally, launch legal cases and (to an extent) organise at the grass-roots. Employing the term 'movement' therefore enables a more holistic appreciation of the diverse tactics which supporters of Israel use. Moreover, the transnational Zionist movement has itself, since its inception, used the phrase 'Zionist movement' self-referentially.[8] Exclusive use of the term 'lobby' – with its connotations of domestic interest groups – would also risk obscuring this transnational context, which remains critical to understanding the Zionist movement in any given country.

Against Israeli apartheid and anti-Semitism

It is precisely because of my commitment to anti-racism that I oppose *both* Israeli apartheid and anti-Semitism. This book aims to help restore a transversal anti-racism as opposed to the selective, zero-sum view of anti-racism currently touted by the Zionist movement – which posits that one can be an opponent of *either* anti-Semitism *or* Israeli apartheid, but not both. It needed to be written first and foremost because apologists for any state practising the crime of apartheid, including Israel, should be exposed and opposed by all who support racial justice. But as well as being written for the right reasons – namely, in solidarity with Palestinians – it also needed to be written in the right way. Anti-Semitism is a very real threat to Jewish communities. The topic of the 'Israel lobby' or 'Zionist movement' requires sensitive handling and respect for the legitimate concerns around anti-Semitism that addressing it can provoke. This requires a degree of empathy and emotional intelligence often lacking in such discussions. It also calls for a clear understanding of how the complex racial politics of Israel/Palestine play out in global contexts. While it is outside the scope of this book to do full justice to this topic, about which whole volumes have been written, it merits serious attention.[9]

As scholars Yasmeen Abu-Laban and Abigail Bakan point out, apartheid Israel has long enjoyed solidarity from the governments of other settler-colonial states like the US, Canada and Australia, as well as former imperial states like Britain and France. All these countries retain huge power in the world and support Israel's apartheid system in numerous ways.[10] Since 1977, Israeli politics has fairly consistently moved to the right, and its current coalition government is the most far right in history. In the post-9/11 era, the opportunistic positioning of Israel as the 'front line' of the 'War on Terror' by many Israeli politicians and significant elements of the Zionist movement has accelerated. This plays into a 'clash of civilisations' narrative preoccupied with a confrontation between 'the West' and 'radical Islam' which greatly appeals to the far right.[11] Perversely, despite the anti-Semitic affinities of far-right authoritarian leaders like Hungary's Viktor Orbán, Brazil's Jair Bolsonaro, India's Narendra Modi and former US president Donald Trump, these men are among those who came to be counted, by Prime Minister Benjamin Netanyahu, as Israel's closest allies.[12]

Simultaneously, the Israeli government and Zionist movement have sought to move away from the broad and long-standing consensus that anti-Semitism is 'hostility to Jews as Jews'.[13] Instead, they have promoted the idea that some types of criticism of Israel or Zionism constitute a 'new anti-Semitism'. As British sociologist Keith Kahn-Harris notes, the term 'new anti-Semitism' is not itself particularly novel, having appeared at least as early as 1967.[14] It gained prominence, however, from around the turn of the millennium – a point at which Zionism, as we will see, entered a period of systemic crisis – as part of an ideological offensive apparently stimulated by that crisis. Scholar Brian Klug explains that the 'new anti-Semitism' thesis cast leftists (alongside Muslims), rather than the far right, as the main perpetrators of this novel form of racism. Meanwhile, its victim – rather than Jewish people – is the state of Israel, understood as 'the collective Jew'. Klug notes the lack of clarity pervading the voluminous literature on 'new anti-Semitism' but discerns that 'on one point there is a virtual consensus: anti-Zionism as such is beyond the pale'.[15]

It is fundamentally important to challenge attempts to conflate anti-Zionism with anti-Jewish racism, a dangerous conceptual move which has, according to the former director of the Institute for Jewish Policy Research, Antony Lerman, become 'a political weapon in a global propaganda battle'.[16] However, it is not necessary to assume bad faith on the part of those alleging (new) anti-Semitism. Klug points out that the notion is rooted in the Zionist belief that a Jewish state was the only solution to historic anti-Semitism:

> As the twentieth century swept on . . . with the rise of anti-Semitic
> parties . . . and the Nazi accession to power in Germany, it appeared
> to many Jews in Europe and elsewhere that there were only two
> solutions to this question: either Herzl's or Hitler's . . . if Zionism is
> seen as the only alternative to anti-Semitism, then it seems to follow
> that hostility to Zionism (or to the State of Israel as the expression
> or fulfilment of Zionism) must be anti-Semitic.[17]

As such, as Bakan and Abu-Laban note, the Zionist movement 'lays
claim to anti-racist ideological space as a response to anti-Semitism'
even while it simultaneously advances 'colonial expansion in the
Middle East'.[18] The deep tensions here were perhaps most vividly
illustrated at the 2001 World Conference against Racism in Durban,
South Africa, when Israel and its allies sought to condemn the
conference itself and withdrew, citing anti-Semitism, while other
delegates conversely sought to condemn Israel for practising apartheid against Palestinians.[19]

Despite its deep flaws, the 'new anti-Semitism' thesis has been
promulgated widely by its advocates and gained considerable institutional acceptance. This process began in 2005, when the EU's
Fundamental Rights Agency – then called the European Union
Monitoring Centre (EUMC) on Racism and Xenophobia – produced
a 'working definition' of anti-Semitism. Author Kenneth Stern, whose
works include a 2004 'Proposal for a Redefinition of Antisemitism'
and the book *Anti-Zionism: The Sophisticated Anti-Semitism*, was
a key influence.[20] While the EUMC working definition gained
limited traction, it soon resurfaced in a strikingly similar document
produced by the International Holocaust Remembrance Alliance
(IHRA), an intergovernmental institution established in Berlin in
1998.[21] The latter has been endorsed by numerous actors – including,
as we will see, the British government.

Both the EUMC and IHRA definitions listed, as potential
examples of anti-Semitism, 'denying the Jewish people their right to
self-determination, e.g., by claiming that the existence of a State
of Israel is a racist endeavor'. This rhetoric of self-determination –
also frequently articulated as Israel's 'right to exist' (as a 'Jewish
state') – is in this case, as writer and activist Dan Freeman-Maloy
points out, 'entangled with the coercive exclusion of Palestinians'.[22]

It perversely implies that calling out Israeli state racism is itself a form of racism. Effectively, such rhetoric silences Palestinians from speaking about the historical fact of their forced expulsion and dispossession during the Nakba (literally 'the catastrophe'). It prevents them from labelling the current settler-colonial reality by pointing out that Israel is practising apartheid, with a network of settler-only roads, a dual legal system, and 'admissions committees' enforcing segregation by keeping non-Jews out of certain towns. And it impedes Palestinians' ability to name the ongoing ethnic cleansing carried out by Israel through a plethora of means including home demolitions, revocation of residency permits and state support for settler-led evictions – all of which attest to the fact that while Israel may be a democracy for its Jewish citizens, it is something quite different for Palestinians. This book, therefore, concurs with the considerable critical literature on the subject, largely produced by Jewish and Palestinian scholars, arguing that the IHRA definition's expansion of the meaning of 'anti-Semitism' illegitimately attempts to protect Israeli apartheid from criticism.[23]

What are the implications of this for writing about the Israel lobby? Maintaining a principled anti-racist position – opposed to both Israeli apartheid and anti-Semitism – can feel at times like walking a tightrope. Leaving aside the IHRA definition, it is vital to acknowledge that *real* anti-Semitism *is* on the rise globally. Furthermore, racist tropes which essentialise and homogenise Jewish people, while attributing to them immense, inexplicable and nefarious powers, have a long and ignominious history. As Brian Klug explains, ideas about a 'hidden hand' of Jewish 'control' over 'banks, commerce and media, manipulating governments and promoting wars among nations' have featured prominently in the history of anti-Semitism.[24] These claims are racist myths, and they cause harm to Jewish communities. Therefore, a critique that addresses the pro-Israel lobby's power in a cavalier fashion or fails to evidence its assertions could easily and justifiably be accused of conspiratorial paranoia, at best, or of feeding anti-Semitic tropes at worst. This is especially the case because historical figures like the Rothschilds – who so often feature in racist fantasies – are mentioned in the book, albeit in passing.

As well as Palestinians, then, I also stand in solidarity with Jewish communities, who should never be the target of collective blame for the actions of the Israeli state. By demystifying, as far as possible, the networks that constitute the Israel lobby, this book aims to challenge *both* efforts to ring-fence pro-Israeli apartheid activism from critical scrutiny *and* anti-Semitic conspiracy theories which 'ethnicise' a fundamentally political issue. In the last analysis, such dangerous fantasies not only breed racism, but also misidentify the problem, creating a sense of impotence which fosters passivity, ultimately decreasing the likelihood of clear-headed engagement and practical solidarity with Palestinians struggling against injustices which are all too real.

In addition to rejecting wholesale any attempt to characterise the Israel lobby as a 'Jewish' lobby, we must also avoid exaggerating the Zionist movement's power. For example, claims like those made by ex-US president and Netanyahu ally Donald Trump that Israel once 'had absolute power over Congress' were rightly met with strong criticism.[25] This book makes no claim of 'control' for the Zionist movement. On the contrary, it demonstrates that although elements of the movement have access to significant resources and can, in certain arenas at specific times, exert influence, pro-Israel actors are very far from all-powerful. Indeed, while most existing studies of the Israel lobby (which are overwhelmingly focused on the US) pay little attention to pro-Palestinian activism, this book emphasises its importance. It shows that the Zionist movement has been profoundly challenged by the grassroots BDS movement and has had to mobilise a backlash *precisely because it lacks control* and because support for Israel *is* vulnerable to erosion through Palestine solidarity activism. The book analyses the strategies and circumstances that lead to both the lobby's successes *and its failures* on a political terrain that is complex and continually contested and in which power is never absolute. It stresses, in particular, the consistent growth of the boycott movement – despite a well-resourced Zionist counter-campaign which has at times succeeded in censoring, undermining and repressing BDS – and in so doing highlights the *limitations* of the lobby's power.

Methods and structure

Undeniably, powerful actors – including nation-states and their supporters – develop strategies to defend their power. They are also, as author Christopher Williams points out, 'almost by definition' likely to 'actively evade being researched'.[26] Moreover, as chapter 2 explains, while the Israeli government and the Zionist movement have often been open about their strategies, at certain times they do seek to operate at least semi-covertly. For example, Israeli politician Gilad Erdan has said explicitly that opacity is critical to the Israeli government's anti-BDS efforts.[27] Similarly, as Steven Rosen, a former director of foreign policy at the major lobby group American Israel Public Affairs Committee (AIPAC), once observed: 'A lobby is like a night flower: it thrives in the dark and dies in the sun.'[28] Indeed, the Zionist movement is not exceptional in this regard. A degree of secrecy is intrinsic to many states' propaganda operations and to *all* lobbying and political influence, from fossil fuels to pharmaceuticals to financial industries.

Importantly, though, the extent to which some pro-Israel campaigning operates behind the scenes should not be misinterpreted, or misrepresented, as indicative of a secret conspiracy. Conspiracy, the Marxist scholar Fredric Jameson argued, 'is the poor person's cognitive mapping', a psychological crutch for a failed attempt to represent a system that cannot be comprehended.[29] The chronic lack of transparency intrinsic to all lobbying and political influence does pose a challenge to research and indeed, the practical difficulties of researching the Zionist movement may be an additional reason that this book is the first of its kind. However, as with other state-centred machinations, from Watergate in the US to the undercover policing scandal in Britain, the power and influence of the Israeli state and the Zionist movement are far from hidden and unknowable. Despite significant barriers to evidence-gathering, the subject has proved amenable to research; journalists, activists and others have often exposed and documented pro-Israel lobbying at work.

This book is based on years of research using investigative sociological methods, appropriate in what anthropologist Joan Cassell describes as 'settings where one is likely to find great discrepancies between frontstage and backstage activities'.[30] As such, this approach is arguably essential for studying lobbying, political influence and state propaganda. While gaps inevitably remain, I used freedom of information requests to overcome the opacity of pro-Israel networks in order to access and gather as much data as possible on activities and conversations taking place behind closed doors. FOIs are a useful tool which scholars have lagged behind journalists in deploying.[31] Not usually crafted for public consumption, documents obtained via FOIs can to a certain extent be viewed, in the words of sociologist John Scott, as 'the objective residue of the past'.[32] They share this trait with much primary archival material, offering 'insider' insight and historical context to the contemporary Zionist movement, on which I draw heavily in chapter 3. Elsewhere, I use other credible, reliable sources, including the Israeli press, data from Companies House and the Charity Commission, statements by Israeli government ministers, materials produced by Zionist groups, and interviews with Zionist movement actors and Palestine solidarity activists. So, rather than needing to construct a juicy conspiracy theory, I instead carefully trace, meticulously reference, and cautiously assess the considerable available evidence.

This book is also informed by power structure research, a specific approach to 'studying up' (the study of powerful, as opposed to weak, actors), which emerged from the work of thinkers like C. Wright Mills and G. William Domhoff. Beginning with organisations as the key to power, power structure research seeks to map out the interconnections between people and organisations constituting a power structure in any given context in order to demystify them. It uses network maps, simplified versions of which are occasionally used in this book, to depict the links between key players. Rather than a monolithic bloc, they enable the Israel lobby to be visualised as a 'they', not an 'it',[33] and illuminate the diverse range of actors involved. Simultaneously, they make the networks visible as a coherent movement due to the complex web of interconnections between individuals and organisations. Mapping out connections within a power structure, when done carefully, ought to be the *antithesis* of conspiratorial thinking, but it can nonetheless be controversial, as shown by the 2022 furore over the Mapping

Project – an initiative that sought to document US-based institutions' links to the colonisation of Palestine.[34] Judgement is required to determine the evidential basis justifying each actors' inclusion and the significance (or otherwise) of specific links.

The first chapter of this book lays the foundations for understanding the backlash against Palestine solidarity today. It explains some key theoretical concepts, looks at historical precedents (including apartheid-era South Africa's own global anti-boycott campaign), grounds the analysis in imperial Britain's history of support for the Zionist project (and ongoing complicity in Palestinian oppression), and briefly describes the early transnational Zionist movement, mapping out the role of the 'national institutions' in pre-state settler colonialism through to Israeli statehood and beyond. Chapter 2 then provides the global context necessary to understand the British Zionist movement, examining Israel's intensifying legitimacy crisis and the Israeli government's global campaign of propaganda and repression to combat so-called delegitimisation and the BDS movement. Highlighting the work of Brand Israel, the Global Coalition for Israel, Kela Shlomo (Concert) and the Ministry of Strategic Affairs, it shows how the civil society–led nature of the boycott movement has heightened the importance of Zionist civil society organisations from the perspective of the Israeli government, leading to increased reliance on state–private networks, in particular in the field of 'lawfare'. It also provides a short overview of the US Zionist movement, pointing to trends and tendencies which are echoed in Britain. In chapter 3, I trace the evolution of the Zionist movement in Britain, charting its history through the lens of its struggle against the Arab League boycott of Israel through to its contemporary anti-BDS campaigning today. This serves as an introduction to some of the key players in the British Zionist movement and demonstrates that – despite considerable tensions and differences – there is historical continuity in the way a wide range of actors work together at critical junctures to pursue common goals (such as opposing boycotts of Israel), including across state–private networks with the Israeli embassy.

The remaining five chapters focus on different arenas of society: Parliament, civil society and the cultural arena; local government and the legal sphere; academia; and the media. Chapter 4 traces the history of the Zionist movement in Westminster, charting the emergence and changing fortunes of Labour Friends of Israel and Conservative Friends of Israel. It highlights these groups' non-transparent and unaccountable modus operandi and the intermittent scandals which occasionally illuminate their activities, as well as the close informal working relationships cultivated by the Israeli embassy. Chapters 5 to 7 are case studies looking specifically at the backlash against BDS. In chapter 5, I describe the Israeli embassy and Zionist movement's efforts to manufacture a 'counter-delegitimisation' network in civil society to combat BDS and the critical role which British government ministers supportive of Conservative Friends of Israel have played in repressing BDS initiatives in the cultural sphere. Chapter 6 focuses on pro-Israel actors' 'lawfare' activities to prevent local government BDS initiatives. It explains how key pro-Israel lawfare initiatives in Britain, such as UK Lawyers for Israel, fit a wider pattern of lawfare coordination across state–private networks and how the British government's efforts to repress local boycott activism chime with its wider authoritarian agenda. In chapter 7, I look at how the Zionist movement has responded to the academic boycott campaign in British universities. As well as scrutinising Zionist philanthropists' efforts to adjust the contours of the academic landscape in Israel's favour – through the fostering of 'Israel studies' and the BIRAX project (a British Council–led anti-BDS collaboration with the British and Israeli governments) – it highlights intensifying efforts to censor and silence scholarship and activism by Palestinians and their supporters. Finally, chapter 8 surveys the media landscape. It examines the various 'carrot' and 'stick' strategies employed by pro-Israel actors seeking to influence the media, emphasising the important role of the Britain Israel Communications and Research Centre (BICOM), and assesses the extent to which the BBC and the British press are swayed by their pressure. The conclusion argues that the backlash against Palestine solidarity and the BDS movement is a testament to their efficacy – and ironically provides hope that through democratisation, empowerment of independent civil society, principled anti-racism and collective liberation politics, current power structures can and will shift.

I

Understanding the 'Israel Lobby'

As a result of Israel's long-standing ethnic cleansing, Palestinians are geographically scattered. Millions live as second-class citizens with Israeli citizenship, subject to a plethora of discriminatory laws.[1] Others are hemmed into the tiny besieged coastal enclave of the Gaza Strip. Still more live under military occupation in ever-shrinking fragments of the West Bank, surrounded by more than half a million Israeli settlers. Finally, there are millions of Palestinians who for decades have been forced to live in exile; they constitute the largest refugee population in the world. In May 2021, in a popular mobilisation on a scale not seen for decades, Palestinians throughout historic Palestine and beyond rose up in united protest.[2] The immediate trigger for these demonstrations was ongoing ethnic cleansing in Sheikh Jarrah, East Jerusalem, including Israeli settlers' attempts to evict twins Muna and Mohammed El-Kurd and their family from their home. Noting that the settlers receive financial support from US-registered companies, Mohammed El-Kurd called Sheikh Jarrah 'a perfect illustration of settler colonialism, a micro-cosm of the reality for Palestinians across 73 years of Zionist rule'. The 'Unity Uprising', he continued, therefore reflected a broader sentiment shared by all Palestinians: a stubborn refusal to silently accept their dispossession under Israeli apartheid.[3]

In at least the fifth intense episode of Israeli state violence in twelve years, the Israeli government deployed its police, army and air force to brutally repress the uprising – killing approximately 250 people, including around fifty children, in just over ten days. In Britain during this time, Israel's friends were making their voices heard. Natasha

Hausdorff, from an organisation called UK Lawyers for Israel, told *Sky News* that 'the lengths the Israeli army goes to [in order] to protect civilian life, [are] unparalleled in the history of warfare'. Palestinian militant group Hamas, she insisted, was actually 'killing its own people', and it was in fact rockets fired at Israel from Gaza, but falling short, that were responsible for Palestinian deaths.[4] Meanwhile, a group called We Believe in Israel urged its supporters to write to their members of Parliament to 'condemn Hamas rocket attacks'. Together with one of Britain's oldest Israel-advocacy bodies, the Zionist Federation, it also announced an event as part of 'Zionism Month' to 'celebrate seventy-three years since the signing of Israel's Declaration of Independence'.[5] Palestinians commemorate this as the Nakba, marking the expulsion of over 750,000 people from the land which became Israel, who have been prevented from returning ever since.[6]

British pro-Israel groups like these have different methods, diverse target audiences and varying degrees of influence. However, together with a host of other actors – chiefly governments – their apartheid apologetics contributes to dampening and counteracting the considerable pressure for change. In solidarity with the Palestinian uprising, hundreds of thousands around the world took to the streets; Britain saw its biggest Palestine protest in history.[7] Yet Britain's Middle East minister, James Cleverly – a strong supporter of Conservative Friends of Israel[8] – merely declared that Israel had a 'legitimate right to self-defence'.[9]

Key concepts

The Zionist movement spans the state/private divide. Groups like UK Lawyers for Israel, as we will see, have a close relationship with the Israeli government – which is increasingly seeking to informally cooperate with pro-Israel civil society actors overseas. Meanwhile, British politicians like James Cleverly are at one and the same time state actors *and* members of the Israel lobby, in their capacity as supporters of groups like Conservative Friends of Israel. It is useful, therefore, to set out some key concepts pertinent to understanding what the Israel lobby is (and isn't) – namely 'social movements from above', 'state–private networks', 'new public diplomacy' and finally 'manufactured civil society'. These concepts underpin the book's analysis of the relationship between the Zionist movement, past and present, and the Israeli (and to a lesser extent British) governments. Placing the Israeli government's contemporary strategy for fighting the worldwide Palestine solidarity movement in context beside its historical precedents, especially the South African apartheid regime's anti-boycott efforts, will also show that this modus operandi is far from unique.

First and foremost, I conceptualise the Zionist movement as a 'social movement from above'. In contrast to dominant theories, which assume that the term 'social movement' solely indicates collective grassroots activism, usually seeking to disrupt existing power structures, researchers Laurence Cox and Alf Nilsen argue that we should not see social movements as limited to a specific level of a fundamentally given socio-political order. They argue, rather, that social movements come from above as well as below. A 'social movement from above' can be defined as 'the collective agency of dominant groups' seeking to defend or enhance dominant power structures, while a social movement from below is 'organised by subaltern social groups' to disrupt power structures.[10] Social movements from above enjoy 'superior access to economic, political and cultural resources' and privileged access to state power.[11] Their strategies frequently include 'ideological offensives'. Critically, movements from above and below tend to emerge and intensify their activities simultaneously, in moments when existing power structures are in crisis. Such oppositional movements decisively shape each others' strategies and should therefore be understood and analysed together.[12]

This framework fits the case at hand well and allows us to situate the Palestinian liberation struggle, BDS campaign and wider Palestine solidarity and anti-apartheid movement – a social movement 'from below' – on the same level as the Zionist and counter-BDS movement – a social movement 'from above'. Again, this should not be misinterpreted as a faux anti-elitist narrative in fact alluding to Jewish people (constructed as 'the establishment' as if working-class Jewish communities somehow didn't exist). Rather, the dominant power structure in question is the Israeli state's apartheid system imposed on Palestinians. The BDS movement comes 'from below' because it seeks to act in solidarity with the oppressed Palestinian people to dismantle this apartheid system. It is also a largely grass-roots initiative. The Zionist movement comes 'from above', even though it has non-elite as well as elite elements, because it defends the dominant oppressive structure of Israeli apartheid. As Cox and Nilsen point out, the 'majority of states in the world today' have themselves 'been made and remade by social movements'.[13] This is certainly true of the state of Israel, which was brought into being in part by the activism of the transnational Zionist movement.

Since then, the Zionist movement has had the nation-state of Israel at its heart. And, like other modern nation-states, the Israeli government today seeks to enlist civil society organisations into its propaganda campaigns. This has implications for how we should understand state power and civil society. Whereas many liberal theorists see civil society, simplistically, as a buffer against government tyranny, Italian Marxist Antonio Gramsci argued that the 'trenches' of civil society are a key arena in which the ruling class reinforces its power using non-violent means. Contemporary scholars have used Gramscian theory to explain the complicated relationship between the state and civil society spheres. Inderjeet Parmar, for instance, argues that 'one of the most significant powers of dominant classes is the ability to establish private institutions that become fundamental to the exercise of state power' and, in turn, 'one of the most significant powers of the modern state' is its power 'to reach deeply into its "own" society and draw upon reservoirs of legitimacy and popular goodwill'.[14] Contrary to liberal theory, then, these connections require us to see civil society as potentially an arena of state power.

In the current era of neoliberalism, anthropologist Janine Wedel argues, such 'blurred boundaries' are even more relevant: ours is an age 'marked by privatization and contracting out, and a resulting fusion (and confusion) of state and private power'. In today's world, 'emergent forms of governing, power and influence' play out 'at the nexus of official and private power'.[15] Both Parmar and Wedel use the term 'state–private networks' to describe the connections between the state and dominant pro-state groups in civil society. Parmar points out that state–private networks reflect 'shared and mutual state–private elite interests',[16] while Wedel draws attention to the fact that, together, these players' ability to straddle the state–private divide and coordinate 'from multiple vantage points' is critical to their modus operandi. Official and private power often reinforce each other, and state–private networks are able to harness the relative advantages of *both* state and non-state actors.[17]

Given the resulting potency of state–private networks, scholars working in so-called new public diplomacy often advocate for governments to utilise state–private networks (though without using the specific term). Like all forms of diplomacy, the field of new public diplomacy seeks to help governments defend and maintain their power. While traditional diplomacy involves the cultivation of relationships between official representatives of two states, public diplomacy 'targets the general public in foreign societies'.[18] In turn, *new* public diplomacy – which gained prominence soon after 2000 – differs in part because it increasingly involves *non-state* actors in this targeting of foreign publics. The key reason new public diplomacy theorists advocate the use of non-governmental actors is that the general public today is often deeply sceptical of state power. Therefore, as leading new public diplomacy scholar Jan Melissen notes, diplomats may not be 'the best messengers' to deliver government messages, since they are identifiable as official 'government representatives'.[19] Shaun Riordan, another scholar working in this field, underlines this point. Diplomats, he notes, can 'lack credibility' and thus from the perspective of governments are 'often not the ideal, or are even counter-productive, agents for engaging with broader foreign civil societies'.[20]

By contrast, civil society organisations tend to be afforded, in the eyes of the general public, a degree of legitimacy widely denied to governments. Civil society actors are often assumed to be independent, democratic and benign. Chiefly for this reason, new public diplomacy scholars argue that governments should seek to make their diplomacy 'more effective' by enlisting the help of 'non-governmental agents of the sending country's own civil society' as well as by 'employing local networks in target countries'.[21] Diplomats must learn, Melissen writes, to 'collaborate with non-official agents' and 'to piggyback on non-governmental initiatives'. Indeed, he claims that this dissolution of boundaries between official state representatives and the civil society sphere is such that 'issues at the grass roots of civil society have become the bread and butter of diplomacy at the highest levels'. He terms this the 'socialization of diplomacy'.[22]

Importantly, leading new public diplomacy scholars stress that the relationships between state and civil society actors must remain at least partially covert. Riordan, for example, explains that being 'seen as too close to, or acting at the behest of, government' would 'undermine the very credibility' which constitutes civil society organisations' 'added value'. He therefore advises against the creation of official government-run committees to facilitate the desired state–private networks, since 'membership of formal government committees may cause significant ethical or political problems for many potential public diplomacy agents'. Instead, he suggests that looser and 'less formal network structures' – implicitly less overtly associated with governments – will be more likely to avoid denting civil society organisations' credibility and 'prove more effective, cost-efficient and less politically sensitive'.[23] Within the type of state–private networks advocated by Riordan, the role of governmental actors in relation to civil society organisations is 'as catalysts, coordinating [civil society organisations'] activities within a broader strategy, encouraging those not already engaged in such activities, and, on occasion, providing discreet technical and financial support'.[24]

At their most 'discreet', such state–private relationships may produce organisations best labelled 'manufactured civil society'. This term, as scholar Lesley Hodgson explains, refers to 'groups that are formed and funded, at least initially, through some type of state initiative'. By dint of being 'orchestrated by government' in this way, 'manufactured' civil society organisations represent the antithesis of that independent, organic self-organisation which is 'the very crux of grassroots initiatives'.[25] The concept of 'astroturfing', more often discussed in relation to corporate marketing campaigns,[26] is very similar and is used to describe ostensible 'grassroots' activities or organisations in fact manufactured by top-down actors.

The South Africa precedent

The strategy of the Israeli government, which will be set out in due course, can be cast in a useful comparative light by way of reference to other examples of governments utilising state–private networks and manufacturing civil society in the ways new public diplomacy theorists advocate. In the domestic arena, for instance, the British government was revealed in 2016 to be disseminating so-called counter-extremism messages through a network of apparently independent grassroots Muslim organisations. These bodies were deemed to be more credible messengers than the government itself.[27] Some of the civil society organisations involved in these state–private networks were willingly co-opted, seeing themselves as part of a 'counter-extremism movement'.[28] However, some employees of other organisations reportedly knew little or nothing about the fact that the British government was funding and directing the covert propaganda campaigns on which they worked.[29] A second national example comes from Turkey, where the government has been accused not only of undermining, co-opting and repressing critical civil society organisations – such as Kurdish groups – but also of manufacturing its own organisations and, in effect, creating what scholar Jessica Doyle calls 'a shadow state-controlled civil-society sector'.[30]

At the transnational level, however, the most pertinent precedent is that of apartheid-era South Africa. The South African apartheid government's decades-long global propaganda campaign has many parallels with the case of Israel. South Africa then, like Israel now, was facing a worldwide boycott campaign by a social movement from below. As journalist Ron Nixon explains in his book *Selling Apartheid*, this campaign consisted of volunteers organising on 'shoestring budgets', who were attempting to isolate South Africa over its discriminatory racial policies, just as the BDS movement hopes to pressure Israeli apartheid today. The South African government's global propaganda campaign in response to this boycott was in large part coordinated by Eschel Rhoodie, secretary of the Department for Information. The counter-campaign was waged by a highly professionalised transnational network with 'massive resources', including numerous PR firms and front groups.[31]

This was the case because Rhoodie, long before new public diplomacy theorists carved out their niche, had recognised that official government representatives 'will always be criticised as . . . paid apologists for the government'. His solution also preempted new public diplomacy. The problem could be overcome, he reasoned, by

> making extensive use of existing goodwill among individuals, companies and organisations and, where they are non-existent, we should look to create our own. Such non-governmental voices, independent, or ostensibly independent, whether South African or foreign, are very often more effective, are listened to and are considered more seriously than our own.[32]

As well as advocating for the manufacture of civil society, Rhoodie also understood the need for state–private networks to remain largely covert. Much of the Department for Information's work was therefore kept secret.[33] In keeping with the prescriptions of new public diplomacy, the South African government assumed a role as catalyst and coordinator, encouraging and often quietly funding civil society organisations' propaganda initiatives which were 'complementary' to official efforts.[34] Soon after the international propaganda campaign masterminded by Rhoodie was publicly exposed, journalists who interviewed him likened the network of global projects supporting South African apartheid to 'dozens of pieces that had been manipulated on a worldwide chessboard'.[35] While in reality, the degree of influence the government exerted on different bodies varied considerably, it is undeniable – as Rhoodie observed appreciatively about a propaganda body called the South Africa Foundation – that such groups sought to 'do on a private basis what the Department of Information [was] doing on an official basis' and that the synergies arising from their informal collaboration across state–private networks were vital to that effort.[36]

The Cold War looms large as another context which exemplifies the instrumentalisation of civil society groups by state powers at the transnational level in a manner which might today be called new public diplomacy. In the latter half of the twentieth century, the 'Big Three' American foundations' – Rockefeller, Carnegie and Ford – were crucial, as Parmar notes, to building 'the infrastructure for continued American hegemony', and their modes of cooperating with the US government across state–private networks blurred the public/private distinction. While these foundations were ostensibly independent – which proved helpful overseas 'in circumstances that made it difficult for the US government to be seen to be too actively involved' – in reality, they often acted, in Parmar's words, 'as unofficial state actors'. The foundations were especially active in re-shaping academic institutions in ways believed to benefit the US.[37]

The cultural realm was also key to the Cold War. The CIA developed a variety of state–private networks, from front organisations like the Congress for Cultural Freedom – which it often covertly funded – to informal cooperative relationships with wealthy arts benefactors like Nelson Rockefeller and John Hay Whitney (both of whom had close links to US intelligence). Within Hollywood, as historian Hugh Wilford notes, the CIA even cultivated 'an informal but powerful group of movie artists and moguls' with a sense of national duty. Indeed, Wilford maintains that joint public–private ventures were 'typical' of CIA operations in the cultural Cold War.[38] Researcher Giles Scott-Smith agrees, noting that the government's Cold War propaganda efforts 'relied heavily on like-minded citizens who were more than willing to fill [the] ideological space and join the contest with the financial and organisational support of the US state'.[39] The Soviet Union engaged in similar activities. As well as funding Communist parties in various countries, it too understood the importance of covert propaganda and cultural production. Historian Sean McMeekin writes that at the peak of his powers, Soviet propagandist Willi Münzenberg 'controlled from his Berlin headquarters a seemingly invincible network of Communist front organizations – charities, publishers, newspapers, magazines, theaters, film studios, and cinema houses – which stretched, on paper at least, from Buenos Aires to Tokyo'.[40]

Britain's historic responsibility

This book shows how the Israeli government, including its embassy in London, seeks to mobilise, coordinate and enhance cooperation with Zionist civil society groups across state–private networks, and even occasionally manufactures them. This modus operandi aligns with the prescriptions of new public diplomacy theorists and strongly echoes the counter-boycott tactics employed in previous decades by the South African apartheid regime and others. Given these empirical realities, it is vital to clearly differentiate the argument of this book from one which implicitly and misleadingly blames 'foreign influence' and, as such, lets the British establishment off the hook for its complicity in Palestinian oppression.

Britain's historic and ongoing role in Palestinian oppression cannot be overstated. In the early years of Zionist settler colonialism, British imperialism had something of a symbiotic relationship with the Zionist movement; indeed, the former nurtured the latter in its formative years.[41] The Balfour Declaration – a short text stating that the British government viewed 'with favour the establishment in Palestine of a national home for the Jewish people' – encapsulates this intimate relationship. Issued by British foreign secretary Arthur Balfour in 1917, it paved the way for the creation of Israel. Though hardly unique, given long-standing imperial practices of carving up territories, the declaration was won in no small part thanks to high-level lobbying by Zionist activists like Chaim Weizmann.

Britain was a hub of Zionist movement activity in the period before the Israeli state was founded. Based in Manchester, Weizmann was president of the Zionist Federation, and later of the World Zionist Organization, before eventually becoming president of Israel. In his early lobbying years, he appealed to British politicians for support, sociologist Paul Kelemen notes, 'largely on the grounds that a Jewish state could render invaluable service to the Empire'.[42] The original foundation, then, of British support for the Zionist project was its usefulness to the British Empire, just as Israel's 'special relationship' with North America today rests, to a very significant degree, on its utility to US imperialism.[43]

Ironically, British politicians' anti-Semitism may have played into the Zionist movement's hands. Foremost among these politicians was none other than Lord Balfour himself, a Conservative who as prime minister had previously introduced the 1905 Aliens Act in order to prevent Jewish refugees fleeing anti-Semitic violence in Russia from settling in Britain.[44] Meanwhile, Labour had declared its support for the Zionist project in its 'war aims' document, issued three months before the Balfour Declaration. The text was drafted by Sidney Webb, a man who once expressed satisfaction that there were 'no Jews' in the Labour Party and was concerned that 'race deterioration, if not race suicide' could result in Britain 'gradually falling to the Irish and the Jews'.[45] Equally, deep-seated Orientalism coloured British politicians' attitudes towards Palestinian Arabs. Labour member of Parliament Josiah Wedgwood, for example, called Palestine 'the Clapham Junction of the Commonwealth', arguing that its native inhabitants 'must suffer as civilisation advances'.[46] Meanwhile, Prime Minister Ramsay MacDonald, under whom Wedgwood served, simultaneously espoused 'vicious anti-Semitic stereotypes' yet held to the paternalistic belief that through the Zionist project, 'the Jewish worker is helping the Arab to raise his standards'.[47]

Less well known than the Balfour Declaration, but equally important, is the later period during which imperial Britain ruled Palestine under the post–World War I mandate. During the mandate, which lasted almost thirty years between 1920 and 1948, thousands of Palestinians were made refugees. Meanwhile, as historian John Newsinger notes, Britain brutally repressed Palestinian uprisings like the 1936–39 Arab Revolt, including through RAF bombing campaigns.[48] In the same period, Britain at times restricted Jewish immigration to Palestine – including in 1939 when Jewish refugees were fleeing Nazi persecution in Europe – and interned tens of thousands of Jews in camps like the one in the coastal town of Atlit. Today, episodes like these are often ignored thanks to Britain's pervasive amnesia about its own colonial history. Yet it is vital to recognise that the contemporary situation in Israel/Palestine is one of many enduring and harmful legacies of the British Empire and that facing up to Britain's significant historic and ongoing role in the injustices inflicted upon Palestinians is part of facing up to our own history.

This book therefore attempts to situate the birth and ongoing activities of the British Zionist movement *within the broader history of British state racism*, which continues to this day. Indeed, British support for Israel can only be fully understood when placed in this wider context. For instance, consider that the same year that Israel was established, the famous passenger liner *Empire Windrush* arrived in Britain bringing West Indian immigrants from Jamaica (at that time still a British colony). The same racist political logic shaped Britain's treatment of colonial populations, from Palestinians to the Windrush generation, and both groups continue to suffer scandalous consequences today. This book shows that Zionist activism is by no means alien to the body politic. On the contrary, it has long been an integral *part of the British establishment*. Former Conservative Party chair Lord Andrew Feldman provides one contemporary example of how Zionist movement players are embedded within wider (mostly, but certainly not exclusively, right-wing) networks of power and influence. At the start of the COVID-19 pandemic in early 2020, he lobbied for companies represented by his PR firm to win contracts to provide personal protective equipment. As chapter 5 explains, only a few years earlier, it appears that he had intervened in a similar manner – in support of Israel against a BDS initiative.

Situating British Zionism as an *example of British complicity* in this way makes the analysis presented here diametrically opposed to other conceptualisations of the Israel lobby which problematically insinuate 'foreign influence'. A famous 2007 study of the Israel lobby in the US by realist international relations scholars John Mearsheimer and Stephen Walt, for example, has rightly been critiqued by Palestinian academic Joseph Massad. The problem with their book, he points out, is that it places so much blame on the Israel lobby that it effectively 'exonerates the United States government'.[49] Similarly, scholar Mark Lacy notes that Mearsheimer and Walt's book appears to emphasise domestic political 'penetration' by foreign actors,[50] and to imply that the Israel lobby matters because it diverts US policy away from America's 'national interest'.[51] Notably, some leftists, too, are tempted to deploy these misguided 'progressive nationalist' narratives, which portray the Zionist movement as a polluting foreign influence corrupting an otherwise-pristine democracy. For example, sociologist James Petras has claimed that

> Americans have a necessity to put our fight against Israel and its Lobby at the very top of our political agenda . . . because of its role in promoting its US supporters to degrade our democratic principles, robbing us of our freedom to debate and our sovereignty to decide our own interests.[52]

Similarly, US representative Ilhan Omar claimed in 2019 that the public should discuss 'the political influence in this country that says it is OK for people to push for allegiance to a foreign country'.[53]

These types of assertions are problematic on several counts. Firstly, by assuming the existence of an objective 'national interest', such discourses treat countries like indivisible 'black boxes'.[54] However, as generations of scholarship has shown, the very concept of a US or British 'national interest' is only ever socially constructed – usually by political elites – and is always subject to dispute. Indeed, it is largely a myth which ignores the conflicting interests of different societal groups according to race, class, gender and other factors. Secondly, Petras's and Omar's rhetoric misidentifies the heart of the issue: the reason the Israel lobby matters is that it helps to maintain the oppressive status quo in Israel/Palestine and thus *harms Palestinians*. Its role is consequential not because it allegedly undermines some coherent American or British 'national interest', but rather because its goals often coincide with the interest of a section of the US or British political elite. Thirdly, reductive interpretations which suggest that a degree of cooperation with Israeli government actors renders Israel's supporters 'foreign agents' or 'assets' denies their agency – and their responsibility. As we shall see, some Zionist organisations' existence *predated* the creation of the state of Israel, meaning the label 'foreign agent' would also be an ahistorical misnomer.

Most importantly, however, such characterisations – rooted in the language of the US Foreign Agents Registration Act, which there have been recent moves to emulate in Britain as part of a new National Security Bill – are also potentially xenophobic in tone. They risk playing into the notion of 'dual loyalty', an erroneous idea

resting on a problematic expectation of undivided patriotic defer-
ence to the authority of a single nation-state. We ought to reject this
idea wholesale. Instead, we should celebrate a world in which people's attachments and solidarities are multiple and cross borders,
while questioning and challenging all allegiances to state power
and nationalism. Use of the concept of state–private networks to
describe the relationships between some supporters of Israel and
Israeli, and sometimes British, government actors provides a
nuanced lens which brings state power back into the analytical
equation – and, in the process, avoids attributing exaggerated
power to pro-Israel lobby groups in civil society. To be clear, then,
with very rare exceptions such as the case of Shai Masot – who was
directly employed by the Israeli government when he was filmed by
undercover journalists plotting to 'take down' a British MP critical
of Israeli apartheid[55] – Zionist activism in Britain should not be
understood as 'foreign interference'. Even in Masot's case, the key
problem is not the 'foreignness' of his activities but their anti-democratic means and their oppressive ends. Furthermore, I am
categorically *not* arguing that British pro-Israel actors are somehow
insufficiently loyal to the British state, which has its own array of
racist and oppressive domestic and foreign policies (in addition to
its support for Israeli apartheid) that should be actively opposed.

Due to the flawed perspectives mentioned, international relations
scholar David Wearing has argued that 'the "Israel lobby" thesis . . .
is one best left to the establishment intellectuals and state loyalists
who originally produced it'.[56] However, this book shows that it is
possible to analyse the British Zionist movement while being
anti-establishment, and indeed anti-state, without implying that 'the
tail is wagging the dog' and without externalising an issue which is
largely *internal*. This requires setting the British Zionist movement
in its proper context and acknowledging not only Britain's historic
responsibility but also its ongoing complicity, alongside contemporary material and geopolitical realities. Primarily, as the Ministry
of Defence's 2021 military strategy says explicitly, it is clear that
Israel is seen as 'a key strategic partner'[57] by the British government
(and is not, as some have incorrectly claimed, a 'hostile foreign
state').[58] Accordingly, the contemporary Britain–Israel alliance
reflects the British foreign policy establishment's *construction* of

the so-called national interest and its economic, commercial and strategic aspects. Despite Israel's systematic denial of Palestinian rights and flagrant violations of international law, Britain collaborates closely with Israel in areas such as cybersecurity, counter-terrorism, intelligence, and military technology. In 2017, Britain issued a record £221 million in arms sale licences to Israel.[59] In 2020, the two countries signed an agreement to 'formalise and enhance' military cooperation.[60] And in 2022, Britain entered negotiations to 'upgrade' its free trade agreement with Israel.[61]

To scrutinise the pro-Israel lobby is not, then, to pretend that wider structures of power built on material interests and long-standing political alliances are anything less than critical. Nor is it to pretend that *without* the activities and influence of the Israel lobby in domestic politics, the British government would suddenly become pro-Palestinian, any more than it would be pacifist without the arms trade lobby or anti-capitalist without financial lobbying. But it *is* to refuse a false dichotomy between structure and agency and, as Cox and Nilsen put it, to 'rethink structure as collective agency'.[62] In other words, it is to acknowledge that power struggles between numerous different actors and interests forge, over many years, contingent structural outcomes: the 'way things are' has been 'consciously produced', though sometimes with unexpected or inadvertent consequences.[63] At the granular level of daily political contestation, pro-Israel organisations contribute to building and maintaining, over time, the geopolitical alliances and constructions of the 'national interest' extant today. These alliances include, of course, our so-called special relationship with US imperialism, which is part and parcel of successive British governments' 'Atlanticist' orientation and a significant lever upholding British support for Israeli apartheid. In turn, as Wearing notes, Israel's value to US imperialism as 'a dependable, militarily powerful ally in a geostrategically crucial region of the world' needs little explanation.[64]

The early Zionist movement

The next chapter explains why, in the era of BDS, the Israeli government is increasingly reliant on local Zionist networks, including those in Britain – and is, in effect, seeking to enlist civil society actors in support of state power. Firstly, however, a brief review of the history of the early transnational Zionist movement is needed, to illustrate that its cooperation with the Israeli state has been long standing.

The Zionist movement is far from a monolithic bloc. Testament to this are the numerous forms of cultural, religious and political Zionism which exist. Even the category 'political Zionism' incorporates a wide gamut of iterations, from the labour Zionism of David Ben-Gurion to the fascist-influenced revisionist Zionism of Ze'ev Jabotinsky.[65] The respective degrees of influence enjoyed by the various different ideological currents have ebbed and flowed over time, and internecine conflict between them is a consistent trait. However, even if they disagree on much – such as where the precise boundaries of Israel should be – all constituent strands of the political Zionist movement share a commitment to the idea of a 'Jewish state'.[66] This idea of Jewish statehood around which political Zionists cohere emerged and came to prominence, write political scientists Yameen Abu-Laban and Abigail Bakan, as a 'conservative ideological response' and proposed solution to European anti-Semitism.[67] Its development in the late nineteenth century followed centuries of anti-Jewish persecution, and its immediate context was a wave of anti-Jewish pogroms in Russia.

Zionism's key proponents were dispersed across countries. Therefore, as scholar Fiona Adamson notes, the Zionist movement necessarily organised across borders and was, from the start, simultaneously a 'transnational nationalist movement' and a settler-colonial project. Often identified as the father of political Zionism, the movement's most influential advocate, Austro-Hungarian journalist Theodor Herzl, wrote *Der Judenstaat* (*The Jewish State*) in 1896. The following year, he helped to convene the First Zionist Congress in Basel, Switzerland. Soon, a 'transnational network of branches' of what would become the World Zionist

Organization, the original umbrella body of the Zionist movement, had been established.[68] Three other so-called national institutions were first founded through the World Zionist Organization at subsequent congresses to help bring the state of Israel into being. Each of these three bodies – the Jewish National Fund, Keren HaYesod and Jewish Agency for Israel – had a network of affiliates overseas and carried out different functions.

The Jewish National Fund, known in Hebrew as Keren Kayemet Le'Israel, was founded in 1901 to acquire land for Jewish colonisation of Palestine.[69] It continues to play this role today. For example, the Jewish National Fund focuses on 'Judaisation' efforts in the Negev desert (or Naqab in Arabic), a key frontier of the Israeli government's ongoing ethnic cleansing[70] where 'unrecognised' Bedouin villages have been repeatedly demolished by the authorities on the pretext they are trespassing illegally on state-owned land. Meanwhile, Keren HaYesod ('the Foundation Fund'), also known as the United Israel Appeal, was set up in 1920, primarily as a fundraising body.[71] It financed the activities of the pre-state *yishuv* (settlement) in Palestine. Finally, the Jewish Agency, principally concerned with facilitating Jewish immigration to Palestine (*aliyah*), was established in 1929 at the Sixteenth World Zionist Congress. Importantly, these organisations were all founded during the period in which imperial Britain ruled Palestine under the mandate, underlining the entwinement of British imperialism and Israeli settler colonialism. Keren HaYesod was in fact launched in London a few years after the Balfour Declaration, and Britain officially recognised the Jewish Agency in 1930, a year after its foundation.[72]

In Zionist mythology, the ancient Jewish connection to the land of Palestine morphed into the claim that Palestine was 'a land without a people for a people without a land'.[73] In fact, the Zionist movement achieved its goal of Jewish statehood in Palestine at the expense of the indigenous Palestinian people. To turn the myth into reality – or at least to engineer the prerequisite Jewish demographic majority – the creation of Israel in 1948 involved the deliberate ethnic cleansing of Palestinians during the Nakba.

After 1948, the relative importance of Britain as a hub of Zionist activism somewhat waned. Unsurprisingly, the movement's centre of gravity shifted to Israel and secondarily to the US, which had

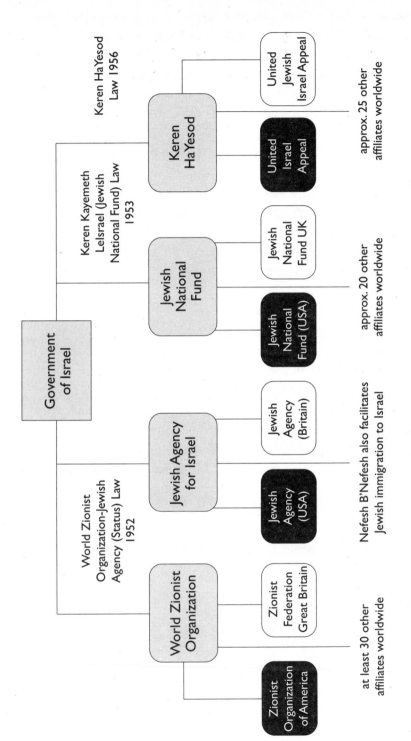

Figure 1.1. Basic structure of the Zionist movement: national institutions and key affiliates

emerged in the post-war order as a far more significant global power. In this critical period immediately after the formation of the Israeli state, the key organs of the Zionist movement which had helped to bring the Jewish state into being were not dissolved. Rather, the newly established Israeli government recalibrated its relationship with the movement. Redefining their roles, the national institutions evolved into quasi-autonomous non-governmental organisations (often called 'quangos'). They shared responsibilities with official state organs, in what the Jewish Agency's website describes as 'a kind of "distribution of labour"'.[74] Fundamentally, though, the transnational Zionist movement continued to play a critical role in enhancing Israeli state power.[75] Moreover, as Israeli historian Evyatar Friesel notes, local Zionist movements around the world still drew their 'raison d'être from being part and parcel of the Zionist movement as a whole'.[76]

Today, the national institutions are all based in the same Jerusalem building complex as the World Zionist Organization.[77] As well as predating the state of Israel, these bodies and their overseas affiliate organisations still constitute the backbone of the contemporary transnational Zionist movement (though supplemented since then by numerous additional groups). Figure 1.1 represents the basic structure of this network, listing each parent organisation in Israel (grey) and their key affiliates in two key Western states allied to Israel, the US (black) and Britain (white). It also indicates how the national institutions' relationships with the newly established government of Israel were first legally defined, for example by the World Zionist Organization–Jewish Agency Status Law, passed in 1952.

Speaking that same year, Israel's first prime minister, David Ben-Gurion (himself a past Jewish Agency president and World Zionist Organization head), said:

> The State of Israel . . . is obliged to operate like every other state, and its capacity outside its borders is restricted. It is the Zionist Organization, built upon the voluntary association and activity, which is able to achieve what is beyond the power and competence of the State, and that is the advantage of the Zionist Organization over the State . . . The State and the Zionist Movement complement each other.[78]

As we will see, Ben-Gurion's articulation of the relative advantages of unofficial Zionist actors operating in civil society, and their complementary relationship to the official organs of the Israeli state, remains key to understanding the role of the Zionist movement today.

2

Selling Apartheid: Israel's Global Propaganda Campaign

In the centre of the occupied Palestinian city of al-Khalil (known in Hebrew as Hebron), armed Israeli settlers – some from the United States – have driven out Palestinian families and taken over their homes. They throw rubbish and human excrement out of their windows onto the Palestinian market below. This happens in plain view of occupying Israeli soldiers, who protect the settlers against any Palestinian retaliation and stand guard at a matrix of checkpoints around the city. One such checkpoint stands at the entrance to al-Shuhada Street, a former bustling market in the Old City from which Palestinians have been banned since 1994, now a virtual ghost town. Graffiti on the walls of the city's Tel Rumeida neighbourhood reads: 'Gas the Arabs.'[1]

In October 2014, British Conservative politician Alan Duncan – who already had a reputation as a critic of Israel, having branded its West Bank wall a 'land grab' in 2011[2] – gave a speech to the Royal United Services Institute, a Whitehall think-tank close to the British military and security establishment. In it, he declared that 'apartheid' was an 'accurate and undeniable' description of the situation in Hebron. 'In South Africa', he said, 'it meant pass cards, no free movement, forbidden areas, and first- and second-class citizens. So it is in Hebron.'[3] Unsurprisingly, this opprobrium concerned the Israeli government and its supporters. In 2017, an employee of the Israeli Embassy in London named Shai Masot was caught on camera by undercover journalists plotting to 'take down' Duncan, widely understood to mean discredit and thus silence him.[4] Masot was disgraced, his employment terminated and he was forced to return to Israel.

But Masot was not some 'bad apple' gone rogue. On the contrary, his actions index a fundamentally anti-democratic effort to constrain the prospects for meaningful Palestine solidarity led by the Israeli government. This chapter provides the global context necessary to understand and make sense of the British Zionist movement, with which the rest of the book deals. It focuses on the global backlash campaign being waged by the Israeli government in an attempt to repress its opponents, especially supporters of the Boycott, Divestment and Sanctions (BDS) movement. It outlines how the BDS campaign and counter-campaign emerged in the context of a profound legitimacy crisis for Israel – brought on by decades of violence, occupation and apartheid – which crystallised around the turn of the millennium and provoked, in 2005, an official propaganda effort called Brand Israel. When this 'nation branding' exercise failed to halt the decline in the country's image while it continued to commit atrocities against Palestinians, it was soon supplemented by other tactics.

The Israeli government's counter-BDS strategy has been influenced by ideas from 'new public diplomacy', discussed in the previous chapter and articulated by think-tanks like the Reut Institute. This strategy involves efforts to construct an 'anti-delegitimisation network' by enlisting, mobilising and coordinating pro-Israel civil society groups via 'state–private networks'. As I will show, these efforts are encapsulated by the Global Coalition for Israel project, a 'public–private partnership' established in 2010. Yet by 2015, with the boycott movement still making strides in global civil society, the Israeli government felt compelled to task its secretive Ministry of Strategic Affairs (where Shai Masot likely worked) with leading Israel's global fight against BDS. As we will see, the ministry employed more offensive and aggressive strategies, including surveillance, intelligence gathering and 'black ops'. Using tactics reminiscent of South African apartheid and Cold War propaganda, it sought to indirectly fund pro-Israel civil society groups through an arms-length body called Kela Shlomo, or Concert, and collaborated with wealthy supporters of Israel. The final sections of this chapter focus on 'lawfare' – describing how the Israeli government and its supporters have sought to both outlaw BDS and prosecute BDS activism – and on the pro-Israel lobby in the US, which warrants special attention due its status as the primary sponsor of Israel and its considerable parallels with Britain.

Crisis, boycott and Brand Israel

For decades, Israel's international image was in slow decline. Amid increasingly right-wing governments, successive wars, entrenched occupation, ongoing ethnic cleansing, and continued colonisation through sprawling settlement expansion, it became increasingly difficult for the Zionist movement overseas to convincingly justify and defend Israel's actions. In the 1990s, the internal challenge from 'post-Zionism' within Israel also reached new heights. By the turn of the millennium, the Zionist project had entered a distinct period of crisis. Analysts from Israel's Institute for National Security Studies, a think-tank close to the country's security establishment, identified the 'failure of the Camp David summit in July 2000 and the outbreak of the Second Intifada in September 2000' as key turning points, triggering a rapid intensification of Israel's PR crisis.[5]

Israeli *hasbara* (pro-Israel PR or propaganda; literally, 'explanation') aims, as anthropologist Miriyam Aouragh observes, to maintain 'the international alliances that protect Israel through the provision of material and diplomatic support'.[6] For this reason, the Israeli establishment viewed the apparent *failure* of hasbara, and the country's deep global-image crisis, in national security terms as a serious threat of an existential nature. Although Israel's military supremacy over Palestinians remained clear, the 'hegemonic place of Zionism in Western ideology' appeared increasingly fragile after the year 2000.[7] Principally due to the scale of the settlement enterprise in the West Bank, Western commentators began to pronounce the two-state solution – long seen as an international consensus – 'dead', 'dying' or 'on life support'.[8] This created space for the re-emergence of discussions about a possible one-state solution, an eventuality which would spell the end of the Zionist project.

All polling showed clearly that Israel's image was in trouble. The Israeli government and Zionist movement were especially concerned by trends in the US – Israel's main sponsor. Commissioned research concluded that growing numbers of young Americans, including Jews, were 'swayable' on Israel[9] and that the country was widely viewed as religious and militaristic.[10] The same study observed that Israel's PR problem was most evident on the left, noting that 'core Israel supporters' were 'older, wealthier, more conservative, whiter Americans', while 'younger [people], minorities, [and] liberals' were 'at risk' of siding with Palestinians.[11] The generational split was confirmed by a 2016 Pew poll which found that although more young people in the US still sided with Israel, support for Palestinians among millennials had tripled in a decade.[12]

Rather than admit that the apartheid system imposed on Palestinians was the reason for Israel's international image crisis, Zionist thinkers stressed the increasing urgency of engaging in a 'battle of narrative' to halt Israel's image decline. Einat Wilf, a former member of the Israeli Knesset (parliament), quipped that Israel needed an 'Intellectual Israeli Defence Force'.[13] In a seminal 2010 report called *Building a Political Firewall against Israel's Delegitimization*, the Tel Aviv–based Reut Institute coined a new term – 'delegitimisation' – to describe the problem Israel was facing. Identifying delegitimisation as a strategic threat to Israel's security, it described the existence of a 'delegitimisation network' in Europe and North America. Although used by some supporters of Israel today to describe almost any criticism of Israel, Reut made clear that it saw 'delegitimisation' as a synonym for 'anti-Zionism'.[14]

Israel's crisis of legitimacy had in no small part been caused by challenges from below, chiefly long-standing Palestinian resistance. It also presented new opportunities. After the turn of the millennium, the Palestinian liberation struggle entered a new phase of non-violent popular resistance. In Palestine, weekly protests in many 'Area C' West Bank villages sprang up and, internationally, the BDS movement emerged. Boycott – *muqata'a* – has a long history in Palestinian resistance.[15] The origins of the BDS movement lay to a considerable extent in grassroots popular committees and in civil society, as opposed to the Palestinian political elite. The attitude of the Palestine Liberation Organization to BDS remained ambivalent; the Palestinian Authority's stance was often hostile.[16]

The official BDS call, issued in July 2005 by 170 Palestinian civil society organisations, 'took disparate campaigns to pressure Israel and united them around three clear demands, with one for each major component of the Palestinian people',[17] namely: for Israel to withdraw from the territories it occupies, end the siege of Gaza and remove the West Bank wall; grant full equal rights to Palestinian citizens of Israel; and respect Palestinian refugees' right of return. Modelled on the international boycott campaign which contributed to ending apartheid in South Africa, BDS is a rights-based movement grounded in international law. It advocates academic, cultural and economic boycotts of, and divestment from, Israel and its institutions, as well as companies involved in violations of Palestinian rights. It also calls for international sanctions on Israel, including an end to military cooperation.

Critically, the BDS call appealed directly to 'international civil society organisations', explicitly on the premise that received institutional channels – such as government-led negotiations – had failed to deliver peace or justice.[18] The civil society–led nature of the BDS movement is important; it is here, in civil society, that the struggle for legitimacy is taking place. Despite its reliance on a highly decentralised network of volunteer activists taking 'bottom-up' action in universities, trade unions, faith groups and local communities, BDS has achieved major victories.[19] Notably, transnational corporations such as Veolia and G4S, in 2015 and 2016 respectively, both pulled out of Israel following global boycott campaigns. As such, BDS poses a profound challenge to Israeli apartheid. Indeed, after its first decade, the growth of the boycott movement (including within some of Israel's key Western allies like the US and Britain), was described by Israeli president Reuven Rivlin as a 'strategic threat of the highest degree'.[20]

While BDS is a social movement 'from below' and is to some extent, even according to its critics, 'connected to opposition to imperialism, neoliberalism and global capitalism',[21] Israel is today aligned with neoliberalism, having broken decisively with the labour Zionism dominant in past decades. Starting in the mid-1980s, as economist Shir Hever explains, the country underwent a 'deep shift . . . from a republican, strong-state model of an ultra-nationalist welfare state, into a new model of neoliberalism, while still keeping the ultra-nationalism'.[22] This turn towards free market economic policies – a 'transformation from corporatist Zionism to neoliberal Zionism'[23] – accelerated in the early years of the twenty-first century, cementing a right-wing realignment whose corollary was the political left's slow disillusionment with Israel.[24] As Israeli scholars Neve Gordon and Erez Tzfadia observe, this means that 'even though Zionism's major goals have not changed, the methods deployed to realise them have been undergoing a radical transformation'. This neoliberal transformation saw the state 'outsourcing more and more of its responsibilities to private firms' and also, as Palestinian scholar Tariq Dana points out, 'underpinned the Oslo process'.[25] During Oslo, Israel's strategy was to seek what Foreign Minister Shimon Peres called 'an economization of politics', instead of a 'politicization of economics', as it characterised boycott initiatives.[26]

The Israel government's hasbara responses to its image crisis – and to the threat of 'delegitimisation', Palestine solidarity and the global BDS movement – have also been visibly shaped by neoliberalism. A key example is the Brand Israel project, launched by the Ministry of Foreign Affairs in 2005. The basic premise of nation branding was that marketing principles could be used to package and sell a state's image – regardless of reality. Leading nation-branding advocates such as Keith Dinnie describe their field as working to help 'erase misconceptions about a country' and 'restore international credibility'.[27] The brainchild of Israel's first 'head of brand management', Ido Aharoni, the Brand Israel project saw the Israeli government contract the services of a number of PR companies on the assumption that private actors would deliver hasbara more effectively than government itself. The professed aim of Brand Israel was to 'broaden the conversation'[28] about the country 'beyond the conflict'.[29] Its strategy was multifaceted and involved highlighting Israel's cultural diversity, LGBTQ+ rights, gender equality and achievements in science and technology. Again reflecting the influence of neoliberalism, Brand Israel sought to position the country as 'the start-up nation'[30] and shift Israel's brand towards 'positive values', said to include 'entrepreneurial zeal'.[31]

The cultural sphere, however, was increasingly viewed, in the words of one commentator, as 'the national brand par excellence'.[32] Accordingly, another significant component of Brand Israel was the government-sponsored promotion of Israeli culture overseas. The aim here, as one official put it, was to 'show Israel's prettier face, so we are not thought of purely in the context of war'.[33] Major budgetary reforms were made within the Ministry of Foreign Affairs' Division of Cultural and Scientific Relations in order to 'significantly augment worldwide exposure of Israeli culture'.[34] Those Israeli artists, musicians, writers and others who received state sponsorship to tour, perform or exhibit overseas were left in no uncertainty about the PR motivation behind the government's financial support. As the contractual terms for one such government-funded trip made clear: 'The service provider is aware that the purpose of ordering services from him is to promote the policy interests of the State of Israel via culture and art, including contributing to creating a positive image for Israel.'[35] Confirming beyond doubt the ministry's instrumental weaponisation of culture, Deputy Director Nissim Ben-Sheetrit declared explicitly, 'We [see] culture as a hasbara tool of the first rank, and I do not differentiate between hasbara and culture.'[36]

As well as promoting Israeli culture, the Israeli government worked to defend Brand Israel against the advances of BDS in the cultural sphere. According to Israeli newspaper *Yedioth Ahronoth*, Israeli embassies around the world have been 'very active behind the scenes when it comes to preventing foreign artists from cancelling performances in Israel'. A Ministry of Foreign Affairs official quoted in the report explains how diplomats work through third parties, noting that 'an Israeli ambassador can't call an artist and say: 'Don't listen to Roger Waters' – the Pink Floyd musician and prominent BDS supporter – 'but he can approach an influential agent and ask him to approach the particular artist and convince him to come to Israel and not give in to the boycott.'[37] Chapter 5 will show this modus operandi in action in the British cultural sphere.

The Global Coalition for Israel

Within a few years of the 2005 launch of the nation-branding campaign, it became apparent that Israel's attempt to generate support through such means had been insufficient to halt the deterioration of the country's image. Instead, the years 2009 and 2010 saw an intensification of Israel's legitimacy crisis. This was a consequence of Operation Cast Lead – Israel's bloody military assault on Gaza, during which it killed well over 1,100 Palestinians – and its attack on the Gaza Freedom Flotilla in May 2010, in which it killed nine peace activists on board the Turkish ship *Mavi Marmara*. On the back of this deadly state violence, the BDS movement made significant advances in global civil society, and as a result, Brand Israel was soon supplemented by new strategies. In particular, this period saw a conscious step-change in the Israeli government's relationships with civil society groups.

Domestically within Israel/Palestine, the Israeli government has long sought to repress critical civil society organisations, notably left-leaning Israeli human rights organisations like B'Tselem and Breaking the Silence. Indeed, it took the latter to court on charges of 'treason'.[38] Repression of Palestinian civil society has always been harshest and has included the use of raids, travel bans, and incarceration targeting lawyers, health professionals and other activists.[39] In 2021, in a move the UN dubbed an 'attack on human rights defenders', Israel designated as 'terrorist organisations' six leading Palestinian civil society bodies – including prisoner solidarity body Addameer, human rights group al-Haq, an agricultural association, a network of women's committees and a children's rights charity.[40] At the same time, the Israeli government has long maintained close, cooperative relationships with a clutch of right-wing Zionist civil society groups, such as NGO Monitor, the Jerusalem Center for Public Affairs, Im Tirtzu, and the Meir Amit Intelligence and Terrorism Information Center. The latter, for instance, is run by a retired lieutenant colonel and staffed by former intelligence officers, has acknowledged receiving government funding, and reportedly maintains an office in the Israeli Ministry of Defense. According to one Israeli journalist, it acts as a 'pipeline' for disseminating information military intelligence 'does not want directly associated with it'.[41]

Overseas, a similar dynamic exists. In response to criticism of Israel and solidarity with Palestinians emanating from numerous civil society arenas, Israel has maintained relationships with many Zionist groups in civil society across loose state–private networks. As the overview of the 'national institutions' in the previous chapter shows, such relationships are nothing new. However, after the turn of the millennium, when Israel's crisis of legitimacy crystallised, these networks have proliferated. For example, Hasbara Fellowships, established in 2001 to work on US university campuses, was set up by religious Zionist organisation Aish HaTorah with seed funding from the Israeli government, with whom it collaborated on early projects.[42] Similarly, StandWithUs, another US-headquartered hard-line pro-Israel body founded in 2001, has 'unusually close coordination with Israel's government', demonstrated by a number of joint hasbara projects and its reported receipt of Israeli government grants.[43]

The Israeli government's strategy has been heavily influenced by ideas from new public diplomacy, outlined in the previous chapter. For example, government hasbara strategy documents cite the work of leading new public diplomacy theorist Jan Melissen, whose ideas were discussed in chapter 1.[44] Another influential voice was that of Tel Aviv think-tank the Reut Institute, which argued that, due to a lack of credibility, 'Israel's governmental agencies will have a hard time dealing effectively with non-governmental organizations that criticize Israel's policies'. Reut advised turning, instead, to pro-Israel civil society bodies, arguing that they were 'more likely to do a better job' and adding that many could be 'mobilized toward this task'. While the government should 'let the local pro-Israel community lead',[45] Reut suggested the state should offer discreet support from behind the scenes. It was not alone in advocating use of state–private networks; also in 2010, several papers presented at the Herzliya Conference – the Israeli establishment's premier strategic gathering – articulated similar ideas. One asserted that 'public relations work does not always have to be done by official Israeli entities' and advocated 'mapping the pro-Israeli and pro-Western NGOs and tapping into their services'.[46]

On the advice of Reut and others, a new initiative seeking to institutionalise cooperation on a global scale between the Israeli government and the transnational Zionist movement was established in December 2010. The Global Coalition for Israel was co-founded by the Israeli government and the World Jewish Congress, an international federation of Jewish community organisations founded in Geneva in 1936, which has long been staunchly Zionist (its co-founder Nahum Goldmann simultaneously served as World Zionist Organization president for over a decade, indicative of the two organisations' close relationship).[47] Reflecting the private sector orientation of much contemporary Zionist activism in the neoliberal era, the Global Coalition for Israel's key architects called it 'a public–private partnership',[48] and the World Jewish Congress described it as 'a cooperative and collaborative global approach to strengthen the position of Israel'.[49] The title of the new venture's inaugural meeting – 'Building Partnerships and Synergies in Countering the Assault on Israel's Legitimacy' – reflected this aim. The event, held in Jerusalem, was attended by over one hundred Zionist leaders from around sixty different organisations based in more than thirty countries, as well as senior officials from seven different Israeli government ministries. Speakers were drawn from both the highest levels of government and the Zionist movement: they included Prime Minister Benjamin Netanyahu and Foreign Minister Danny Ayalon, Jewish Agency chairman Natan Sharansky and World Jewish Congress secretary general Dan Diker.[50]

At the Global Coalition for Israel's third conference, held in Jerusalem in February 2016, Israeli minister Gilad Erdan quoted verbatim from Reut's influential report when he declared, with reference to combating the decentralised BDS movement, 'It takes a network to fight a network.'[51] He also alluded to ideas from Reut which were aligned with new public diplomacy theory. Just as the think-tank had argued that the government must 'let the local pro-Israel community lead', Erdan remarked that 'in this battle [against BDS], cooperation between Israel and the pro-Israel community is not just a good idea but a necessity'.[52] In further comments, which recall David Ben-Gurion's emphasis on the complementary role of the Zionist movement in relation to the Israeli state, Erdan explained precisely why the civil society organisations' role was so critical:

It's not necessarily good that the government is at the front of this battle . . . BDS brings in civil society, labor organizations, student organizations, private businesses, so it's better that the response comes from civil society . . . there are organizations that have been doing great work for years, whether it's the Jewish Agency or Stand-WithUs or Israel on Campus Coalition . . . They need to see where we can help them in the government . . . to strengthen their actions and harness the government's advantages.[53]

As we will see, the nature of the 'help' given by the Israeli government to Zionist civil society organisations has included considerable semi-covert funding. But the Global Coalition for Israel also facilitated the flow of information across state–private networks, enabling the government to seek to keep its supporters 'on message'.[54] Because the coalition was a supposedly 'secret' project, details of the project remain obscure – although reported on by the press, its gatherings were described as 'closed conferences'.[55] Table 2.1 shows all known participants in its meetings since it was founded in 2010.[56]

As well as seeking to mobilise and coordinate existing Zionist groups through hubs like the Global Coalition for Israel, the Israeli government has also sought to supplement its support networks by helping to create new 'manufactured civil society' organisations. Such tactics were advocated by some Zionist strategists at the aforementioned 2010 Herzliya Conference: 'NGOs can be established', they pointed out, to advance the Israeli government's hasbara goals.[57] And, according to an in-depth 2012 study by Israeli think-tank Molad, the Israeli government had acted on this advice. Clearly influenced by new public diplomacy thinking, Molad's report noted that governments 'are not generally good persuasive agencies' and are therefore more likely to achieve their objectives 'by working through parties and organizations trusted by people in the target country' and building 'cooperative networks' involving 'organizations in the private, non-governmental sector'. Effective public diplomacy, Molad argued, 'passes through a network of private, non-governmental organizations who benefit from broad public legitimacy in the target country'.

Israel, Molad asserted, had absorbed and implemented these ideas, based on a 'working assumption' that civil society organisations 'have access to key resources and players that the state is denied, and thus have an ability to advance Israeli interests reaching beyond the power of the state'.[58] The Israeli government, it stated had 'established organizations in various countries throughout the world whose purpose is to deliver hasbara messages through "indirect channels" without officially identifying themselves as such'.[59] Corroborating this account, in 2011, the Reut Institute hailed the 'successful creation of a global "anti-delegitimization network"' in global civil society — and credited the 'critical contribution' made by the Israeli government to its construction.[60]

Organisation	Type	Country	Representative(s)
American Jewish Committee	Civil society	US	David Harris
B'nai Brith	Civil society	US	Dan Mariaschin
Board of Deputies	Civil society	Britain	Vivian Wineman
British parliament	State	Britain	Alistair Burt
Canadian parliament	State	Canada	Irwin Cotler
Conference of Presidents	Civil society	US	Malcolm Hoenlein
Fair Play Campaign Group / Israel Advocacy Forum	Hybrid forum	Britain	Arieh Kovler
Israel on Campus Coalition	Civil society	US	Stephen Kupperberg
Israeli Ministry of Foreign Affairs	State	Israel	Danny Ayalon
Israeli Ministry of Strategic Affairs	State	Israel	Yosef Kuperwasser
Israeli Prime Minister's Office	State	Israel	Benjamin Netanyahu
(+ four more Israeli government ministries)	State	Israel	-
Italian parliament	State	Italy	Fiamma Nirenstein
Jerusalem Center for Public Affairs	Civil society	Israel	Dore Gold
Jewish Agency for Israel	National institution	Israel	Natan Sharansky
Jewish Federations of North America	Civil society	US	William Daroff
Jewish Leadership Council	Civil society	Britain	Jeremy Newmark
World Jewish Congress	Civil society	US / global	Dan Diker & Maram Stern

Table 2.1: Bodies known to have participated in the Global Coalition for Israel

Concert and the Ministry of Strategic Affairs

In 2015, the Israeli government gave its Ministry of Strategic Affairs – following a turf war with the Ministry of Foreign Affairs – overall responsibility for leading the global fight against BDS.[61] Initially granted an annual budget of £20 million (NIS 100 million),[62] the sum allocated by the Israeli government to the ministry's global anti-BDS fight would rise to more than £50 million by 2017.[63] The Strategic Affairs Ministry had close links to Israeli intelligence. Early director general Yosef 'Yossi' Kuperwasser, also a key figure in the Global Coalition for Israel, was formerly head of research at Israel's military intelligence body Aman – historically the largest of the country's intelligence agencies.[64] At Aman, Kuperwasser had supported the 2011 establishment of a department reportedly tasked with 'monitor[ing] Western groups involved in boycotting Israel' and gathering information about their activities.[65] At the Strategic Affairs Ministry, he continued this work, conceiving a plan for 'aggressive legal and media campaigns'. Meanwhile, Israeli politician Gilad Erdan, who served as minister for strategic affairs between 2015 and 2020, met with senior officials from Israel's Mossad intelligence agency – known for its extensive and often brutal covert activities, including targeted assassinations – to discuss 'the struggle against the boycott'.[66]

The reason Israel was turning to a range of darker, more offensive strategies was in part that increased funding for propaganda had, on its own, proven insufficient to stem the growth of the BDS movement. A leaked 2017 report, for instance, noted that despite a twentyfold increase in money spent on combating the Palestine solidarity movement over six years, 'results remain elusive.'[67] The Reut Institute and others advocated for Mossad-style tactics, calling on the Israeli government to 'sabotage' BDS movement 'catalysts'.[68] Sure enough, the ministry adopted an increasingly aggressive approach involving surveillance and intelligence gathering, compiling blacklists of BDS supporters to be denied entry to Israel,[69] buying anti-BDS coverage in newspapers,[70] and – according to veteran Israeli intelligence analyst Yossi Melman – so-called black ops too.[71] Specifically, Melman has claimed that the ministry's work likely includes harassment, defamation campaigns and infringing on the privacy of BDS activists, as well as cyber-attacks on pro-Palestinian websites. Even the possibility that death threats made to Palestinian human rights activists were the Israeli government's doing, he claims, 'cannot be ruled out'.[72] There may even have been a link to the machinations in Britain in which Shai Masot schemed to 'take down' members of Parliament critical of Israel, since some sources – notably the Israeli Embassy in London itself – suggested he had been working for Erdan's ministry at the time.[73] It is also known that as well as authorising the Israeli spyware firm NSO to sell its technology to human rights–abusing states around the world, from Saudi Arabia to Mexico, the Israeli government itself deployed the tool against Palestinian human rights defenders.[74] It is possible the spyware technology has also been used against BDS activists overseas.

Unsurprisingly given its tactics, the Strategic Affairs Ministry operated with a high degree of secrecy. Its location and staff members – mostly former intelligence officials – remained a state secret.[75] Kuperwasser's successor, former military intelligence brigadier general Sima Vaknin-Gil, said she hoped most of the ministry's work would stay 'under the radar' and remain 'classified' because of its 'sensitivities'. 'If you want to win the campaign you have to do it with a great deal of ambiguity,' she declared.[76] Erdan, too, felt the ministry's activities should remain opaque and exempt from freedom of information legislation. He spelt out why at a July 2017 plenum in the Israeli parliament:

> One of the principles for success is keeping our methods of action secret . . . Since most of the ministry's actions are not of the ministry, but through bodies around the world who do not want to expose their connection with the state, we must protect the information whose exposure could harm the battle.[77]

Many of the bodies concerned with keeping their ties to the ministry under wraps were civil society organisations cooperating with the Israeli government across state–private networks. The government, it soon transpired, had been channelling funds to many pro-Israel groups, in a manner reminiscent of South African apartheid, via a dedicated anti-BDS company called 'Concert'.

Originally named Kela Shlomo ('Solomon's Sling'), Concert was first established in 2017 and rebranded soon after. Yet again, former ministry director-general Yossi Kuperwasser was, as a co-founder, centrally involved. Like the Global Coalition for Israel before it, the company was described by its leading personnel as a 'public–private partnership'.[78] In practice, though it had an independent board, the Ministry of Strategic Affairs director-general chaired its steering committee.[79] Concert's purpose was to serve as a mediating buffer so that the Israeli government could provide grants to pro-Israel civil society bodies but do so *indirectly*. As an Israeli government report noted, civil society groups' pro-Israel propaganda was 'seen to be independent and authentic' rather than an 'element of the government's activity'. Since perceived independence was 'a factor that determines the effectiveness of the Hasbara', it observed, 'third parties abroad may prefer to avoid direct engagement with the government'.[80]

Collaboration with wealthy supporters of Israel was an established pattern. Echoing some of the US government's Cold War tactics, the Israeli government had long co-funded the pro-Israel group Birthright – which offers free trips to Israel for young Jewish people – in partnership with businessmen Michael Steinhardt and Charles Bronfman.[81] Similarly, the Ministry of Strategic Affairs openly teamed up with the now-deceased casino magnate and billionaire Sheldon Adelson – in his lifetime a donor to the election campaigns of both Donald Trump and Benjamin Netanyahu – to produce an app called Act.IL which 'game-ified' internet Israel advocacy for its users in order to influence online discourse.[82] In June 2015, after consulting with Israeli officials, Adelson also hosted a private Las Vegas fundraising meeting. The gathering, at which Netanyahu spoke, was also attended by entertainment mogul and Democratic donor Haim Saban and real estate developer Adam Milstein, and raised £15–40 million for fifty Zionist advocacy groups.[83]

Concert, however, aimed to take such collaborations to new heights and was less transparent. The company is known to have distributed around £7.8 million to Zionist groups over three years.

Over half of this went to US-based groups, including $1 million each to Christians United For Israel and the aforementioned Hasbara Fellowships, with most of the money reportedly earmarked to fund chartered trips to Israel. However, although the Strategic Affairs Ministry pledged to match-fund contributions up to approximately £30 million (NIS 128 million) over four years, as a public–private partnership Concert was expected to raise half its own budget and struggled to do so.[84] Nonetheless, the company outlived the Ministry of Strategic Affairs, which was wound down when the Israeli government gave the anti-BDS remit back to the Ministry of Foreign Affairs in late 2021. In January 2022, Israeli investigative journalism site *Seventh Eye* reported that Foreign Minister Yair Lapid planned to inject new funding into Concert and keep the project alive until at least the end of 2025, led by Deputy Foreign Minister Idan Roll.[85] Outgoing director-general Tzahi Gavrieli declared, 'We have to keep fighting . . . we have to operate civil society networks,' while Foreign Ministry spokesperson Lior Hayat said the Israeli government would continue 'promoting partnerships with civil society in Israel and around the world'.[86]

Anti-BDS 'lawfare'

In their struggle to counter the BDS movement, the Israeli government and its friends in the Zionist movement have often deployed 'lawfare' – a term used in this book to refer to a wide range of legal means to achieve repressive political goals. Sketching out the global context for pro-Israel lawfare initiatives will help to make sense of their deployment in Britain, scrutinised in chapter 6. Two key lawfare fronts which have been advanced around the world are examined here: firstly, attempts to outlaw BDS and, secondly, efforts to prosecute BDS supporters in court.

Since at least 2010, Zionist movement strategists contemplated working to pass new anti-boycott laws to counter BDS. One strategy document presented at the Herzliya Conference that year advocated the mobilisation of 'existing friendly NGOs' to engage in 'efforts to amend current legislation'.[87] Similarly, in 2011, Israel's Institute for

National Security Studies called for 'undermining and blocking BDS activity through national legislation' in the US and Europe.[88] And at the Global Coalition for Israel in 2014, World Jewish Congress president Ronald Lauder declared, 'We will draft and lobby for legislation.'[89] As American Zionist campaigner Noah Pollack, of the Emergency Committee for Israel, explained, 'Part of the idea behind moving the battleground to state legislatures is to find more favorable turf.' While Israel was losing the debate in civil society, for instance among young people on university campuses, the Zionist movement – as a social movement from above – enjoyed superior access to state power compared to the BDS movement. Sneering at BDS activists, Pollack added: 'While you were doing your campus antics, the grown-ups were in the state legislatures passing laws that make your cause improbable.'[90]

In February 2016, Strategic Affairs Minister Gilad Erdan declared that the battle against BDS was about to become 'a whole new ball game'.[91] That same month, a Foreign Affairs spokesperson stated that the government had 'stepped up our efforts directly and indirectly, dealing with friends of Israel in a variety of countries in which we have the BDS movement, fighting it with legal instruments'.[92] In other words, pressure for anti-BDS legislation was being pursued on two fronts. On the one hand, the Israeli government itself was lobbying allied governments around the world to implement new laws. On another, parallel track, 'friends of Israel' made similar calls 'indirectly' from the sphere of civil society. Some of the groups lobbying for anti-BDS legislation, such as Christian Zionist organisation Proclaiming Justice to the Nations – reportedly 'the driving force' behind anti-BDS legislation in Tennessee, the first US state to pass such a law in April 2015 – had received funding, via Concert, from Israel's Ministry of Strategic Affairs.[93]

This two-pronged lobbying effort proved highly effective. In the space of eighteen months, a flurry of national and regional governments passed new measures to make holding Israel accountable through boycotts or divestment harder. By October 2017, more than twenty US states had enacted legislation which either blacklisted, divested from or barred from public contracts any company deemed to be complying with BDS.[94] By July 2020, that number had risen to thirty – a development for which Erdan explicitly claimed credit.[95] A range of other powerful Western states, including Canada, Germany and France, also implemented various anti-BDS measures.

Meanwhile, each of these countries also witnessed an uptick in another type of lawfare: direct legal attacks on BDS supporters. The evidence shows that state–private networks and outsourcing to the private sector are key traits of this second type of contemporary pro-Israel lawfare, which emerged initially as a counter-terrorism strategy.[96] As American legal scholar Orde Kittrie explains, 'public–private lawfare partnerships', which have been 'typical' of contemporary Israeli lawfare are, 'at their most effective, from the perspective of the government, when the instigating government's hand is relatively hidden'. Accordingly, he observes, the Israeli government 'has rarely, if ever, been at the forefront of an offensive lawfare deployment', yet 'Israeli officials have sometimes quietly (but on the public record) provided information to private sector litigators'.[97] This way of working combines the resources and power of government with the access and flexibility of private actors, while simultaneously transferring risk away from officials and making such actions deniable. The state's 'most prominent partner' in this type of lawfare has been Shurat HaDin, an Israeli law firm with 'deep ties to the Israeli government'.[98]

Established in 2003, Shurat HaDin is arguably the prototype for state–private cooperation on contemporary Zionist lawfare. The law firm counts right-wing philanthropist Adam Milstein and Christian Zionist pastor John Hagee among its US donors, but from its inception – as cables published by WikiLeaks revealed – the firm 'took direction . . . on which cases to pursue' from Israeli intelligence agencies.[99] Interestingly, Shurat HaDin's own account of its utility to the Israeli government echoes very closely David Ben-Gurion's observations about the value of the Zionist movement vis-à-vis the Israeli state and Strategic Affairs Minister Erdan's comments about relative advantages of state and non-state actors. The firm's director, Nitsana Darshan-Leitner, noted at a 2012 Washington, DC, event that the Israeli government 'has some constraints . . . and they cannot do what private lawyers can do'.[100] By contrast, as a non-governmental organisation operating in the private sector, Shurat HaDin was positioned to undertake actions that the Israeli government is unable to formally engage in. We are not constrained by political pressures, diplomatic relations, nor international treaties. As such, we are able to act unapologetically against the enemies of the Jewish State.

The firm's notable early work involved bringing cases against alleged funders of terrorism – 'bankrupting terrorism one lawsuit at a time'. By its own account, it became involved in this work after being 'approached' by operatives from Tziltzal ('Harpoon'), a secretive anti-terror financing operation founded by ex–Mossad director Meir Dagan in the Prime Minister's Office.[101] A case against the Bank of China, for example, was said to have been 'initiated following an Israeli government request'.[102] However, as well as targeting alleged terrorists and their funding networks, Shurat HaDin soon began specialising in targeting advocates of the non-violent BDS movement and other supporters of Palestinian rights.

In 2011, Shurat HaDin worked with the Israeli Prime Minister's Office to impede a flotilla of ships on a solidarity mission aiming to break the siege of Gaza, successfully preventing all but one of the boats from leaving Greek ports.[103] In 2018, the firm sued the home-sharing platform Airbnb after it removed listings located in illegal West Bank settlements, eventually prompting the company to reverse its decision.[104] Then, in 2019, the Ministry of Strategic Affairs – with whom Shurat HaDin has confirmed it collaborates[105] – claimed credit for the closures of thirty pro-BDS organisations' bank accounts, or other financial services, in the preceding two years.[106] Shurat HaDin had helped in the case of the Palestinian Boycott National Committee, which had its online fundraising platform shut down following legal allegations of links to terrorism, documented in a report produced by the ministry called *Terrorists in Suits*.[107] However, while it was the most prominent pro-Israel lawfare actor, Shurat HaDin was by no means alone.

As early as 2011, StandWithUs reportedly held a coordinating meeting with Israeli officials in its legal case against a Washington State food cooperative boycotting Israeli goods.[108] In 2016, Shurat HaDin held a Jerusalem seminar 'to train lawyers from abroad to litigate BDS' and disseminate its honed techniques to other pro-Israel actors.[109] In 2015, another significant lawfare contractor, the International Legal Forum – which has been directly funded by the Ministry of Strategic Affairs – brought legal action against several Spanish cities which had passed resolutions supporting BDS and secured the rollback of two such decisions.[110] Subsequently, the Ministry of Strategic Affairs announced that it would fund the law firm to establish the 'Legal Network Initiative', through which grants of up to £143,000 would be disseminated to other actors bringing anti-BDS actions.[111] Thus, revelations published in *Haaretz* in 2017 that the Israeli government had for some time been 'outsourcing' counter-BDS legal work in Europe and North America to private law firms were consistent with an established pattern, to which we will return in the British context in chapter 6.[112]

The US Zionist movement

The final stop on this tour of Israel's global backlash campaign against Palestine solidarity requires a brief visit to the US, which deserves specific scrutiny due its status as the primary sponsor of Israel and the considerable parallels with the Zionist movement in Britain.

The US Zionist movement has a strong track record of cooperation with Israel across state–private networks. The best-known group, AIPAC, was founded in 1951 by Isaiah Kenen, a former Israeli Ministry of Foreign Affairs representative. It has played a key role in cultivating bipartisan support for Israel on Capitol Hill and draws many members of the American political elite, including US presidential hopefuls, to its annual conference, alongside thousands of activists. During the mid-1970s, when combating the Arab League boycott of Israel, the Israeli government's strategy was 'not to act, but to activate'[113] civil society bodies, in line with the principles of new public diplomacy. Economic scholar Gil Feiler records that AIPAC was among the US pro-Israel bodies that the Israel government 'decided . . . to mobilize' to this end.[114] Similarly, when fighting the BDS movement today, the Ministry of Strategic Affairs has held discussions about whether to 'activate' AIPAC and other pro-Israel US lobby groups.[115]

Other contemporary US pro-Israel groups with varying degrees of closeness to the Israeli government include StandWithUs, which coordinates closely with the Israeli government; the Israel Project, a now-defunct body whose vice-president was former Israeli diplomat Lior Weintraub; Hasbara Fellowships, a project of religious Zionist body Aish HaTorah supported by Israeli government funding; and HonestReporting, also established by Aish HaTorah with support from Israeli ambassador Lenny Ben-David.[116] Meanwhile, the Israel on Campus Coalition, which boasts that it models its work on counterinsurgency strategy, a military doctrine first developed by British colonial leaders, says it 'communicates' with the Ministry of Strategic Affairs.[117] It has adopted some of the ministry's murkier tactics, such as reportedly gathering intelligence on student pro-Palestine activists and creating anonymous websites to smear young BDS advocates.[118] Likewise, a group called Canary Mission – which has never confirmed its funders but also says it 'coordinates' with the Israeli government[119] – runs a notorious McCarthyist blacklist website smearing BDS-supporting students as 'racist' in an effort to harm their job prospects.[120]

There have also been tensions across the state–private network. Israeli academic Natan Aridan argues that the Ministry of Foreign Affairs has, since its inception, 'refused to endorse pro-Israel organizations it has deemed either ineffective or unwilling to be "instructed" by Israel's diplomatic representatives'. He cites an example from 1956, where the group American Friends of Israel was informed at a meeting with Israeli diplomat Abba Eban that 'the Government would have to insist on coordination with itself', since 'it was inconceivable that a body organized with the name of Israel should undertake action without reference to the information, the advice and views of the Government of Israel'.[121] Due to its uncooperative attitude, Israeli officials refused to endorse the group, effectively marginalising its Israel-advocacy efforts. This episode was uncannily similar to the treatment of J Street, a liberal Zionist group founded in 2007. In 2009, J Street was put in its place when Israel's Washington, DC, embassy very publicly declined an event invitation, seemingly to express disdain for even the very mild criticisms of Israeli settlements voiced by the group.[122]

In Washington, the Israel lobby 'spends heavily to influence US policy' – according to the *Guardian*, an estimated £16 million ($22 million) on lobbying and campaign contributions in the 2018 election cycle, channelled through political action committees. While far below that spent on lobbying by many sectors of big business, few other nation-states have comparable levels of activity.[123] Yet despite this long-standing pattern of Capital Hill financial contributions – more of which goes to Democrats than Republicans – cracks have nonetheless started to appear in the long-standing bipartisan pro-Israel consensus. This is partly a sign of wider political polarisation. The changing political landscape is perhaps best illustrated by the 2018 election of two Democrats to the House of Representatives who openly endorse the BDS campaign – the first federal elected officials to do so.[124] At the other end of the political spectrum, many pro-Israel groups' have found their support base narrowed to the radical right within the Republican Party, alongside the evangelical Christian Zionist movement. A significant section of the US Zionist movement enthusiastically embraced ex-president Donald Trump, despite his anti-Semitic statements – a development symptomatic of the toxic racial politics at play in contestation over Israel/Palestine today and very pronounced in the US context.

Right-wing Zionism in the US overlaps considerably with the organised Islamophobia movement. Some of the groups implicated include lawfare bodies such as the Lawfare Project, whose director, Brooke Goldstein, has provided legal advice to Dutch politician and notorious Islamophobe Geert Wilders.[125] Other groups deploying racial narratives include some funded by the Ministry of Strategic Affairs, or its front company Concert. For example, the Israel Allies Foundation, a body which has received Israeli government funding and promoted anti-BDS laws in the US, describes itself as promoting support for Israel on the basis of 'Judeo-Christian values'.[126] More explicitly, Laurie Cardoza-Moore, president of Proclaiming Justice to the Nations, has called Islam a 'political system of global domination' and claimed that 30 per cent of American Muslims are terrorists.[127] Meanwhile, organisations like the Institute for the Study of Global Antisemitism and Policy – which in 2018 received Israeli government funding accounting for almost 80 per cent of its annual revenue – have promoted the 'new anti-Semitism' thesis, which conflates criticism of Israeli apartheid or Zionism with anti-Semitism.[128]

Simultaneously, Jewish communities in the US, as in Britain, are increasingly turning away from Israel. Some established Jewish community organisations continue to argue that lobbying for Israel is part of their mandate; notably, the Conference of Presidents of Major American Jewish Organizations, an umbrella body bringing together more than fifty American Jewish and Zionist groups.[129] However, support for Israel has been evaporating rapidly among younger generations, a shift indicative of the crisis of Zionism discussed earlier. The growth of pro-Palestinian group Jewish Voice for Peace – which has explicitly critiqued Zionism[130] – and the emergence in 2021 of the 'Open Hillel' movement, a counterweight to the explicitly pro-Israel politics of the mainstream Jewish student group Hillel, illustrate the growing disillusionment of younger American Jews with Israel.

Palestinian liberation has, meanwhile, become a central pillar of progressive movements in the US, making it increasingly untenable today to be progressive 'except for Palestine'.[131] While Israel advocacy, as a social movement from above, is strongly aligned with other conservative causes – and some pro-Israel donors also fund climate change denialism and anti-LGBTQ+ activism[132] – Palestine solidarity is deeply embedded in wider anti-racism and social justice struggles. Notably, in 2016 the Black Lives Matter movement made condemnation of Israeli apartheid a key plank of its internationalist global agenda and officially endorsed BDS, building on a rich lineage of Black–Palestinian solidarity.[133]

Having mapped out the global and US contexts, this book now turns to British pro-Israel activism. We will see how the crisis of Zionism expresses itself domestically in similar ways, and how civil society actors working across state–private networks are key to the backlash against the BDS movement, including its lawfare elements. The next chapter traces the evolution of the British Zionist movement over time, through the lens of its struggle against the Arab League boycott.

3

Evolution of the British Zionist Movement

'Jaffa is beautiful . . . There's nothing else like it,' says Palestinian Salwa Naser, recalling her family's seaside home in the Ajami neighbourhood of the port town Jaffa. 'Our house was right next to the sea . . . We'd play by the sea every single day.' Now an elderly woman, Salwa was six years old when she and her family were forced to flee their home in the 1948 Nakba. 'I remember when the violence all started,' she says, explaining that one morning, an explosion shattered the windows of her classroom. 'I'm still sad about my school . . . the food was good, our uniforms were cute.' After the bombing near the school, Salwa's father decided there was no option for the family but to leave, via boat, to Lebanon. 'I remember it like it was yesterday. We left in the middle of the night. My mother walked us down the stairs to the port to a boat. There were tens of other families doing the same thing.' As they boarded the boat, Salwa's mother began to cry. 'When we asked her what was wrong, she said: "We're leaving . . . I just will miss our home," and then leaned over to my oldest brother and said "I'm not sure we'll ever see home again."' As they made it further out to sea, the boat stopped. The city was on fire. 'That's when my mother really started crying.' Salwa now lives in a small breeze-block room in the Shatila refugee camp in Lebanon. Built in 1949 and originally intended as temporary housing for around 3,000 people, it is now home to over 20,000 people – three generations of Palestinian refugees who Israel has prevented from returning. But, Salwa explains, 'Jaffa will always be home.'[1]

Over 750,000 Palestinians like Salwa and her family were ethnically cleansed from historic Palestine.[2] Their dispossession was necessary from the point of view of the Zionist military forces intent on ensuring a Jewish demographic majority in the new state of Israel. However, the lobby group Britain Israel Communications and Research Centre (BICOM) tells a different story, promoting the Nakba denialism still common today within Israel itself. In 1948, the British pro-Israel organisation agrees, 'the Arab population of Palestine left in large numbers for neighbouring Arab states'. But, it claims, 'there was no deliberate, coordinated Jewish policy to expel the Arabs'.[3] As well as undermining Palestinian refugees' right to return, BICOM also calls Jerusalem 'the capital of Israel', rejecting the notion that Israel should relinquish control of any part of the city – which it wholly occupied in 1967 and annexed in 1980. Taking the Israeli government position that the occupied territories are merely 'disputed',[4] BICOM refers to illegal settlements built on stolen Palestinian land in the West Bank as 'communities' or 'neighbourhoods', rejecting the idea that they should be dismantled. The group justifies these positions by saying that 'most Israelis would not be willing to contemplate' such moves, despite the fact that international law (the Fourth Geneva Convention) proscribes the transfer of a civilian population into occupied territory. On legalised discrimination against Palestinians, BICOM merely concedes that 'as in other societies, minority groups still suffer from inequalities'.[5] BICOM is an important British pro-Israel lobby group, but it is only part of a wider network of Zionist organisations in Britain which seek to defend and uphold Israeli apartheid.

Fighting the Arab League boycott

Just as the pro-Israel movement in Britain can only be properly understood by way of reference to the wider Israeli government and Zionist movement strategies mapped out in the previous chapter, it is equally important to situate the lobby historically. In order to grasp how the infrastructure of the British Zionist movement has developed over time and how various actors have both competed and cooperated, it is useful to use a case study – and in the process introduce some key pro-Israel groups. Since contemporary support for Israel often expresses itself through work to undermine and repress the BDS movement (examples of which later chapters will explore in depth), it is instructive to examine how the British Zionist movement organised against a boycott of Israel from a previous era.

The so-called Arab boycott was initiated in 1945, when states from the recently established Arab League, including Egypt, Syria, Jordan, and Lebanon, began boycotting products made by the *yishuv* in Palestine. In 1951, the Arab League states tightened their boycott of the newly founded state of Israel.[6] This boycott campaign, then, was a top-down, state-led initiative enforced by governments, sometimes using punitive means. It focused almost exclusively on impacting Israel economically and succeeded, for years, in reducing foreign investment to Israel. In the early 1990s, the Federation of Israeli Chambers of Commerce estimated the forty-year cost of the boycott to Israel at $45 billion.[7] However, it had little influence beyond the Middle East, and on occasion it was expressed in anti-Semitic ways, leading to the targeting of individuals because of their Jewish identity. As such, the Arab League boycott was a very different creature to the contemporary BDS movement, which is a bottom-up, civil society–led initiative instigated by Palestinians themselves, based on moral persuasion and founded on firmly anti-racist principles. The respective Zionist counter-campaigns, then and now, however, exhibit distinct parallels. In particular, they show consistent cooperation between a clutch of key organisations across state–private networks.

One such organisation was the Board of Deputies of British Jews (henceforth 'the Board'), Britain's oldest Jewish political organis-ation, founded in 1760.[8] The Board has over 300 member organisations who democratically elect representatives, known as 'deputies'.[9] As former president Vivian Wineman puts it, the Board seeks to act as a 'parliament for the [Jewish] community'. Indeed, it is important to acknowledge the positive work that the organisation does for British Jewish communities.[10] Yet, despite Zionism's status as an increas-ingly divisive issue within the Jewish community, and despite a major study by the Institute for Jewish Policy Research finding that 'extremely few' British Jewish respondents felt communal bodies 'should regularly make representations to the British government on Israel's behalf',[11] the Board's leadership today also actively supports Israel. In its 2020 trustees report, the Board described having a 'close working relationship with the Embassy of Israel in the UK . . . and strengthened links to the Israeli Ministry of Strategic Affairs and the IDF [Israel Defense Forces]'.[12] Its current constitution commits it to advancing 'Israel's security, welfare and standing', and its 'International Division' is principally concerned with Israel advocacy. As recent Board president Jonathan Arkush states explicitly: 'We lobby unashamedly for Israel.'[13] On this basis, the Board can be considered part of the contemporary British Zionist movement that contributes to the maintenance of Israel's apartheid policies.

Originally, however, the Board was critical of Zionism. As sociologist Keith Kahn-Harris explains, 'anti-Zionism was once a commonly held, respectable position in Anglo-Jewry'.[14] The Board's leadership remained ambivalent or even hostile towards the Zionist movement for several decades and opposed the Balfour Declaration in 1917[15] (as did the only Jewish member of the cabinet, Edwin Montagu).[16] From the 1930s onwards, though, in the wake of growing persecution of Jews in Europe culminating in the Nazi Holocaust, the appeal of Zionism's promise of a Jewish state as a safe haven unsurprisingly grew more attractive.[17] By World War II, the Board took an 'unequivocally pro-Zionist' stance and, according to Kahn-Harris, the Zionist movement 'effected the "capture" of the Board at its triennial elections of June 1943'[18] (though other sources date this shift to 1939).[19] What non-Zionists called the 'Zionification' of the Board was certainly firmly consolidated by the time Israel was established in 1948.[20]

The Board's archives in London contain documents charting the history of its involvement in the Zionist counter-campaign against the Arab League boycott. These records show that in 1956, a few years after the Israeli government established a dedicated unit within the Ministry of Foreign Affairs focused on combating the boycott, the Board called a meeting of British pro-Israel groups in London. As a result, a coordinating body called the 'Special Purpose Committee' was established to counter manifestations of the boycott in Britain. Mapping out the members of this committee provides insight into the interlocking institutions at the heart of the British Zionist movement during this period. Table 3.1 shows the key organisations represented.

Organisation	Type	Country	Representative(s)
Anglo-Israel Chamber of Commerce	Civil society	Britain	Allan Burke
Board of Deputies	Civil society	Britain	Barnett Janner, Sidney Salomon, Martin Savitt, John Dight
Israeli embassy	State	Britain/ Israel	Michael Palgi
Jewish Agency	National institution affiliate	Britain/ Israel	Schneier Levenberg
Labour Party (MPs)	State	Britain	Maurice Orbach, Barnett Janner
Poale Zion (Great Britain)	Civil society	Britain	Maurice Orbach, Schneier Levenberg
Trades Advisory Council	Civil society	Britain	Maurice Orbach
Zionist Federation	National institution affiliate	Britain/ Israel	Barnett Janner, Monty Schaffer

Table 3.1. Members of the Special Purpose Committee circa 1956

As well as four representatives from the Board, affiliates of two of Israel's 'national institutions' – which, as chapter 1 explained, form the backbone of the Zionist movement – sat on the Special Purpose Committee. One was the Zionist Federation of Great Britain and Ireland, formed in 1899, shortly after its parent body, the World Zionist Federation – partly because Theodor Herzl's first two visits to England failed to win significant support from the leadership of Anglo-Jewry. It was to the Zionist Federation, over a century ago, that British foreign secretary Arthur Balfour asked Lord Rothschild to communicate the seminal Balfour Declaration, signalling the British government's support for Jewish statehood – a goal which the organisation played a pivotal role in achieving.[21] One of the Zionist Federation's earliest presidents, Manchester-based Chaim

Weizmann, went on to become president of the World Zionist Organization and later of Israel itself.[22] Today, while the organisation remains active and relevant due to its close ties to Israel across state–private networks (it often organises events jointly with the World Zionist Organisation or Israeli Embassy in London),[23] its own members have dwindled from 120 organisations to thirty, and its importance in the British pro-Israel landscape has diminished relative to newer groups. Nonetheless, it is active in combating BDS today as it was in combating the Arab League boycott in the era of the Special Purpose Committee. Meanwhile, the Jewish Agency's British affiliate on the committee was Schneier Levenberg, also at the time a prominent member of Poale Zion (a precursor of the Jewish Labour Movement, described in chapter 4).

Two Labour members of Parliament – Maurice Orbach (also of Poale Zion) and Barnett Janner (simultaneously president of both the Board and the Zionist Federation) – were also involved in the Special Purpose Committee. In 1957, Orbach and Janner would become, respectively, a founder and key member of Labour Friends of Israel (also described in chapter 4).[24] Other members of the committee included representatives of the Anglo-Israel Chamber of Commerce (a precursor of the contemporary body UK Israel Business) and the Trades Advisory Council, a body set up in 1940 by the Board to combat anti-Semitism in business. Finally but significantly, a representative from Israel's London embassy also sat on the Special Purpose Committee. Minutes of the committee's meetings show that close communication across the state–private network occurred, yet considerable tensions were experienced too.

Records of the committee's meetings show that Zionist civil society groups were often frustrated with the Israeli embassy, since it was – perhaps surprisingly – seeking to *restrain* rather than mobilise anti-boycott activism in Britain during this period. The Board's John Dight complained that the embassy had imposed 'virtually an embargo on anti-boycott action by the Committee', and the Zionist Federation's Monty Schaffer lamented that 'cold water was thrown upon every move made in the direction of countering the Arab-boycott' by the embassy.[25] Israeli officials, economic scholar Gil Feiler explains, were wrestling with a dilemma: on the one hand, they 'did not want to create the impression that the Arab boycott was more than a minor irritant, by giving publicity to its successes', yet on the other, they 'could not ignore the real economic damage'.[26] The Israeli embassy's apparent diffidence, therefore, was likely a strategic calculation about how best to combat the boycott without running the risk of increasing its potential impact. It favoured discrete, targeted interventions but sought to restrain the London-based committee from autonomous anti-boycott campaigning. For instance, minutes of a June 1959 meeting at the embassy record that the embassy proffered advice to Dight and fellow Special Purpose Committee representative Sidney Salomon on which companies should – and should not – be lobbied.[27]

The notes of these meetings suggest that Special Purpose Committee members demonstrated considerable willingness to defer to the government of Israel's representatives in London. There appears, then, to have been a degree of informal, unspoken hierarchy in the state–private relationship. Indeed, Feiler mentions a British anti-boycott outfit established in 1956 which operated 'under the guidance' of the Israeli Embassy in London, possibly a reference to the Special Purpose Committee.[28] It bears repeating here that this cooperation does not render Israel's British supporters 'foreign agents'. It affirms, however, historian Natan Aridan's point, cited previously, that the Israeli government has always held the power to legitimise and empower certain cooperative pro-Israel groups, while also being ready and willing to marginalise or undermine the Israel-advocacy efforts of other actors.

The Prittie and Nelson programme

Thanks to its alignment with Western imperialism, Israel had significant capacity to withstand the economic war of attrition waged by Arab League states through their boycott campaign. Indeed, by the time Labour leader Harold Wilson condemned the boycott in 1964, Zionist concern about the campaign had significantly subsided. Moreover, the subsequent period between 1967 and 1973 was a time of 'unprecedented economic prosperity' for Israel, as it developed an economy which could flourish even in near-permanent war, including major arms industries.[29] However, in the mid-1970s – following the 1973 oil price crisis, when oil-rich nations wielded heightened economic power – there was a renewal of intense Arab League boycott activity.

In 1975, the Israeli government responded by establishing an 'Economic Warfare Authority' which had staff in both Israel and the US. Its role, according to legal scholar Dan Chill, was to 'coordinate international political, economic, and communal reaction to the boycott's efforts throughout the world'.[30] As such, it was arguably the precursor to the Ministry of Strategic Affairs, which, as chapter 2 explained, has played the same role in recent years coordinating international efforts to counter the BDS movement. The unit was linked to a hybrid 'public committee' made up of state and non-state actors, including representatives of industry and officials from the Ministry of Foreign Affairs, which to a lesser extent bears some resemblance to the Global Coalition for Israel.[31] According to Danny Halperin, one of the Economic Warfare Authority's leading figures, its core strategy was 'not to act, but to activate'. In other words, it worked to mobilise Israel's friends in civil society.[32]

In the US, this anti-boycott strategy proved effective. The Zionist organisations which led the campaign formed a 'united front',[33] constituting an effective coalition that managed to advance anti-boycott legislation.[34] In Britain, by contrast, anti-boycott progress remained minimal. For instance, in April 1975, when a delegation from the Board including Barnett Janner and Schneier Levenberg – who nineteen years earlier had been founding members of the by-now-defunct Special Purpose Committee – lobbied the secretary of state for trade on the issue, the minister would merely reiterate the British government's nominal opposition to all boycotts other than those sponsored by the UN.[35] Here, then, the pro-Israel lobby's efforts proved ineffective. British Zionist campaigners rightly concluded that their government did not want to jeopardise its trade interests in the Arab world 'or impede the flow of Arab capital into Britain'.[36] The problem was certainly *not* that British Zionist campaigners had failed to show a united front of their own.

In 1975, a body called the Anti-Boycott Co-ordinating (ABC) Committee, was established. A direct descendant of the Special Purpose Committee, it was modelled on the blueprint the latter had provided for collective anti-boycott organising. By bringing together key players from the major British Zionist organisations, the ABC Committee constituted the institutional power base for concerted action against the Arab League campaign in this period. Table 3.2 enumerates these people and organisations. The network reveals a considerable degree of institutional continuity in the British Zionist movement. Collaboration between pro-Israel civil society organisations and the Israeli embassy across the state–private networks persisted, and six organisations which had been represented on the Special Purpose Committee in the 1950s – the embassy, the Zionist Federation, the Board of Deputies, Poale Zion, the Anglo-Israel Chamber of Commerce, and the Trades Advisory Council – were represented on the ABC Committee too.

Also present at early ABC Committee meetings were B'nai B'rith, a Jewish organisation founded in 1843 which describes itself as a 'staunch supporter and defender of Israel';[37] the Institute for Jewish Affairs, set up by the World Jewish Congress; the British Overseas Trade Group for Israel; the Histadrut, Israel's national trade union body; and finally an ardent Christian Zionist named Terence Prittie. A former *Guardian* journalist turned PR professional, Prittie was the editor of the pro-Israel publication *Britain and Israel* and would play a critical role in formulating the ABC Committee's strategy for action.[38]

Through *Britain and Israel*, Prittie contracted the services of an American PR consultant named Walter Henry Nelson to help combat the boycott. Introducing him to the ABC Committee, Prittie described Nelson as 'eminently suited' to carrying out the work required.[39] Notably, the transferable experience Nelson brought to the role included formerly working in US military intelligence.[40] During that time, Nelson had reportedly co-founded Radio Free Europe, the partly CIA-funded Cold War–era psy-ops propaganda station.[41] Together on the ABC Committee, the pair developed a plan, referred to as the 'Prittie and Nelson Programme', in close cooperation with the Israeli embassy. Prittie told the committee that 'the full blessing and cooperation of the Israeli government, and of its representatives in London' would be needed for the plan to succeed.[42] That approval was given formally at a 12 June 1975 meeting of the ABC Committee – though Nelson had already discussed Prittie's plan with the embassy before presenting it to the committee.[43]

Organisation	Type	Country	Representative(s)
Anglo-Israel Chamber of Commerce	Civil society	Britain	Harry Schwab, Justin Kornberg, Lewis Goodman, Allan Burke
B'nai B'rith (Great Britain)	Civil society	Britain	Hayim Pinner, Fred Worms
Board of Deputies	Civil society	Britain	Martin Savitt, Jacob Gerwirtz
Britain & Israel	Civil society	Britain	Terence Prittie, Walter Henry Nelson
British Overseas Trade Group for Israel	Civil society	Britain	Lewis Goodman
Histadrut	Civil society	Israel	B. Wangar
Israeli Embassy	State	Britain/ Israel	Amos Lavee, T. Kaddar
Poale Zion (Great Britain)	Civil society	Britain	Hayim Pinner
Trades Advisory Council	Civil society	Britain	Jacob Gerwirtz
World Jewish Congress / Institute of Jewish Affairs	Civil society	Global/ Britain	Stephen Roth
Zionist Federation	National institution affiliate	Britain/ Israel	Zvi Reisman

Table 3.2. Members of the Anti-Boycott Coordinating (ABC) Committee circa 1975

The Prittie and Nelson programme was a plan to combat the boycott in all of Britain's key political arenas. A principal tactic was 'steady and persistent canvassing' of MPs and 'mobilising our friends' in parliament, especially the Labour, Liberal Democrat and at that point recently founded Conservative Friends of Israel groups.[44] Also in the committee's sights, however, were academia, churches, think-tanks, trade unions and the press; the plan listed in minute detail how to approach targets in each key sphere of society. To execute their strategy, the groups represented on the ABC Committee agreed upon a division of labour: the Board would carry out legal and parliamentary work; the Britain and Israel office assumed responsibility for public relations; and B'nai B'rith was to use its branches throughout the country as 'listening posts' for information about boycott activities. The cost was also shared. Prittie estimated that establishing the new PR bureau would require 'at least £10,000 per annum[45] (equivalent to around £75,000 today). Towards this, five key Zionist groups on the ABC Committee (the Zionist Federation, the Board, the Anglo-Israel Chamber of Commerce, B'nai B'rith and *Britain and Israel*) agreed to raise £2,000 each.[46]

While the ABC Committee's individual member organisations – spanning the gamut of British Zionist institutions – commanded varying financial resources, the committee as a whole enjoyed the support of some prominent businessmen. ABC meetings would sometimes be held at Michael House on Baker Street, the London headquarters of retailer Marks & Spencer, which was run by two prominent Zionist families, the Sieffs and the Marks. It was during this same period of intense anti-boycott organising that two men closely connected to Marks & Spencer, Lord Sieff and Michael Sacher, helped to initiate and fund a new pro-Israel body to augment the efforts of the ABC Committee's member groups. Sacher was president of the United Jewish Israel Appeal (originally founded in 1920 as the United Palestine Appeal, then known as the Joint Israel Appeal). With Sieff, he set up BIPAC (the British-Israel Public Affairs Committee) in May 1976, intending for it to emulate AIPAC in the US. BIPAC's first chair was Eric Moonman, who – like Barnett Janner before him – was a Labour MP and well-connected Zionist leader, simultaneously serving as Zionist Federation chair.[47]

Yet, however strategic and zealous the activities of the ABC Committee and BIPAC were, they were ultimately far less signi-ficant than geopolitical events in determining the fate of the Arab League boycott. In 1979, Israel brokered a peace treaty with Egypt, considerably diminishing the impact of the campaign. The sense of urgency around the ABC Committee's activities waned correspondingly. Yet more significantly, an increasingly influential strand of the Zionist movement had begun calling for a peace process, recognising that reducing the 'political stigma' attached to Israel would help to further normalise economic relations. While the Oslo process that ensued in the early 1990s delivered neither justice nor peace – and the situation for Palestinians in fact significantly *deteriorated* during the talks – the negotiations nonetheless achieved a huge amount from Israel's perspective. Those who had spoken of a 'peace dividend' turned out to be right.[48] Foreign direct investment to Israel increased sixfold between 1991 and 1995, and the Arab League boycott was rendered virtually irrelevant.[49]

Similarly in the mid-1990s, the Britain-Israel relationship deepened. Conservative prime minister John Major's administration ended the arms embargo that had been implemented by his predecessor Margaret Thatcher, alongside other European states, following Israel's 1982 invasion of Lebanon.[50] Trade ties and arms industry links blossomed, and Major's government called for increased bilateral investment. Together with Israeli prime minister Yitzhak Rabin, shortly before his assassination, Major established the Israel-Britain Business Council (another forerunner of UK Israel Business), a private sector–driven body supported by the British and Israeli governments which worked to promote economic ties between the two countries.[51] In 1996, British Foreign Office minister Jeremy Hanley told the House of Commons that the government was 'actively encouraging businessmen to ignore the [Arab League] boycott', which, he added, was 'withering on the vine'.[52]

The Oslo process had also precipitated a bifurcation of the British Zionist movement. While BIPAC had flourished in the 1980s, undergoing a process of professionalisation,[53] by the early 1990s it was starting to lose the support of key donors due to its hard-line stance against the negotiations. In contrast, an increasingly influential business-oriented wing of the Zionist movement in tune with Israel's neoliberal turn, including bodies like the British-Israel Chamber of Commerce (as the Anglo-Israel Chamber of Commerce was renamed in 1980), supported the Oslo talks. BIPAC eventually closed in 1999, leaving a significant gap in pro-Israel infrastructure. When the Second Intifada broke out in 2000, that gap was filled, as we shall see, by new groups like BICOM and the Jewish Leadership Council, just as a new and different boycott movement – BDS – was emerging, prompting a renewed wave of anti-boycott organising from British Zionist groups.

A 'big tent for Israel': Fighting BDS

While today less important than the US, Britain is still a critical ally to Israel. Therefore, the consistent growth in British support for Palestinians, noted by postcolonial scholar Bashir Abu-Manneh, has been a cause of considerable concern to Israel.[54] This applies particularly to the growth of the BDS solidarity movement, which academic Arun Kundnani calls the 'largest anti-colonial movement in Britain today'.[55] Indeed, Israel's strategic affairs minister Gilad Erdan has described Britain as 'the world centre' of the BDS campaign, while the Reut Institute think-tank calls London the 'mecca of delegitimization' and stresses the city's 'significant global influence'.[56]

There is little weight to claims made by some commentators that the BDS movement is merely a continuation of the Arab League boycott.[57] Besides their common target and tactic, four major dimensions – normative, geographical, strategic and structural – differentiate BDS. Normatively speaking, the latter explicitly rejects all racial discrimination, including the anti-Semitism which was sometimes a feature of Arab League boycott activities. BDS targets institutions, rather than individuals; and whereas the Arab League boycott was 'not focused on the rights of Palestinians or on international law', BDS is a rights-based movement grounded in international law.[58] In terms of geographical scope, the BDS movement is 'global' and has emerged prominently in Western countries, where the Arab League boycott remained limited to those states.[59] Strategically, as well as advocating economic and trade boycotts to make an impact at the material level, BDS emphasises academic and cultural boycotts, partly as an educational device. Finally, structurally speaking, BDS is a decentralised, civil society–led movement rather than a state-led initiative and has been called for directly by Palestinians themselves.[60]

Despite these significant differences between BDS and the Arab League boycott, the strategies employed by Israel and its supporters to combat it have been remarkably similar. As in previous eras, a centralised hub to coordinate the pro-Israel counter-campaign has been convened. Such bodies speak to the importance of Zionist unity – or at least cooperation – in the face of BDS, which is stressed by several strategists. For example, the challenge of BDS, it was noted at a conference convened by the Israeli Ministry of Foreign Affairs in 2009, 'draws a line in the sand'.[61] In other words, it serves in some ways as a unifying agent among Zionist actors from a wide range of perspectives who disagree on much – but nonetheless all oppose the BDS movement. Similarly, the influential Reut Institute identified the need for a 'broad tent' within the Zionist movement, incorporating different strands of opinion yet with clear 'red lines' around it.[62] This unified bloc, it explained, would allow the Zionist movement to 'drive a wedge' between mere critics of Israel's policies and the so-called extremists – such as advocates of BDS – who were delegitimising Zionism.[63]

Despite antagonisms between different wings of the British Zionist movement, this metaphor for Zionist unity proved popular in Britain. Events organised under the 'big tent for Israel' banner were held in both Manchester and London.[64] And when, in 2006, the university lecturers' union began discussing a potential boycott of Israeli universities – a seminal moment which chapter 7 examines further – key British Zionist bodies responded by establishing a new coordinating hub that same year called the Fair Play Campaign Group (since renamed the Israel Advocacy Forum). Fair Play's two co-founding organisations, whose senior figures served as joint chairs, were the Board and the Jewish Leadership Council.[65]

Founded in the wake of Zionism's post-2000 crisis, the Jewish Leadership Council was established in 2003 with the support of a number of men the *Jewish Chronicle* described as 'undeniably influential, wealthy . . . figures who have in the past lacked the patience for the tiresome business of wider consultation and accountability'.[66] They included Tony Blair's chief fundraiser, Michael Levy, through whom it was deemed possible to access and lobby Downing Street.[67] The involvement of several donors to the major British political parties – including private-equity pioneer Ronald Cohen and former mining magnate Mick Davis – helped the Jewish Leadership Council secure high-level, bipartisan political access, such as an annual 'community' meeting with the prime minister – usually involving explicitly pro-Israel organisations like BICOM as well as Jewish groups.

As an umbrella body loosely modelled on the American Conference of Presidents, the Jewish Leadership Council, like its US counterpart, counts a combination of Jewish groups and Israel-advocacy groups among its thirty affiliated members.[68] The organisation's activities include laudable work raising funds for Jewish charities and schools. However, another significant aspect of its self-declared mission is to foster a community 'confident in its support for Israel', and recent CEO Simon Johnson states that the organisation 'reflect[s] the community's pride in and support for Israel as actively as any organisation'.[69] Moreover, the Jewish Leadership Council says it works 'closely' with US Zionist group AIPAC[70] and with the Israeli government 'to ensure continual sharing of successful techniques and intelligence'.[71] Cooperation across state–private networks also includes holding 'regular liaison meetings' with Israel's London embassy.[72] It is in this sense that it also functions to prop up Israeli apartheid. Despite this, the Jewish Leadership Council has been criticised from the right for being insufficiently supportive of Israel and, separately, for its perceived attempt to usurp the role of more long-standing, democratic organisations like the Board of Deputies.[73] To legitimise itself in the face of this criticism, the organisation has provided significant funding for pro-Israel activism. For instance, in 2014, it donated funds for a Global Coalition for Israel event held in London,[74] and in 2015, it gave £100,000 to 'grassroots' pro-Israel groups.[75] The Jewish Leadership Council's financial accounts also show that it provided significant financial support for the Fair Play Campaign Group (including after the body was renamed the Israel Advocacy Forum).[76]

The aim of the Fair Play Campaign Group was 'bringing together those committed to opposing anti-Zionist activity and boycotts' targeting Israel.[77] It was intended to serve as 'a co-ordinating hub and early warning system' and 'provide a coordinated approach to combating anti-Israel campaigns'.[78] Reportedly, Fair Play assisted in a number of battles against BDS and Palestine solidarity, including boycott initiatives within professional bodies such as the National Union of Journalists, the Royal Institute of British Architects, the British Medical Association, and the University and College Union.[79] In the early days – echoing the ABC Committee of the 1970s – participating members of the Fair Play group were each expected to pay a £5,000 subscription fee.[80] Though not a particularly transparent body, the identity of Fair Play's other members can be gleaned in part from *Jewish Chronicle* reports. BICOM, the Zionist Federation, the Union of Jewish Students and the British-Israel Chamber of Commerce are all mentioned as participants.[81] In the spirit of building the 'big tent for Israel', Fair Play simultaneously involved hard-right group StandWithUs UK[82] and, at least at one stage, the minor left-leaning group Brits for Peace Now.[83] Trade Union Friends of Israel – founded in 1983 but by 2005 reportedly 'largely defunct' – was at some point rejuvenated and participated in the network.[84] Former Board president Vivian Wineman, who says meetings took place 'about every five or six weeks', also lists Labour Friends of Israel, the Community Security Trust (described shortly) and the Israeli embassy as Fair Play participants.[85] Communications consultant Arieh Kovler coordinated the group.

As well as involving the embassy, Israeli Foreign Affairs representatives – including Amir Ofek, the official at one stage responsibility for combating BDS – were at various stages affiliated to the Fair Play Campaign Group.[86] By facilitating collaboration across state–private networks in this way, the group was, functionally speaking, the direct descendant of the 1950s Special Purpose Committee and the 1970s Anti-Boycott Co-ordinating Committee. All three chimed with the strategies advocated by new public diplomacy theorists, as articulated by the Reut Institute and others. They combine the relative advantages of state and non-state actors by 'letting the local pro-Israel community lead', while also enabling state actors' consistent contact with Zionist civil society groups, providing the latter with regular opportunities to play a supporting role as 'catalysts' and attempting to coordinate them within an overarching strategy. Indeed, just as building 'partnerships and synergies' between the Israeli state and Zionist non-state actors was the aim of the transnational Global Coalition for Israel project described in chapter 2, Fair Play arguably performs the same function on a domestic level. It is a loose, informal and partially covert network structure, rather than a formal government committee of the kind which new public diplomacy scholar Shaun Riordan points out could be 'politically sensitive' and jeopardise civil society organisations' credibility.[87] (Such political sensitivities have not always been avoided, however: in 2016, a leaked Israeli embassy cable accused the Ministry of Strategic Affairs of 'operating' British organisations 'directly from Jerusalem', without coordinating with the embassy and in ways which could violate British charity law, though no specific groups were named.)[88]

At least four of the same key organisations involved in the Special Purpose Committee and the ABC Committee were also involved in Fair Play: the embassy, the Board, the Zionist Federation, and the British-Israel Chamber of Commerce. And, like its predecessors, Fair Play served as a backbone for the Zionist movement, seeking to ensure an efficient division of labour and a smooth flow of communication while pooling and distributing resources between different pro-Israel actors in Britain. For example, it hosted fundraising events to facilitate relationship building between pro-Israel philanthropists and more 'grassroots' groups.[89] It also provided a forum via which more liberal organisations like the Board could work at arm's length with hawkish groups such as the Zionist Federation and StandWithUs on common goals like combating BDS, while still maintaining a respectable distance from the latter's more stridently right-wing politics such as explicit support for settlements. Table 3.3 shows all organisations, as of the time of writing, known to have attended meetings of the Fair Play Campaign Group. As this is a fluid and fairly opaque body, it may not be a complete or up to date representation of the hub's members. In 2022, the group, now known as the Israel Advocacy Forum, was co-chaired by Keith Black and Hilda Worth, both from the Jewish Leadership Council (and the latter also deputy chair of Conservative Friends of Israel, making it another likely participant, alongside its Labour counterpart).[90] Today, there are very few public mentions of the Israel Advocacy Forum's activities, but its work quietly coordinating UK Zionist anti-BDS campaigns is still underway.

Organisation	Type	Country
Academic Friends of Israel	Civil society	Britain
BICOM	Civil society	Britain
Board of Deputies	Civil society	Britain
British-Israel Chamber of Commerce	Civil society	Britain
Community Security Trust	Civil society	Britain
Friends of Israel Academic Study Group	Civil society	Britain
Israeli embassy	State	Britain/Israel
Jewish Leadership Council	Civil society	Britain
Jewish National Fund UK	National institution affiliate	Britain/Israel
Labour Friends of Israel	State	Britain
Trade Union Friends of Israel	Civil society	Israel
Union of Jewish Students	Civil society	Britain
Zionist Federation	National institution affiliate	Britain/Israel

Table 3.3. Bodies known to have participated in the Fair Play Campaign Group / Israel Advocacy Forum

The contemporary pro-Israel landscape in Britain

British pro-Israel organisations vary widely in size and function, and span the gamut of political persuasions within the Zionist spectrum. It is vital to acknowledge the existence of tensions and rivalries between them, rather than regard them as a homogeneous bloc. Indeed, the differences between liberal and right-wing Zionists are the fault-lines beneath some very considerable internecine antagonisms. That said, there are significant overlaps between some groups in terms of board memberships and donors. Moreover, as the Israel Advocacy Forum shows, on critical issues – such as opposition to BDS initiatives targeting Israel – a wide range of organisations work together towards common goals and coordinate across state–private networks.

Table 3.4 provides basic data on twenty key organisations in the British Zionist movement today. The amount of missing data is symptomatic of the lack of transparency surrounding many organisations, including those working in Parliament. Among the institutions listed, this chapter has already discussed the Board of Deputies, the Zionist Federation and the Jewish Leadership Council. Chapter 4 will offer a more fulsome introduction of key Westminster groups Conservative Friends of Israel and Labour Friends of Israel, as well as the Henry Jackson Society and Jewish Labour Movement. In chapter 5 we will meet some groups active within civil society, most importantly We Believe in Israel and Campaign Against Antisemitism but also StandWithUs UK and a host of hyper-local 'Friends of Israel' groups. Chapter 6 introduces key lawfare groups UK Lawyers of Israel and Jewish Human Rights Watch and in chapter 7 we meet bodies active in the university sphere including the Union of Jewish Students. Finally, in chapter 8 we more thoroughly examine BICOM, the most important pro-Israel group focusing on media influence. The remainder of the groups listed below are less significant but described in what follows here in the interests of contextualising the contemporary pro-Israel landscape in Britain.

Name	Established	Approx. annual income (£)	Employees
BICOM (Britain Israel Research and Communications Centre)	2001	2,000,000*	7
Board of Deputies of British Jews	1760	1,250,000	16
Campaign Against Antisemitism	2014	800,000	4
Christian Friends of Israel	2004	470,000	-
Christians United for Israel	2015	-	-
Community Security Trust	1994	11,310,000	93
Conservative Friends of Israel (CFI)	1974	-	7
Henry Jackson Society	2005	790,000	13
Jewish Human Rights Watch	2015	-	-
Jewish Labour Movement	2004	-	-
Jewish Leadership Council	2003	2,450,000	26
Jewish National Fund UK	1901	15,410,000	28
Labour Friends of Israel (LFI)	1957	-	-

* The figure of BICOM's expenditure at approximately £2 million dates from 2010: Mills et al., *Giving Peace a Chance?*, 54.

StandWithUs UK	2010	120,000	-
UK Lawyers for Israel	2010	-	-
Union of Jewish Students (UJS)	1973	-	13
United Jewish Israel Appeal (UJIA)	1944	8,210,000	61
We Believe in Israel	2011	-	2
Yachad	2011	220,000	4
Zionist Federation of UK & Ireland	1899	-	4

Table 3.4. Basic data on key British pro-Israel organisations[91]

The Jewish National Fund UK is the British affiliate of the Israeli national institution of the same name which has been a pivotal organisation in the historic and ongoing colonisation of Palestine. In 2021, the main focus of the British group was, in its own words, 'seeking to make a real difference' in the southern Negev region of Israel, an area which the Israeli government is seeking to 'Judaise' and ethnically cleanse of Palestinians.[92] Perhaps unsurprisingly, the group epitomises the toxic racial politics found in the right wing of the Zionist movement, and its senior leadership have openly expressed racist views. Chair Samuel Hayek caused outrage in early 2022 when he claimed Muslim immigration posed a threat to British Jews.[93] Though the organisation itself claimed to disavow this perspective, its deputy president Gary Mond was accused of Islamophobia just a few weeks later when social media posts surfaced in which he appeared to suggest the West is 'at war with Islam', forcing him to resign as senior vice-president of the Board of Deputies.[94] Remarkably, the Jewish National Fund UK has registered-charity status and boasts former prime ministers Tony Blair and Gordon Brown among its patrons.[95]

The United Jewish Israel Appeal (UJIA – the British affiliate of another of Israel's national institutions, Keren HaYesod) focuses, like its parent body, on fundraising. As such, it performs little to no straightforward 'lobbying' but is still an important organisation in the British Zionist movement, closely connected to other pro-Israel organisations. Since the UJIA wants members of the British Jewish community to have 'a lifelong commitment to Israel', a key aspect of its work involves efforts to cultivate a strong Zionist mindset among young British Jews.[96] It does this by funding Zionist youth movements and 'Israel education' as well as offering free trips to Israel via schemes such as Birthright, which is partly funded by the Israeli government.[97] In 2017, then Prime Minister Theresa May was guest speaker at a UJIA dinner marking the seventieth anniversary of the foundation of Israel.[98]

Beyond these key Zionist groups, which predate the state of Israel itself, the picture is more complex. The Community Security Trust, established in 1994, is an example of a Jewish group which, like the Board of Deputies and Jewish Leadership Council, also involves itself in Zionist activism. The organisation was set up by right-wing business tycoon Gerald Ronson, a supporter and donor to Israeli prime minister Benjamin Netanyahu and strong critic of ex–Labour leader Jeremy Corbyn (who Ronson alleged posed a threat to Jews 'far more subversive than the danger posed by Nazis').[99] The Community Security Trust primarily works to monitor and counter anti-Semitism but has also been involved in efforts to counter anti-Zionism and the BDS movement, and on this basis can be considered part of the Zionist movement. For example, the group has been involved in the Fair Play Campaign Group / Israel Advocacy Forum, described earlier, and was also involved in campaigning to amend legislation and outlaw local-authority boycott initiatives.[100] The organisation frequently attracts senior politicians to its annual dinner.[101]

At the other end of the political spectrum sits Yachad ('Together'), founded in 2011 to express 'a more critical attitude towards Israel' taking shape 'within the mainstream of the [British Jewish] community'.[102] Yachad describes itself as 'pro-Israel, pro-peace' and took inspiration from American liberal Zionist group J Street; but, as in the US, the liberal Zionist politics it represents constitutes a minor and fairly marginalised current. Yachad acknowledges that 'Israel has ruled over another people for more than two thirds of its young history', criticises the occupation and calls for a withdrawal 'close to the pre-1967 lines' – principally because it believes a two-state solution represents 'Israel's best hope for safety and security'.[103] The group organises trips to visit the occupied West Bank, draws attention to Israel's demolition of Palestinian homes and has openly criticised the Board of Deputies – for example, in May 2021 for failing to condemn violent far-right nationalists who marched through Jerusalem chanting, 'Death to the Arabs'.[104] It is silent, however, on Palestinian refugees' right of return and states that it opposes the BDS movement for which Palestinians have called.[105] Nonetheless, Yachad's stances have caused tension within the Zionist movement. Although it was permitted to join the Board of Deputies in 2014, the previous year the Zionist Federation rejected its attempt to affiliate. And in 2016, the Israeli embassy let it be known it had declined an invitation to speak at a Yachad event.[106]

While the logic of Zionism dictates that Israel should receive automatic support from Jewish communities on the basis of ethno-religious identity, we have already seen that British Jewish support for Zionism has always been historically contingent and was never a consensus issue. Mirroring Zionism's wider crisis of legitimacy, Jewish communities' support for Israel has incrementally declined, and explicit challenges to the status quo have grown more numerous. In 2007, for instance, anti-war British Jews who felt alienated by the Board's call for 'solidarity' with Israel during the second Israel-Lebanon war formed Independent Jewish Voices.[107] In 2010, a survey found that 72 per cent of British Jews categorised themselves as Zionists, but five years later another study put this number at just 59 per cent.[108]

Over time, deep community divisions have become increasingly prominent, reflecting wider political polarisation. As in the US, younger generations within the British Jewish community (and beyond it) are increasingly turning away from Zionism. Newer groups Jewdas and Na'amod, comprising mostly younger members, assert a strong Jewish identity while simultaneously rejecting leading communal bodies' pro-Israel stance. The latter has staged protests at events held by right-wing pro-Israel groups such as the Zionist Federation, StandWithUs UK and UK Lawyers for Israel. In response to subversive activism like this, some Zionist movement actors have increasingly sought to intimidate, marginalise, and silence Jewish dissent.

To reiterate, then, a key point made in the introduction to this book: support for Israel is a fundamentally political question, rather than synonymous with ethno-religious identity. The role of Christian Zionist groups underlines this. The Christian Zionist scene in

Britain, as in the US, is a deeply conservative space. Christian Friends of Israel, founded in 1985, has held joint events with the Israeli embassy and also works closely with the Zionist Federation.[109] Since the late 1980s, the two groups have jointly organised an annual lobby of Parliament. This was supplemented in 2015 by the establishment of Christians United for Israel UK, a branch of the US-based organisation, founded by John Hagee, which calls itself the 'largest pro-Israel grassroots organization in the United States' and has, as the previous chapter noted, received funding from Israel's Ministry of Strategic Affairs. Grassroots pro-Israel activism in Britain is increasingly reliant on (often evangelical) Christians, who make up the majority of the activist base of We Believe in Israel and a significant proportion of the hyperlocal 'Friends of Israel' groups we will meet in chapter 5.[110] First, however, we turn to the elite sphere of Westminster.

4

Insulating Parliament

On 29 December 2008, an Israeli military drone dropped a missile that struck a flat-bed truck outside the Samur family's metal shop in Jabalya, in the northern Gaza Strip. Later that day, Israeli Defense Forces captain Elie Isaacson announced that his unit had 'struck a Hamas vehicle loaded with dozens of Grad type missiles'. As Human Rights Watch has documented, these were in fact oxygen canisters used for welding, about half the length of the Grad rockets used by Hamas and recognisably different, especially viewed through the advanced imaging equipment on board Israeli drones. Eighteen-year-old Palestinian Basil Nabil Ghabayen told Human Rights Watch that he had been getting equipment from the shop when the missile hit: 'I heard the sound of the drones flying overhead but [since this is common in Gaza] I did not pay much attention to them.' After the missile hit, he continued, 'I went out to see what happened [and] found my brother and four of my cousins and their friends burnt and lying in a pool of blood and flesh.' Another survivor of the attack, Muhammad Sa'di Ghabayen, also eighteen years old, told Human Rights Watch: 'I saw horrible scenes. Three canisters were already on the truck and five gallons of benzene ... the oxygen and the benzene burned and also burned the bodies of the dead.'[1]

Israeli arms company Elbit Systems produces many of Israel's armed drones, like the ones that launched the attack that day. After Amnesty International highlighted the fact that Elbit drone engines used in military assaults on Gaza are manufactured in Britain,[2] each fresh Israeli assault on Gaza has seen Elbit subsidiaries in

Britain targeted with direct action by activists who say the factories are 'directly linked to the butchering of children in Gaza'.[3] However, Elbit has long employed the services of professional lobbying firms to maintain its brand among those in power. At one stage it hired LLM Communications, whose co-founder Jonathan Mendelsohn was a key figure in Labour Friends of Israel (LFI).[4] During another period, Elbit hired lobbying firm The Westminster Connection (since renamed TWC Associates), run by Stuart Polak – a key figure in Conservative Friends of Israel (CFI).[5] Despite their affiliations to opposing political parties, together Mendelsohn and Polak serve as co-directors of Cedarsoak Ltd, a company which provides the secretariat for the Britain-Israel All Party Parliamentary Group (APPG), a type of informal cross-party grouping providing a less-than-transparent backdoor for influence in Parliament.[6] Using their Westminster access, the pair lobby for Israeli apartheid alongside Israeli arms companies like Elbit. Notably, each has received a peerage from their respective party. This chapter charts the history of Zionist activism in Parliament, in particular tracing the role of Labour Friends of Israel and Conservative Friends of Israel – often alongside the Israeli embassy – in ensuring British government support for Israeli apartheid.

Friends of Israel, old and new

Imperial Britain played a critical role in nurturing the Zionist movement and its quest for statehood in its early years – partly on the basis of the perceived utility of the Zionist project to the British Empire and partly due to senior British officials' colonial arrogance and racist attitude towards both Jews and Arabs, as chapter 1 explained. In contrast, as we shall see, to the extent that a few disparate organisations can be said to constitute a small 'pro-Palestine lobby' in Britain, these groups have never been fostered in the same way nor enjoyed comparative strength, access or influence in the corridors of power, since they have little instrumental purpose to British elites.

Foreshadowing the contemporary era, the Balfour Declaration was achieved in part thanks to arms trade connections: one reason

Chaim Weizmann had the ear of senior politicians was his work as a biochemist, in which he developed new techniques for producing acetone, which proved useful in World War I and were highly valued by the British arms industry.[7] His discreet, high-level lobbying of government ministers is also a practice which – although tested over the years by intermittently occurring scandals – remains a hallmark of the lobby's tactical approach today. Leading Zionist strategists have long observed that 'political elites . . . are much more tolerant towards Israel's policies than the wider public'.[8] Indeed, based on the belief that public opinion 'does not influence foreign policy', key pro-Israel groups have therefore adopted a strategy of 'insulating policy-making environments'.[9] It is a sad indictment of British democracy that, as we will see, by and large this strategy has succeeded, and that growing public support for Palestinians has rarely been reflected in Westminster.

The organisation Poale Zion, which we encountered in the previous chapter, played a significant role in cultivating early support for Zionism within the Labour Party. As sociologist Paul Kelemen notes, despite identifying as 'Marxist-Zionist', Poale Zion privileged 'ethnic over class solidarity'.[10] Nonetheless, it constituted a crucial link between the Israeli and British left after its British branch first affiliated to Labour in 1920. Remarkably, this alliance produced a call for a transfer of population in Palestine from Labour's National Executive Committee some years *before* the creation of Israel and the Nakba. 'Let the Arabs be encouraged to move out, as the Jews move in', declared the Labour Party leadership in a report called *The International Post-War Settlement*, issued shortly before the 1945 election. Although, once in office, Labour abandoned this position – a stance more extreme than even the fascist-influenced revisionist Zionists[11] – it was a Labour government which, in March 1950, first officially recognised the new state of Israel in the wake of precisely this form of ethnic cleansing perpetrated against over 750,000 Palestinians.

It was from this landscape that Labour Friends of Israel emerged in 1957, a new bridge between Labour and David Ben-Gurion's Mapai party in Israel, on 'the initiative of Poale Zion leaders' and with the support of forty members of Parliament.[12] Early anxieties about the potential impact of the Arab League boycott during this period played a part. But the more immediate and important trigger was the 1956 Suez crisis. After Britain's Conservative-led government colluded in Israel's attack on Egypt, the subsequent Anglo-French invasion was condemned by the leadership of the Labour opposition, testing the party's pro-Israel tendency in that period[13] and provoking fury from Israel's political elites.[14] LFI was, then, founded defensively in a moment of weakness. Yet the fact that its existence long predated the establishment of its Conservative counterpart illustrates the point that at this historical juncture, and for some years after, support for Zionism was far more entrenched on the left than the right.

Israel's occupation of East Jerusalem, the West Bank, Gaza and the Syrian Golan Heights in 1967 did not trigger an immediate haemorrhaging of Labour support. This was thanks in part to pro-Israel apparatus like LFI and the strength of Zionism on the left, but also rested on several leading British politicians' close personal relationships with Israeli politicians – often undergirded by shared colonial mentalities. For example, Labour leader and two-time British prime minister Harold Wilson counted among his friends the Israeli prime minister, Golda Meir, said to have possessed towards Palestinians a 'colonial settler's attitude' similar to 'that of British settlers in East Africa'.[15] Likewise, when delivering a memorial lecture for his ally Chaim Weizmann, Bevanite MP and ardent Zionist Richard Crossman once even lamented that settlers' 'right, or indeed their duty, to civilize [other] continents by physically occupying them, even at the cost of wiping out the aboriginal population' was, in the twentieth century, being questioned.[16]

Attitudes were, indeed, slowly changing. As historian John Newsinger observes, after 1967 large sections of the British left were beginning to grow disillusioned with Zionism, having realised that 'far from being a socialist enclave surrounded by menacing fascist Arabs, Israel was a powerful, militarily aggressive state'.[17] Israel's rightward shift and the slow 'implosion of Labour Zionism' made the country's nationalism clearer and the promise of socialist development more tenuous. Meanwhile, as movements for decolonisation advanced around the world, anti-racism and the emerging post–World War II human rights agenda were increasingly being centred in left-wing politics.[18]

This was the milieu from which a small but unprecedented pro-Palestine lobby of sorts emerged, as allies of the Palestinians for the first time began to organise earnestly in Parliament.[19] The cross-party Council for the Advancement of Arab–British Understanding (CAABU) was founded in 1967, and the Labour Middle East Council (LMEC) was set up two years later. The LMEC included left-wing members of Parliament like Michael Foot but also had an influential centrist wing led by figures like Christopher Mayhew, known for his involvement in the Information Research Department, a Cold War anti-Communist propaganda unit in the Foreign Office.[20] Notably, the group was prevented several times from officially affiliating to Labour by the latter's National Executive Committee, and the balance of power within the party remained tilted in Israel's favour. In 1967, LFI could boast a membership of 300 MPs, while in comparison LMEC could by 1972 count only 160 MPs as supporters.[21] However, LMEC's call for a 'radical reappraisal' of Labour's position on Israel carved out some, albeit limited, space within the mainstream of the party for criticism of Zionism.[22]

In 1973, following the October War between Israel and several of its Arab neighbours, Edward Heath's Conservative government imposed an arms embargo on all parties involved in the conflict.[23] Journalist Robert Philpot writes that Labour leader Harold Wilson – who 'behind a cloak of official neutrality . . . strongly supported Israel' – stayed 'in daily contact with the Israelis via the London Embassy' at this time and, at their request, called on the government to lift the arms embargo.[24] According to a letter sent by an official at the Israeli embassy, as part of the Zionist movement's long-standing strategy of targeting 'opinion-making' groups, as opposed to 'every man in the street', more than one hundred British MPs were canvassed.[25] In the House of Commons, Philpot notes, Wilson argued that Israel was a 'socialist country' and 'by any test . . . the only democracy in the region'.[26] Yet despite Wilson remaining committed to Zionism – while simultaneously opposing apartheid in South Africa – the left's broad-based support for Zionism was eroding. For the first time, a major disconnect between the Labour leadership and the wider party on the issue of Palestine became apparent, as illustrated by what Newsinger calls a 'significant revolt' against Wilson's pro-Israel stance.[27]

During this same period, the ascendant Tory right was starting to identify more with Israel, admiring the country's military power and viewing it, according to the *Jewish Chronicle*, as a 'vital outpost of the free world in the Middle East'.[28] The very same 1977 election which saw Likud right winger Menachem Begin sweep to victory in Israel, disenchanting British leftists, simultaneously enthused conservatives. Indeed, as Israeli politics shifted right, encompassing the embrace of neoliberal economics, support for the country in Britain increasingly became the preserve of conservative forces, given their 'elective affinity with military bellicosity and orthodox views on the economy', in political commentator Richard Seymour's words.[29] Conservative Friends of Israel was founded in 1974. In part a response to Heath's arms embargo, as well as the second wave of intense anti–Arab League boycott organising, its establishment was also indicative of this wider trend. Michael Sacher, the president of the Joint Israel Appeal and vice-president of retailer Marks & Spencer (as well as a founder of BIPAC around the same time, as chapter 3 noted) contributed funds to CFI. So too did Community Security Trust founder Gerald Ronson and motor industry magnate Trevor Chinn, both today associated with the Jewish Leadership Council.[30]

CFI's founder, former MP Michael Fidler, espoused a deeply conservative revisionist brand of Zionism as part of a more generalised hard-right world view. Tellingly, according to his biographer, Fidler's attitudes were akin to those of another British Conservative politician, Enoch Powell – notorious for his racist, anti-immigration 'Rivers of Blood' speech. Alongside his work on Israel, Fidler campaigned to 'strictly enforce' Britain's racist immigration legislation.[31] Despite these origins, or perhaps because of them, CFI expanded rapidly. Eighty Conservative MPs, including Margaret Thatcher, joined up the year it was founded, and just one year later it was already reportedly bigger than LFI. By 1978, CFI was said to be the largest grouping in Westminster.[32]

By contrast, at the end of the 1970s, although 140 of Labour's 268 MPs were still members of LFI – compared to LMEC's fifty-five – LFI's general secretary, Martin Cohen, was concerned that the group might need funding from the Israeli embassy in order to survive.[33] The subsequent 1982 Israeli invasion of Lebanon, as well as the Sabra and Shatila massacre of the same year, precipitated a further significant left-wing shift away from Zionism.[34] Social scientist June Edmunds writes that signs of fracture at the top of Labour – such as MP Tony Benn's departure from LFI – reflected a growing 'bottom-up movement' in rank-and-file solidarity with Palestinians among the wider party membership, especially noticeable in London and Scotland.[35] While pro-Israel groups continued to lobby Labour leaders like Neil Kinnock, they were battling a 'sea change in international opinion' on Palestine, precipitated by a wider 'leftward shift' within the party and a domestic context in which the party's 'ethnic constituency' had changed, with predominantly Black and brown first- and second-generation immigrant communities growing in importance as a voting bloc.[36]

Edmunds suggests that Israel's supporters felt it necessary, during this period, to 'copy some of the tactics' of Palestine solidarity activists. For the first time, pro-Israel campaigners abandoned their prior exclusive focus on the Parliamentary Labour Party, seeking instead to organise 'in the constituencies and the trade unions' as well. This 'counter movement' was reflected, for example, in the 1983 establishment of Trade Union Friends of Israel, a response to the threat posed by the founding of Trade Union Friends of Palestine in 1980.[37] As chapter 5 will describe, this would not be the last time that the strategy of insulating parliamentary elites would start to appear insufficient in the face of increased support for Palestinians, stimulating a wave of pro-Israel institution building.

During the 1980s, then, the question of Palestine was becoming, on both the left and the right in Britain, a means of 'forging political identities'.[38] Margaret Thatcher's premiership saw the pro-Israel position cemented on the right (during the same period, notably, that her party was notoriously hostile to Nelson Mandela and the African National Congress fighting apartheid in South Africa). Thatcher was already president of the Anglo-Israel Friendship League in her local Finchley constituency when she became party leader in 1975.[39] She reportedly saw Israel as 'a lone bulwark of democracy' in 'a pretty unpleasant area' and visited Israel three times before becoming prime minister in 1979, at the height of renewed Cold War tensions.[40] Although her government, alongside other European countries, upheld an arms embargo on Israel following its 1982 invasion of Lebanon, she later became the first serving British prime minister to visit the country in 1986.[41]

Meanwhile, within the Labour Party, despite clear differences between the centre left and radical left, by the dawn of the 1990s a 'new consensus' had emerged – one which was more pro-Palestine than ever before.[42] However, Labour had by this time languished in opposition for some years. Hungry for a stint in government, the party soon chose a leader who would usher in a transformative era of New Labour government and, in the process, help to secure more than two decades of renewed support for Israel – at the top of the party, at least.

Blair, Brown and the New Labour 'bag man'

At a time when the general trajectory of the left was one of incremental dissociation from Zionism, one of Tony Blair's first acts upon becoming an MP was to join Labour Friends of Israel in 1983. A decade later, Blair developed what Toby Greene, former director of research for the Britain Israel Communications and Research Centre (BICOM) and LFI, calls a 'fervent interest' in Israel after visiting the country on an Israeli embassy–organised trip.[43] In 1994, the year he became Labour leader, Blair met multimillionaire music industry entrepreneur Michael Levy at a dinner party hosted by Israeli diplomat Gideon Meir. Levy would become a key influence on Blair's Middle East stance and, more broadly, a key figure in the New Labour project upon which Blair was embarking.

As Blair's chief fundraiser, Levy raised many millions for New Labour – efforts which, according to the *Sunday Times*, earned him the nickname 'Mr Cashpoint'.[44] This fundraising was critical to Blair's ability to transform Labour, since it allowed the party to develop financial independence from the trade unions.[45] Levy was the 'bag man' for Blair's Labour Leader's Office Fund, a blind trust to which donors could give anonymously. Among the pro-Israel figures later revealed as donors were the millionaire industrialist

Sir Emmanuel Kaye and Sir Trevor Chinn – noted previously as an early backer of Conservative Friends of Israel.[46] Several of the new donors were closely associated with the Jewish Leadership Council, set up, as the previous chapter explained, partly in order to enable lobbying access to Blair via Levy, the latter seen as a 'gatekeeper to Downing Street'.[47]

During the Blair years – arguably the heyday of elite consensus on Israel in Britain – LFI came in from the cold, following a period in the relative wilderness. In the Blair era, LFI could boast 'some of the most generous donors to party funds', such as Baron David Sainsbury, great-grandson of the supermarket founder.[48] And the political clout which such financial muscle afforded Levy, as well as the other pro-Israel figures who became critical to the health of the party's coffers, was considerable. As Blair's tennis partner and friend, Levy spoke to the party leader almost weekly, and the pair reportedly often discussed Israel.[49] According to one commentator, there was a 'tacit understanding that Labour would never again . . . be anti-Israel'.[50] After Blair won the 1997 election in a landslide, Levy was made a life peer. Years later, he was arrested and questioned twice in connection with the cash-for-honours scandal – in which major donors allegedly made large loans to the party, instead of donations which would need to be declared, in return for peerages – but he was never charged.

Levy had flourished in the context of Blair's infamously impe-rial style of premiership. Decision-making was centralised, Parliament side-lined, and policy was frequently hammered out by a small coterie of advisers around the prime minister. Blair's strongly pro-Israel stance, reflecting his Atlanticism, was at odds with increasingly pro-Palestinian public sentiment; hence, a yawning gap in perspective became apparent. Indeed, if pro-Israel politics became, in the Blair years, part of the 'identity of the "modernizing" wing', as Greene puts it, the issue of Israel/Pales-tine within the party more broadly came to be 'emblematic of ideological rifts between New Labour and the Labour left'.[51] Yet the democratic deficit around foreign policy, correctly identified by Israel lobby strategists, meant grassroots opinion mattered little. This was starkly illustrated elsewhere in Middle East policy by the decision to invade Iraq – based on flawed intelligence and in the face of massive public opposition.

According to Labour lobbyist Jonathan Mendelsohn, Blair had 'attacked the anti-Israelism' in the party and re-entrenched Zionism so that the ideology was once more 'pervasive'.[52] And when his period as prime minister ended, the Labour left remained marginalised. Where Blair had relied on Levy, his New Labour successor Gordon Brown appointed Mendelsohn – a former Blair adviser, LFI chair and ex-director of the New Labour pressure group Progress – as his chief fundraiser. Under Brown, Mendelsohn helped to ensure that the party leadership's line on the Israel/Palestine question remained intact.

Financial scandals linked to key players in LFI continued. In 2007, major Labour donor David Abrahams, once called 'Mr Big in LFI', was revealed to have given large sums to the party illegally via proxies, including his builder and his secretary.[53] Also implicated in similar practices were LFI supporters Willie Nagel, a diamond dealer, and Isaac Kaye, a South African businessman and erstwhile supporter of the South African apartheid regime.[54] Mendelsohn, who reportedly knew about some of these practices, had himself been caught up in the so-called lobbygate affair. He and colleagues were secretly recorded by an undercover reporter posing as a businessman boasting that they could get access – for a fee – to the most senior government ministers.[55] Yet Mendelsohn, like Levy, was later made a Labour peer.

Cash-for-access and undisclosed meetings

For a quarter of a century, one man was at the heart of CFI's parliamentary lobbying. After becoming CFI director in 1989, Stuart Polak reportedly 'had the ear of almost every senior Tory since Margaret Thatcher's premiership'[56]; after all, having a close relationship to CFI, as the BBC has noted, could be a valuable tool for politicians to gain the support of 'wealthy party donors'.[57] Polak – though never seeking to be a headline-grabber or have a public profile[58] – has played a key role in quietly facilitating donations from pro-Israel donors to Conservative MPs. Veteran political journalist Peter Oborne describes how this works:

One Tory MP . . . before he stood in the 2005 election . . . met Stuart Polak, who put Israel's case to him strongly at a social event. Towards the end of the meal, Stuart Polak asked if his campaign needed more money. Sure enough, weeks later two cheques arrived in the post at the Conservative office in the constituency. Both came from businessmen closely connected to the CFI who the Tory MP says he had never met before and who had never, so far as he knew, ever stepped inside his constituency. Another parliamentary candidate fighting a marginal seat . . . had gone to see Stuart Polak, where he was tested on his views on Israel. Within a fortnight a cheque from a businessman he had never met arrived in his constituency office.

Substantial sums have indeed been donated, both to the party and to individual pro-Israel MPs, such as former CFI political director Robert Halfon and Michael Gove, whose clash-of-civilisations book, *Celsius 7/7*, was for a while given away free with CFI membership. According to Oborne, three CFI-supporting donors – Trevor Pears, Michael Lewis and Poju Zabludowicz – were at one stage 'the driving force' behind both CFI and BICOM. Zabludowicz (who, like BICOM, will reappear in chapter 8) had a personal relationship with David Cameron, and the pair met for coffee when the latter was planning his party leadership bid.[59] Since 2000, five influential donors and CFI supporters – Howard Leigh, Stanley Kalms, Richard Harrington, Mick Davis and Stanley Fink – have served as Conservative Party treasurer, and the latter alone has donated a total of £1.75 million to the party.[60]

In a 2009 *Dispatches* documentary, Oborne claimed to have detected a pattern of electoral donations – often channelled through companies, making them hard to trace – connecting CFI-linked figures to around £10 million in donations over eight years. Former British ambassador Sir Richard Dalton claims this amounts to Israel's supporters using 'financial pressures' to effectively 'censor' politicians.[61] Importantly, though, financial contributions are not always necessarily connected to Israel, nor do they automatically sway politicians in a pro-Israel direction. In 2008, for example, Gerald Ronson donated to Ken Livingstone, at that time the mayor of London and a long-standing critic of Israel.[62] Moreover the

British electoral system is somewhat less dependent on money than US politics. However, if such donations had no influence, it would be hard to explain the existence of networks such as the Conservative 'Leader's Group', an elite dining club exposed in 2019,[63] or the party leadership's 'Advisory Board' of super-rich donors exposed in 2022 – whose members typically give in excess of £250,000 in return for privileged direct access to the prime minister.[64] Advisory Board members include not only those with much-publicised close ties to the Putin regime in Russia, such as former banker Lubov Chernukhin, but also supporters of Israel such as property investor Leopold Noé. For over a decade, the committee on standards in public life has been calling for fundamental changes, including a £10,000 limit on donations, to end this political influence culture – but to no avail.

Precisely how much funding bodies like CFI have is difficult to determine, since their legal status and the poverty of parliamentary regulation in this area allows their finances to remain opaque. Nevertheless, we can say with certainty that pro-Israel lobbying within Westminster today remains well funded. Members of Parliament are, at least, obliged to declare expenses-paid trips hosted by groups like CFI – disclosures which show that since 2004, more than 160 Conservative politicians have been taken to Israel on visits worth at least £370,000.[65] In fact, in 2016, Israel was reportedly the destination travelled to *most* by British MPs. We also know that these visits are sometimes partly or wholly funded by the Israeli government: Israel's Ministry of Foreign Affairs has openly co-funded some trips, and more recently Israel's Ministry of Strategic Affairs has indirectly donated via third-party groups it funds, such as the Israel Allies Foundation.[66]

While not all visits go smoothly – in 2004, for instance, Conservative MP Crispin Blunt was shot at in error by Israeli soldiers – in general, such trips are 'powerful and persuasive' in fostering positive affinities with Israel.[67] For example, former prime minister Boris Johnson has reminisced fondly about how on a CFI-sponsored trip to Israel, he 'got very, very drunk' with fellow MPs in Tel Aviv and had 'an extraordinary evening of merriment', which former chancellor George Osborne recalled ended with the group 'singing Israeli resistance songs in a karaoke bar'.[68] Commercial interests intertwine with political interests during these junkets to Israel. For instance, in 2011, MPs on a CFI-sponsored trip visited the head-quarters of arms company Elbit Systems.[69] The following year, Elbit's British chairman, Richard Applegate, was exposed by the *Sunday Times* bragging that Stuart Polak's lobbying firm The Westminster Connection 'piggybacked' on Conservative Friends of Israel on behalf of its client Elbit, in order to 'gain access to particular decision makers'.[70]

In 2011, Conservative defence minister Liam Fox was revealed to have been pursuing, in effect, a freelance foreign policy, accompanied by a close friend and unofficial adviser, the Scottish businessman Adam Werritty. The pair made visits to Israel, Iran and Sri Lanka, many of which were funded by the charity Atlantic Bridge and a private company called Pargav.[71] These bodies shared several donors in common, including former Conservative Party treasurer and Jewish Leadership Council chair Mick Davis, Poju Zabludowicz, and Michael Lewis, the latter two identified by Peter Oborne as critical to both CFI and BICOM.[72] While the affair briefly shone a light on the potential influence of unaccountable private networks, forcing Fox to resign his ministerial post, a few years later he was made trade secretary. And, soon after, an even bigger scandal involving CFI was exposed.

Priti Patel, a former professional lobbyist with PR firm Weber Shandwick, has – according to the *Jewish Chronicle* – long been 'cultivating contacts in the pro-Israel community', especially during her time as CFI vice-chair.[73] In 2013, she travelled to Washington, DC, to attend the annual conference of pro-Israel lobby group AIPAC, at the expense of the Henry Jackson Society[74] – a neoconservative think-tank tied into US funding streams on the more Islamophobic wing of the American Zionist movement. The Henry Jackson Society hosts Israeli political and military figures in Westminster and pushes for draconian US-style counter-terrorism measures domestically.[75] Its prominent parliamentary supporters include senior Conservative Michael Gove, while co-founder and director Alan Mendoza is simultaneously vice-chair of the Jewish National Fund UK, a body whose toxic racial politics the previous chapter discussed.[76] In 2016, the Henry Jackson Society and Conservative Friends of Israel hosted a joint event with the Gatestone Institute, a virulently Islamophobic New York think-tank.[77]

In the summer of 2017, while serving as international development secretary, Priti Patel held twelve secret meetings while supposedly 'on holiday' in Israel.[78] Stuart Polak – who in 2015 had been given a peerage for his services to the Britain-Israel relationship – arranged these unofficial meetings, about which Foreign Office officials were not informed, and attended the vast majority himself. He claimed, too, that it was mere coincidence he was in Israel at the same time. Among Patel's undisclosed meetings were top Israeli politicians including Prime Minister Benjamin Netanyahu and Strategic Affairs Minister Gilad Erdan, the man in charge of countering the global BDS movement. Patel also visited an Israeli army field hospital in the occupied Syrian Golan Heights, where she was treated to a showcase of hi-tech medical equipment produced by a client of Polak's lobbying firm The Westminster Connection.[79] Having already frozen British aid payments to the Palestinian Authority – something for which CFI had long lobbied – Patel now mooted the idea of channelling British 'aid' to this Israeli army base on supposedly humanitarian grounds.[80] But when the scandal of her secret meetings broke, she was forced to resign from the cabinet. Less than two years later, however, she returned to the heart of government as home secretary under Boris Johnson, where she went on to initiate schemes like the attempted deportation of asylum seekers to Rwanda. Polak also weathered the scandal to continue his work promoting Israel in Parliament.

The first rule in politics

In early 2017, Qatari-owned broadcaster Al Jazeera released an investigative documentary based on footage obtained by an undercover journalist. Entitled *The Lobby*, its biggest revelation concerned the activities of a man named Shai Masot. As chapter 2 noted, Masot was working at the Israeli Embassy in London when he was filmed talking to Maria Strizzolo, an aide to leading pro-Israel MP Robert Halfon, about the need to 'take down' Alan Duncan, a Conservative MP critical of Israel. Masot also described another

MP, Crispin Blunt, as being on a 'hit list', while Strizzolo speculated upon the need for 'a little scandal'.[81] These machinations cost the pair their jobs. An official apology from the Israeli ambassador followed, characterising Masot's plotting as the rogue behaviour of a bad apple. In defiance of Labour calls for an immediate inquiry, then foreign secretary Boris Johnson declared the matter closed.

Yet even after Masot returned to Israel, questions remained about precisely what role he had played and on whose orders. For instance, while the embassy described him as 'junior', his business card bore the title 'senior political officer'.[82] Strategic affairs minister Erdan claimed Masot had 'no connection' to his work, yet evidence of a 2016 meeting between Erdan, Masot and CFI executive director James Gurd soon surfaced.[83] Indeed, the London embassy itself suggested Masot had in fact been working for Erdan's ministry at the time.[84] Former diplomats, meanwhile, argued that Masot was 'highly unlikely to be operating without authority'.[85]

The explosive documentary highlighted the state–private networks in which both Labour Friends of Israel and Conservative Friends of Israel participate, examples of which abound. For instance, Erdan briefed members of both groups together during a September 2016 visit.[86] It emerged, too, that Masot had organised a trip for key donors to both groups to the annual AIPAC conference in the US, reportedly to get 'ideas for Britain'.[87] And in 2018, the Israeli embassy co-hosted a joint CFI–LFI event on the plight of Jewish refugees from Arab countries (a topic cynically exploited by the Zionist movement in its attempts to rebuff calls to respect Palestinian refugees' right of return).[88] One former minister in David Cameron's government has alleged anonymously in the press that 'for years the CFI and LFI have worked with – even for – the Israeli embassy to promote Israeli policy' and to thwart 'the actions of ministers who try to defend Palestinian rights'.[89] To say such actors work *for* the Israeli embassy would, as previously discussed, be a reductionist denial of their own agency and responsibility. However, the extent of their cooperation *with* the embassy, across state–private networks, was confirmed by another revelation in Al Jazeera's exposé.

According to ex–Labour MP Denis MacShane, a former member of LFI's policy council, holding a role within LFI was previously 'seen as a kind of stepping-stone to promotion' by ambitious young members of Parliament.[90] Therefore, in the era of Blair and Brown, MPs signed up to LFI in large numbers, bucking the trend on the wider left. However, reflective of the crisis of Zionism which was particularly apparent on the left, after the New Labour years there were indications that the cosy pro-Israel consensus at the top of the party was faltering. In 2017, Masot was filmed by Al Jazeera's undercover reporter speaking privately, in concerned tones, about one such trend:

> For years, every MP that joined the parliament joined the LFI. They're not doing it any more in the Labour party. CFI, they're doing it automatically. All the 14 new MPs who got elected in the last elections did it automatically. In the LFI it didn't happen.[91]

The solution Masot proposed to rectify this generational problem was telling: it suggested that close – but covert – collaboration between Israeli government representatives and LFI was de rigueur. Masot encouraged the undercover reporter, who he believed to be a pro-Israel activist, to establish a new 'Young LFI' group but also urged him not to reveal the embassy's instrumental role in its creation. He explained: 'LFI is an independent organisation. No one likes that someone is managing his organisation. That really is the first rule in politics.'

In the same documentary, staff member Michael Rubin – who subsequently became LFI director – was filmed speaking about the group's state–private cooperation. While warning that LFI needed to be 'careful that we're not seen as Young Israeli Embassy', he confirmed:

> We do work really closely together, it's just publicly we just try to keep LFI as a separate identity to the embassy . . . Being LFI allows us to reach out to people who wouldn't want to get involved with the embassy. Ultimately, we want the same end goal of getting more people to be pro-Israel.

Rubin added that LFI 'work[ed] with the [Israeli] ambassador and the embassy quite a lot' and that the organisation's then chair, MP

Joan Ryan, spoke to Masot 'most days'. These revelations prompted one pro-Palestinian journalist to ask whether LFI was merely 'an Israeli embassy front'.[92]

Masot and Ryan were also filmed discussing 'more than 1 million pounds' in funding from the Israel embassy in connection to a list of 'names that [LFI] put into the embassy' – an apparent reference to people recommended for sponsored trips to Israel.[93] LFI would subsequently declare that this trip was not an LFI parliamentarians' delegation. It denied ever receiving, or being offered funding for its own trips and called Al Jazeera's documentary 'a combination of lies, insinuations and distortions . . . [which] attempted to construct a vast conspiracy involving hidden power, money and improper influence – typical anti-Semitic tropes'.[94] Broadcasting regulator Ofcom received a handful of complaints about the programme, including allegations of bias and anti-Semitism from supporters of Israel, but cleared Al Jazeera on both counts.[95]

The Corbyn catastrophe

During the New Labour era, and for some years beyond it, British public opinion on Palestine never seemed likely to translate into government policy. However, in September 2015, following Ed Miliband's defeat in the general election of that year, an earthquake hit the Labour Party. Left-wing backbencher MP Jeremy Corbyn, widely considered a no-hoper in the party's leadership election, pulled off a shock victory. Corbyn coming to power as Labour leader was, Irish writer David Cronin observes, a 'nightmarish scenario' for the Israel lobby.[96] A long-standing patron of the Palestine Solidarity Campaign, Corbyn had also voiced support for key elements of the BDS campaign, such as imposing an arms embargo on Israel.

Backed by campaign group Momentum, the Corbynite offensive was about much more than Palestine. It was concerned with democratising the Labour Party and reducing economic inequality in Britain by challenging neoliberal politics. Yet Corbyn's record as an anti-racism activist and as an anti-war, internationalist MP – including his commitment to justice for Palestinians – was a key aspect of what marked him out as drastically different from the New Labour politicians who had held sway in the party for so long. And very soon, Corbyn's drastically different approach on Israel/ Palestine became evident.

Where virtually every previous Labour leader had made a political occasion of their appearances at LFI, Corbyn snubbed the organisation's 2017 party conference gathering altogether.[97] Soon after this, he declined to attend an event celebrating the one hundredth anniversary of the Balfour Declaration.[98] Just as worrying for the Israel lobby was the broader transformation of the Labour Party, which Corbyn's victory both expressed and strengthened. Membership of the party rocketed as those disillusioned by New Labour returned, and new members, previously unenthused by mainstream politics, joined up. By late 2016, some were already claiming that Corbyn's Labour was the largest left-wing party in Europe.[99] By threatening to turn growing public pro-Palestinian sentiment into policy, democratisation and an engaged left-wing membership spelled serious trouble for the lobby and its strategy – heretofore relatively successful – of insulating parliamentary elites.

However, almost immediately after Corbyn became leader, Labour began lurching from scandal to scandal concerning alleged anti-Semitism. Much ink has been spilled on this prolonged crisis, about which views are deeply polarised. Many of the interpretations proffered and defensive postures assumed are deeply misguided. It is not correct, for example, to paint Labour as an inherently anti-racist party. Indeed, as we have seen, in figures like Sidney Webb the party has a long history of anti-Semitism; Clement Attlee's Labour government even interned Jewish Holocaust survivors in concentration camps in Cyprus.[100] Labour has also passed discriminatory anti-immigration legislation, not to mention voting in support of the contemporary expansion of detention centres and Islamophobic counterterrorism policies such as Prevent.[101]

Nor should Labour's anti-Semitism crisis be reduced to an Israel-lobby-manufactured 'smear', as some have labelled it.[102] It is true that some complaints of anti-Semitism came from actors with links to pro-Israel activism. These included former BICOM intern Alex

Chalmers and former MP Ruth Smeeth, once an employee of the same organisation,[103] as well the Israel Advocacy Movement and Campaign Against Antisemitism, both groups with deeply questionable anti-racist credentials, as Chapter 5 will explain. Another notable actor was the Jewish Labour Movement, as Poale Zion (which fell into dormancy for many years with the rise of LFI) was renamed in 2004. Resurrected in earnest in 2015, one of the Jewish Labour Movement's explicit aims is to 'promote Labour or Socialist Zionism', and it is affiliated to the British Zionist Federation and the World Zionist Organization.[104] Among its senior staff, there is also something of a revolving-door with pro-Israel advocacy. For instance, Jeremy Newmark was involved in the Fair Play Campaign Group and the Global Coalition for Israel, while Ella Rose previously worked for the Israeli embassy.[105]

None of this, however, renders anti-Semitism within Labour a myth. While there was *one* documented instance of anti-Semitism being fabricated – involving LFI's Joan Ryan at a Labour Party conference[106] – to deny the very real presence of anti-Semitism within Labour would be deeply irresponsible. Indeed, around 30 per cent of all adults in Britain are believed to hold at least one anti-Semitic attitude.[107] The left is not immune. It is vital to recognise, then, that Labour's crisis uncovered the expression of ideas which where were genuinely abhorrently anti-Semitic *by any definition*. The response of a small section of the left – including figures like former Labour MP Chris Williamson and former London mayor Ken Livingstone – who verged on denying any problem of anti-Semitism in the party, was therefore unhelpful and potentially very dangerous. Moreover, while Israeli officials like Masot have, as outlined, been caught plotting to 'take down' British politicians and the Israeli government certainly had an interest in stigmatising Corbyn, when one senior Labour national executive committee member unwisely speculated in 2019 that the Israeli embassy was behind some of the anti-Semitism allegations, he could not point to a shred of evidence.[108]

Claims made at the *opposite* extreme – that Corbyn was presiding over a party attracting Jew-haters 'like flies to a cesspit' – were also incorrect.[109] The truth is that real anti-Semitism was to a considerable extent 'weaponised', as the Jewish Socialists Group put it, in a very cynical way: as a tool in a factional power struggle by a coalition of actors to the right of Corbyn.[110] These actors were much broader than the Zionist movement alone, including the right wing of Labour (which fought bitterly against what it saw as a hard-left capture of the party), the 'hard centre of the British press', and wider conservative forces looking to discredit the party.[111]

The response of the Labour leadership and a broad section of Corbyn's allies was to acknowledge the problem of anti-Semitism but to emphasise its small scale and – in the face of absurd comparisons with Nazi Germany – to call for perspective, given the very real global rise of the far right.[112] However, even when high-profile figures like Livingstone were quietly shown the door, this was read by some as evidence of the depth of the problem, rather than proof that the issue was being dealt with. As such, Labour was caught in a cyclical crisis characterised variously by political commentators as 'intrinsically geared toward perpetual escalation', and 'designed to feed on itself' in a manner reminiscent of a moral panic.[113]

Why was this? Underlying the affair were questions not only about the *scale* of anti-Semitism, or even its weaponisation, but about the very *nature* of anti-Semitism itself. Ideas about Israel and Zionism played an extremely prominent role in the saga. And the culmination of the entire affair was the adoption of the International Holocaust Remembrance Alliance definition (already endorsed by Theresa May's Conservative government in 2016), which redefines anti-Semitism to include certain criticisms of Israel and Zionism.

Labour's adoption of the IHRA definition, deconstructed in the introduction of this book, was first and foremost a travesty of justice for Palestinians; indeed, it was arguably only possible because of anti-Palestinian racism entrenched so deeply within the party as to be virtually invisible. Although Labour's National Executive Committee tried to propose an alternative code, there was a concerted push by the Parliamentary Labour Party – MPs and peers – for the IHRA definition and its problematic accompanying examples to be adopted in full in July 2018.[114] This meant the inclusion of 'examples' of potential anti-Semitism such as calling the state of Israel 'a racist endeavour'. As if to demonstrate the perversity of this erasure of Palestinians' lived experience, that same month the Israeli government passed the Nation-State Law, an unambiguously racist piece of legislation which declared Israel to be the nation-state of the Jewish people alone (*not* a state of all its citizens), further codifying the apartheid system imposed on Palestinians.

Worsening matters further, the adoption of the IHRA definition was also a tragedy for the hopes of building anti-racist solidarity between Jewish communities and other racialised groups. Sadly, the 'historical parting of ways' between movements against anti-Semitism and wider anti-racism struggles, described by Ben Gidley and other scholars, is long standing.[115] The role of Israel and Zionism in creating distance between these struggles is not insignificant, and the IHRA saga demonstrates why. As a letter from a group of Palestinian academics, journalists and intellectuals noted, not only does the IHRA definition prevent Palestinians from naming their oppression and fighting it; the doctrine also 'conflates Judaism with Zionism' and suggests that the state of Israel 'embodies' all Jewish people.[116] Thus, by positioning Jews in opposition to Palestinians' critique of Israeli settler colonialism and apartheid, it creates a zero-sum game in which one cannot be opposed to *both* Israeli apartheid and anti-Semitism – precisely the principled anti-racist position for which the introduction of this book called.

Since it holds important lessons about anti-racism today, the Labour anti-Semitism episode should be situated within the wider context of British state racism. Notably, the Equality and Human Rights Commission (EHRC), a body created by the government in 2006, found the Labour Party to be responsible for harassment and discrimination under the Equality Act.[117] While important, many Jewish activists rightly remained suspicious of the EHRC's highly performative war against anti-Semitism.[118] Notably, just two weeks after the organisation's anti-Semitism ruling, David Goodhart – a journalist who supports the British government's racist 'hostile environment' policies and calls Black Lives Matter's complaints of systemic racism 'statistically naive' – was appointed as an EHRC commissioner.[119] At the same time, a parliamentary committee concluded that the EHRC had 'been unable to adequately provide leadership and gain trust in tackling racial inequality'.[120] The organisation even abandoned an investigation into Islamophobia in the Conservative Party, despite a dossier of evidence submitted by the Muslim Council of Britain.[121] Sociologist Nasar Meer pointed out: 'Few race-equality stakeholders feel connected to [the EHRC], something typified by its nearly all-white board of commissioners. That it has not one black commissioner is a disgrace, and itself evidence of a profound institutional failure on race equality.'[122] The EHRC symbolised and articulated, as a non-departmental public body, a liberal, state-led anti-racism agenda. This type of anti-racism, intellectual historian Barnaby Raine observes, treats racism as a fringe issue of the far left (Corbyn's Labour) or far right (the British National Party – the only other political party the EHRC had investigated), rather than a central feature of British governance. That the EHRC's interventions positioned the state as *protector from*, rather than *perpetrator of*, racism was perhaps unsurprising given that its commissioners are appointed by the government.[123] More recently, the EHRC has also been criticised for failing to uphold the human rights of disabled people and transgender people.[124]

In the context of British racial politics, the Labour anti-Semitism crisis and adoption of the IHRA definition was tragically divisive. Rather than building solidarity, it created a sense of competition and the perception of a 'hierarchy of racism', within Labour and beyond, with Black, Muslim, Palestinian and other groups believing *their* experiences were not taken seriously.[125] The Forde inquiry, an independent investigation commissioned by the party's National Executive Committee, later demonstrated this. Articulating this sentiment, a letter from a long list of self-identifying BAME (Black, Asian and minority ethnic) and community organisations lamented the IHRA definition's effective erasure of Palestinians' history of colonial oppression. It pointed to the Grenfell Tower fire and the Windrush scandal as examples of 'the dangers of silencing migrant and BAME communities' and rendering them 'invisible', precluding contestation of 'the active legacies of British colonialism'.[126] Therefore, while certain sections of the white pro-Palestinian left reduced the IHRA issue to one of 'free speech', the debacle spoke to a wider – arguably global – phenomenon in which, as scholar Liz Fekete observes, 'the nature of anti-racism itself' had 'emerged as the key site of struggle'.[127]

For Fekete, the 'professionalisation of anti-racism' in the era of neoliberalism has seen racism 'redefined solely as [individual] [inter] personal hate, prejudice and bigotry', as opposed to social, institutional and systemic.[128] This attenuated understanding, constructed over decades, poses a threat to anti-racism. Writing in early 2020, she noted presciently that a defining trait of contemporary racism was how it operated as 'a system of denial': 'institutional racism today is held in place by policies, institutions and government spokespeople that deny it exists at all – and this is part and parcel of a new common-sense racism.'[129] Sure enough, a year later, the landmark Sewell report on racial 'disparity' by the Commission on Race and Ethnic Disparities, set up by 10 Downing Street, claimed that Britain was 'no longer' institutionally racist.[130] Widely condemned, one critic dubbed it a 'masterclass in gaslighting'.[131]

Seen in this light, the fact that the Labour anti-Semitism crisis culminated in the adoption of the IHRA definition fits a pattern. The agenda of the Israeli government and its supporters in the British Zionist movement to deny the Nakba and Israeli apartheid aligned neatly with the pre-existing agenda of the British government, the right and much of the British media to deny institutional racism in Britain. This widespread denial and redefinition of racism is catastrophic: for Palestinians, for whom merely speaking about the material reality of their oppression under Israeli apartheid could see them branded anti-Semitic; for Jewish communities, effectively positioned by the IHRA definition as human shields to protect Israeli apartheid from criticism; for the Labour left and Corbyn, who lost the 2019 election to Boris Johnson – a man who had called Muslim women 'letterboxes' and Black people 'piccaninnies' – and for all racialised groups and all anti-racists who believe the fight against all forms of racism must be indivisible.[132]

Two parties of passionate Zionists?

In May 2018, the ongoing oppression of Palestinians momentarily pierced the Westminster bubble. Weekly 'Great March of Return' protests by Palestinians in Gaza, which had been taking place at the border fence since March, were repeatedly violently repressed by the Israeli military. Most brutally, on 14 May 2018 – the seventieth anniversary of the Nakba and the day that Donald Trump's administration moved the US embassy from Tel Aviv to Jerusalem, disdaining international consensus – more than sixty Palestinians were killed.[133] In response, two erstwhile supporters of Labour Friends of Israel asked for their names to be removed from the group's list of parliamentary patrons, and Jeremy Corbyn, at that time still Labour leader, labelled the killings 'an outrage'.[134] Within a few days, Israeli Labor party HaAvoda severed ties with British Labour.[135]

In response to this state violence, and seemingly in defiance of the Parliamentary Labour Party's support for redefining criticism of Zionism as anti-Semitism, Labour members passed an unprecedented pro-Palestine motion at the party's annual conference in late September 2018. It called for an immediate two-way arms embargo with Israel and recognised the Nakba, despite reported behind-the-scenes attempts to have the word removed by shadow foreign secretary Emily Thornberry – who, incidentally, claims to be related to Herbert Samuel, the first British imperial ruler of Palestine.[136] There was also, for 'the first time in recent memory', no LFI stall at all at the 2018 Labour conference.[137]

However, after Corbyn suffered a humiliating electoral defeat to Boris Johnson in 2019, the Labour leadership's stance on Israel/Palestine changed dramatically. Keir Starmer's leadership campaign included the explicit pronouncement, 'I support Zionism without qualification.'[138] Starmer's support for Israel was long-standing: in 2011, as director of public prosecutions, he had blocked an international arrest warrant for ex–Israeli foreign minister Tzipi Livni. Notably, Starmer received a £50,000 donation from pro-Israel donor Trevor Chinn for his bid to become leader (and later a further £20,000).[139] He set up a 'Rose Network' of donors and under its banner saw Blair-era supporters return to the Labour fold. Among them was David Abrahams, once known as 'Mr Big in LFI', whose allegedly Islamophobic online statements prompted calls for his money to be returned.[140]

Yet following Starmer's ascendancy, anti-Semitism did not miraculously disappear. Indeed, Conservative minister Michael

Gove sought to keep wielding it as a political weapon, writing to Starmer to ask why he had previously agreed to serve in Corbyn's cabinet.[141] In turn, Starmer set about proving his credentials. He cancelled his attendance at an Iftar dinner after a pro-Israel activist raised concerns about an organiser's support for BDS, implicitly associating the boycott movement with anti-Semitism.[142] In November 2021, he made a speech to LFI In which he referenced the colonial trope that Israeli settlers 'made the desert flower'.[143] And soon after that, despite his background in human rights law, Starmer declared that he disagreed with human rights group Amnesty International's finding that Israel was committing the crime of apartheid against Palestinians.[144] At the same time, Starmer dismissed the idea of defunding the police – a key demand of the Black Lives Matter movement – as 'nonsense' and condemned the way protestors in Bristol forcefully tore down a statue of former slave trader Edward Colston, fuelling concerns that other forms of racial oppression, particularly anti-Black racism, were also being ignored.[145]

At the 2021 Labour conference, LFI once more came in from the cold, returning to what it called 'capacity crowds'.[146] However, the mood among Labour members had changed less dramatically than the rhetoric at the top of the party, and fundamental solidarity with Palestinians had not gone anywhere. At the very same conference, delegates passed a hard-hitting motion condemning the 'ongoing Nakba in Palestine', asserting that 'Israel is practicing the crime of apartheid' and calling for sanctions and an arms embargo. Kamel Hawwash, chair of the Palestine Solidarity Campaign, said the move demonstrated 'the strength of solidarity with the Palestinian people amongst Labour's grassroots members and within the trade union movement'.[147] Conversely, Luke Akehurst of We Believe in Israel, who sits on Labour's National Executive Committee and describes himself as a 'passionate Zionist', called the motion 'disgusting' and a 'possible breach of IHRA'.[148] An uneasy stalemate was thus reached in Labour, albeit one which, in the face of bottom-up pressure, called into question the sustainability of the strategy of insulating political elites.

Nonetheless, at the time of writing, an elite pro-Israel consensus has been restored. While within Labour, the split between the centrist leadership and the more left-leaning membership on the Palestine issue remains a serious ideological rift, the topic has proven highly toxic. In the Conservative Party, support for Israel remains, as political journalist Martin Bright observes, strong 'at the very top'.[149] It is axiomatic that the party leader will attend the annual CFI Business Lunch, not least because a number of its keenest supporters are also significant party donors. Former prime minister Boris Johnson also describes himself as a 'passionate Zionist',[150] and around 80 per cent of Conservative MPs are believed to be members of CFI.

CFI is an 'ingrained part of the Westminster social scene' and enjoys 'superb contacts at the very top of British politics', calling upon these friends to act at critical moments. For example, CFI was a key player in the British government's decision to oppose a UN resolution endorsing the Goldstone Report, which accused Israel of committing war crimes during its 2008–9 bombing of Gaza. Foreign Minister William Hague was reportedly lobbied about it personally by Andrew Feldman, a former party chair and friend of ex–prime minister David Cameron.[151] As we shall see, CFI has also influenced changes in the law around universal jurisdiction and has long campaigned for BDS initiatives emanating from local councils to be outlawed – legislation which, in late-2022, Conservatives were still pledging to table.

It is difficult, in short, to disagree with the *Financial Times* assessment that CFI is 'very influential'.[152] Writing in 2009, Oborne and Jones went further, calling it the 'best connected and probably best funded' lobby group in Westminster. Former Conservative minister Michael Mates concurs, dubbing CFI 'the most powerful' lobby in British politics – effective, he claims, because its lobbying is 'done very discreetly, in very high places'.[153] Hyperbole or not, the organisation's reputation is such that in recent years it has spawned copycat groups like Conservative Friends of India and Conservative Friends of the Chinese. While a few pro-Palestine organisations such as CAABU and Medical Aid for Palestinians also organise trips for MPs – in essence, seeking to rival LFI and CFI, though on a much-smaller scale – change will not come from Westminster without relentless pressure from civil society. It is to this arena that the following chapter turns.

5

Manufacturing Consent

On 8 July 2014, Israel launched a bombing campaign code-named Operation Protective Edge, its third major military assault on the Gaza Strip in five years. As Palestinian analyst Mouin Rabbani notes, the fact that these regular attacks on Gaza are referred to by the Israeli military as 'mowing the lawn' gives us a sense of how routine and banal they are. The grass in this analogy, he notes, 'consists overwhelmingly of non-combatant Palestinian civilians, indiscriminately targeted by Israel's precision weaponry'.[1] Over fifty-one days in summer 2014, the Israeli military killed more than two thousand Palestinians – the majority of them civilians, including approximately five hundred children. In the same period, Hamas killed seventy-three people, all but six of whom were Israeli soldiers. Yet, in Britain, Prime Minister David Cameron merely declared that he 'strongly condemned the appalling attacks being carried out by Hamas' and 'reiterated the UK's staunch support for Israel . . . and [its] right to defend itself'.[2] Opposition leader Ed Miliband condemned this response to the massacre, declaring that Cameron's 'silence on the killing of hundreds of innocent Palestinian civilians caused by Israel's military action will be inexplicable to people across Britain and internationally'.[3] It even provoked tensions within Cameron's own Conservative cabinet. Several weeks into the bombing campaign, Foreign Office Minister Sayeeda Warsi resigned in protest, calling the British government's stance on the attack 'morally indefensible'.[4]

All over the world, huge protests in solidarity with Palestinians erupted. While those at the very top of the most powerful governments were intent on granting Israel impunity, ordinary people wanted to do what they could to end the violence and suffering. Midway through the sustained bombardment on 26 July 2014, a small theatre in north London called the Tricycle decided it did not wish to be associated with this gratuitous state violence. As it prepared to host the UK Jewish Film Festival, the theatre chose to ask for the Israeli embassy's logo to be removed from promotional materials, offering to reimburse the small amount of sponsorship money involved to ensure that the festival could still go ahead. But festival organisers, outraged, refused the request and soon the story was splashed across all major British press and broadcast media. Just days later, the theatre made a dramatic U-turn.

How, in the intervening period, had this change of direction come about? This chapter tells the story of what happened behind the scenes. It situates the episode within the context of larger battles within the cultural arena: firstly, Israel's attempts to manufacture consent via the Brand Israel programme, versus the Boycott, Divestment, Sanctions movement's efforts to denormalise ties with Israeli apartheid; and, secondly, the British government's broader political agenda to limit the independence of civil society institutions. It shows that grasping the full extent of pro-Israel activism in Britain today means looking beyond traditional lobbying activities in Westminster, where support for Israel is strong, to civil society, where pro-Palestine solidarity initiatives tend to emerge. The Tricycle Theatre saga also reveals a considerable amount about the relatively *minor* role pro-Israel actors in civil society sometimes play compared to the critical role of state actors, including the Israeli embassy and British government ministers supportive of Conservative Friends of Israel. Before that, however, the chapter examines another facet of Israel's attempts to influence wider publics: the 'manufacturing' of civil society.

Building a British 'counter-delegitimisation network'

Israel's government, as chapter 2 explained, has absorbed the ideas of 'new public diplomacy' theorists in its battle against the BDS movement. Like the South African apartheid regime before it, it seeks to enlist civil society organisations to help wage its propaganda war, believing their Israel-advocacy work to be complementary to official efforts – and very likely more effective. As well as mobilising pre-existing Zionist groups, and sometimes discreetly supporting them with direct or indirect funding, the Israeli government has also sought to supplement its support network. Zionist think-tanks note that the Israeli government has 'established organizations in various countries throughout the world' to 'deliver hasbara messages through "indirect channels" without officially identifying themselves as such' and praise it for making a 'critical contribution' to the construction of 'a global 'anti-delegitimization network"'.[5]

Britain is one of the countries which has seen a proliferation of pro-Israel groups founded since Israel's crisis of legitimacy sharpened in 2010 following Operation Cast Lead and the attack on the *Mavi Marmara*, and especially after summer 2014, when Israel's deadly bombing of Gaza provoked renewed outrage. The emergence of these new groups should be understood in this context of growing anxiety in pro-Israel circles about overwhelming public support for Palestinians. Outgoing Israeli ambassador Ron Prosor acknowledged this in 2011, observing that 'in the penthouse – that is to say, on a government level – things are good . . . but unfortunately, lower down, there is serious damage and leaking in the basement'.[6] In other words, the strength of the Palestine solidarity movement in civil society was such that Israel's supporters felt the country could no longer afford to ignore this sphere and concentrate solely on insulating parliamentary elites (and thus foreign policy) from public opinion. With that strategy under strain, renewed efforts to influence wider publics became necessary.

The evidence suggests that many of the hyperlocal 'Friends of Israel' groups which emerged post-2010 were at least partially created by the Israeli embassy, in collaboration with pre-existing pro-Israel civil society groups. This is consistent with the Israeli government's practices around the world and confirms that 'issues at the grass roots of civil society have become the bread and butter of diplomacy at the highest levels', as new public diplomacy scholar Jan Melissen has argued.[7] While often referred to as 'grassroots' bodies, having been co-created by the embassy, these groups are effectively 'manufactured civil society' and are therefore more appropriately termed 'astroturf' groups.[8]

As Israeli newspaper *Haaretz* reported in 2016, Israel's London embassy has played a key role in the creation, since around 2012, of 'a network of more than 40 pro-Israel organizations throughout Britain'. The paper noted that the embassy's approach to the struggle against BDS in Britain was to treat it like a war. It described the office of one Israeli diplomat stationed in London, in which there was 'a map of Britain hanging on the wall . . . like the war room of a brigade on the Lebanese border . . . [which] shows the front – the main campuses, the deployment of pro-Israel activists and the location of the "enemy forces"'.[9]

More evidence of the Israeli government's part in manufacturing pro-Israel groups in civil society came from Al Jazeera's 2017 documentary *The Lobby*. In the film, Shai Masot, the Israeli official who was disgraced after being filmed discussing ways to discredit members of Parliament critical of Israel, unwittingly revealed to an undercover reporter that he was planning to establish a group called City Friends of Israel, the aim of which was to foster support for Israel within London's financial district in a similar way to the Wall Street network fostered by AIPAC in the US. On his LinkedIn profile, Masot boasted that his work in Britain had included 'founding several political support groups in the UK to maximise the Israeli "firewall"' (a term lifted from an influential Reut Institute report). 'It's good', he explained to an undercover Al Jazeera reporter, 'to leave those organisations independent but we help them, actually'.[10]

Further confirmation of the Israeli government's role in manufacturing civil society groups comes from its London embassy's director of public diplomacy, Rony Yedidia-Clein.[11] In a 2016 speech to Zionist activists, she lauded the fact that a network of pro-Israel organisations was springing up across Britain, from Jersey to Inverness. Echoing the *Haaretz* report, she cited the figure of forty new groups, going on to describe the collaborative public–private partnership model behind the cultivation of this new organisational infrastructure. 'We have people here in the room who have helped me at the embassy . . . because it's not just me, we're a whole team', she said appreciatively, 'to set up friends of Israel organisations around the country'.[12] Two of the pro-Israel civil society organisations which appear to have helped the embassy co-create this new network of local groups are the Board of Deputies and We Believe in Israel.

At the Board, Stephen Jaffe worked as a 'grassroots consultant' (work partly funded by the Jewish Leadership Council) and was instrumental in co-producing the pro-Israel 'counter-delegitimisation' network. In a 2014 article hailing what he called the 'growing army of grassroots groups working to defend Israel', he mentioned several such groups, including Friends of Israel chapters active in London and Newcastle. Jaffe also stated that such groups are provided with 'practical support' by both the Israeli embassy and 'national pro-Israel organisations', listing StandWithUs, the Zionist Federation, Christian Friends of Israel and the Union of Jewish Students.[13] At least two self-declared 'grassroots' groups are known to have received thousands of pounds of funding. North West Friends of Israel, active in the Manchester area, was financially supported by the Jewish Leadership Council.[14] After receiving explicit endorsements from Israeli government ministers no less prominent than Prime Minister Benjamin Netanyahu and Strategic Affairs Minister Gildan Erdan, it was also able to attract the chairs of both Labour and Conservative Friends of Israel to speak at its event.[15] Meanwhile, Sussex Friends of Israel, based in Brighton, received funding from an Israeli Zionist organisation called Over the Rainbow, which describes the Israeli government as a 'partner', and used the money to organise anti-BDS activism alongside the Israeli embassy, Board of Deputies and Zionist Federation.[16] Sussex Friends of Israel was also mentioned by Israeli diplomat Shai Masot in Al Jazeera's 2017 investigative documentary as one of the groups *directly* supported by the Israeli Embassy in London.[17]

We Believe in Israel began life as a conference organised by BICOM – with the support of the Israeli embassy and Zionist Federation – in 2011. A rare attempt to mobilise grassroots support in the face of Israel's crisis of legitimacy, the event was originally entitled 'Winning Britain Back for Israel'.[18] Later rebranded as 'We Believe in Israel', it led to the establishment of the organisation by the same name which today holds events such as an annual 'Zionism Month', intended to 're-establish . . . the core case for the Zionist project'.[19] We Believe in Israel director Luke Akehurst formerly worked for lobbying firm Weber Shandwick, where he helped arms companies sell weapons to the Ministry of Defence. A secretary of Labour First, a faction on the right of Labour, Akehurst was elected to the party's National Executive Committee in 2020. He has argued that the Fourth Geneva Convention does not apply to Israel's illegal West Bank settlements, claiming it was designed to stop 'forced deportations', whereas Israeli settlers have 'moved voluntarily'.[20] The consensus among scholars of international law says otherwise.

Implicitly acknowledging the Zionist movement's limited ability to mobilise at the grassroots compared to its excellent access to political elites, Akehurst has said: 'The pro-Israel community in the UK has always been good at top level stuff with politicians. My job is building campaigning infrastructure for ordinary people at local level.'[21] He has confirmed that We Believe in Israel supported 'the development of about 40 local action groups plus sector specific groups' (the latter category includes Local Government Friends of Israel, discussed in the next chapter).[22] And, though he declined to say how often, Akehurst has also confirmed that We Believe in Israel stays in touch with Israeli embassy officials, saying, 'We keep them updated on our work and seek their views.'[23] Many of the new friends of Israel groups hosted an Israeli embassy representative as a keynote speaker at their launch events, often alongside Jaffe and Akehurst.[24] Indeed, the centralisation and homogeneity of the network was such that in 2019, Akehurst estimated that he himself had spoken at 145 out of the 149 events held by local pro-Israel groups in the whole of Britain that year.[25] Similarly, in Scotland, just one person (a man called Nigel Goodrich) was reportedly responsible for establishing at least seven of the country's new pro-Israel groups.[26]

This tells us that although the existence of these local friends of Israel groups is designed to give the impression that support for Israel runs deep within civil society, in reality this is largely an illusion. The fact that support for Israel in civil society has had to be engineered, in a top-down way, illustrates that it has not been spontaneously forthcoming, or at least not on a mass scale. It is also important to note the constituencies in which the Israeli embassy and its allies are able to mobilise. We Believe in Israel's survey of its own activist base revealed that the majority were not drawn from the Jewish community but instead identified as Christians, and a significant proportion of local friends of Israel groups' members are of the same faith.[27] Moreover, as journalist and analyst Ben White observes, the Israeli embassy is increasingly resorting to collaboration with right-wing activists accused of Islamophobia, such as Sharon Klaff and Ambrosine Shitrit, and grassroots support for Israeli apartheid is 'fast becoming the preserve of an extremist few'.[28]

Culture clash: Brand Israel versus BDS in Britain

Alongside the creation of manufactured or astroturfed civil society bodies, a second element of Israel's attempt to manufacture consent beyond the parliamentary sphere has been the weaponisation of culture. The Brand Israel project, as chapter 2 explained, sought to 'show Israel's prettier face' to the world in order to 'broaden the conversation' about the country 'beyond the conflict'.[29] Central to the scheme was the government-sponsored promotion of Israeli culture overseas. And Britain – seen as a key 'hub of delegitimisation' – has been an important target for Brand Israel projects.[30]

A range of Israeli artists, musicians and writers have received state sponsorship to tour Britain. For instance, the classical musicians of the Jerusalem Quartet, who boast that they also perform for the Israeli army, played pieces by Mozart and Ravel at the Edinburgh Festival in 2008 and later at London's Wigmore Hall in 2010. Subsequently, Israel's national theatre company, Habima, performed Shakespeare's *The Merchant of Venice* in Hebrew at the Globe Theatre in London in 2012. The company, which has performed in illegal Israeli settlements, called the invitation to act at the Globe 'an honourable accomplishment for the State of Israel', and Israeli ambassador Daniel Taub attended the play.[31] Rarely, if ever, do state-sponsored Israeli artists produce cultural outputs which are overtly political, let alone nationalistic in themselves. Yet due to their state funding (and vocal support for Israeli apartheid), both these groups' events attracted pro-Palestine protests. Following the disruption of a Jeruslaem Quartet concert by BDS activists,

Taub's predecessor, Ron Prosor, declared, 'We must not give in to the attempts to sabotage the marketing of Israeli art and culture in Britain.'[32]

This clash between Brand Israel and the BDS movement has seen a number of events explicitly celebrating Israel staged in Britain. Such events – for example 'Israel Expo', first organised by the Israeli embassy and Zionist Federation in London in 2002 – certainly predate the Brand Israel programme. But, as Israel's image crisis deepened in the decade after 2010, they appeared to increase in frequency. In 2016, a festival called 'Shalom' ('peace') was staged at the Edinburgh Festival for the first time. It was organised by Stand-WithUs UK, the British branch of the right-wing, pro-settlement Zionist group whose close ties to the Israeli government were noted in chapter 2. It is not known whether the UK branch, established in 2010, received Israeli government funding as its parent body did.[33] Reports about whether Shalom, specifically, received state sponsorship were contradictory.[34]

What we do know is that StandWithUs UK had previously been condemned by the majority of Israeli students at Oxford University's Israel Society, who complained that their student group had been 'co-opted from a cultural society to a hard-line political advocacy group' through its constitutionally mandated relationship with the group, which also reportedly provided funding.[35] In addition, the Shalom festival's chief executive was none other than Nigel Goodrich, the man who had helped establish at least seven pro-Israel groups in Scotland. Goodrich, for his part, claimed that Shalom was an 'apolitical celebration of Israel's cultural diversity'.[36] Yet, alongside more anodyne programming such as an Israeli cooking demonstration, it also featured artwork made from 'rockets fired into Southern Israel' and a film about why media reports from Gaza are biased against the settler-colonial state.[37] In 2019, Goodrich's credentials as an apologist for Israeli apartheid were corroborated when he was exposed as a member of a racist online group called 'Jewish Defence Forces'.[38]

Also in 2017, an event called TLV in LDN ('A Celebration of Tel Aviv culture in London') was openly marketed as a collaboration between the Israeli embassy, Zionist Federation, United Jewish Israel Appeal and other sponsors. An additional key partner was

Marc Worth, a multimillionaire internet entrepreneur. Between 2011 and 2015, Worth had chaired UK Israel Business, a body established in 2011 by the merger of the Israel-Britain Business Council and the British-Israel Chamber of Commerce. While not involved in straightforward 'Israel advocacy', the organisation exists to foster business between Britain and Israel and therefore naturally has an interest in undermining the BDS movement. As we saw in chapter 3, one of its precursor bodies, the Anglo-Israel Chamber of Commerce, played a part in combating the Arab League boycott of Israel. Worth was also the husband of Hilda Worth, an important figure in Conservative Friends of Israel and the Jewish Leadership Council as well as the co-chair of the Fair Play Campaign Group/Israel Advocacy Forum, which coordinates anti-BDS activism in Britain as chapter 3 explained.[39]

Speaking to Israeli media outlet *Ynet*, Marc Worth explained how the TLV in LDN festival came about. He described how 'the cultural department at the Israeli Embassy told me they had a "top secret project" that they wanted my advice on' to 'provide a strong response' to the BDS movements.[40] Such cooperation between the state and pro-Israel elites was by no means unique to Brand Israel efforts in Britain. In 2008, Amir Gissin, an Israeli consular official in Toronto, Canada, praised the efforts of local businessmen who were 'not afraid to combine their businesses with their love for Israel' after they helped to fund similar pro-Israel cultural events.[41] These collaborations across the state–private network echo philanthropists' collaboration with the US state in the cultural sphere during the Cold War, as noted in chapter 1. In 2019, the format of the TLV in LDN festival was reversed, becoming a celebration of London staged in Tel Aviv.

Alongside the promotion of Israel through culture, pro-Israel actors have pushed back strongly against BDS initiatives in the cultural sphere. In February 2015, for example, more than 1,000 artists and performers based in Britain issued a pledge to culturally boycott Israel and by October of that year, a response letter had appeared. It described cultural boycotts of Israel as 'discriminatory' and declared support for a new (but ultimately short-lived) network called Culture for Coexistence. Documents obtained via a freedom of information request suggest that BICOM spin-off We Believe in

Israel played an instrumental role in the 'Culture for Coexistence' initiative, just as it helped to build the 'counter-delegitimisation network' in Britain.[42] Signatories to the letter published under the Culture for Coexistence banner included cultural figures like Harry Potter author J. K. Rowling, but also at least twenty signatories with strong links to Conservative Friends of Israel and *no* obvious links to the cultural sphere. One such name was that of multi-millionaire Stanley Fink, the so-called godfather of the hedge fund industry. A Conservative peer and a former party treasurer, he was both chief fundraiser to ex–prime minister David Cameron and the man who, according to the *Jewish Chronicle*, 'bankrolled' Boris Johnson's bid to become London mayor.[43] The inclusion of names like Fink's likely reflected the role of Baron Andrew Feldman, former Conservative Party chair and another former Cameron fundraiser, as well as his friend and tennis partner. Documents released under freedom of information legislation suggest that in 2015, Feldman circulated the Culture for Coexistence anti-BDS letter to senior Conservatives, encouraging them to sign.[44]

Efforts to police the cultural sphere to stamp out criticism of Israel are long-standing. In 2005 London's Royal Court Theatre was attacked by the Zionist Federation for staging *My Name Is Rachel Corrie*, a play about an American Palestine solidarity activist killed by an Israeli military bulldozer in Gaza in 2003. Then in 2008, the Israeli embassy and others complained about Central London's Barbican Centre hosting the annual Palestine Film Festival and a photography exhibition about the Nakba called *Homeland Lost*.[45] More recently, the Whitworth Gallery in Manchester ended up forcing out its director following a 2021 debacle in which the gallery pulled a statement of solidarity with Palestine from an exhibition. The decision to remove the statement, later reversed, was initially made on the back of a complaint from UK Lawyers for Israel.[46] Eyal Weizman, the Israeli architect and scholar who co-founded Forensic Architecture, the group behind the original exhibit, declared that the incident 'makes clear yet again that the anti-colonial struggle in support of Palestine and elsewhere has to be fought within and sometimes against our public institutions, including universities and art and cultural spaces'.[47]

As noted in a report published in the Israeli paper *Yedioth Ahronoth*, when it comes to opposing BDS initiatives, Israeli embassies are themselves 'very active behind the scenes'.[48] An instructive example from the British cultural sphere took place during the Tricycle Theatre controversy of 2014, discussed above, at which we now take a deeper look.

The Tricycle Theatre affair

The UK Jewish Film Festival, founded in 1997, is predominantly an important Jewish cultural event. However, according to its chair, the festival had also been 'associated' with the Israeli embassy since its establishment.[49] Although the Israeli embassy's sponsorship reportedly totalled just £1,400 in 2014, the festival programme explicitly incorporated a focus on Israel which chimed neatly with the aims of the Brand Israel strategy, showcasing a range of 'feature films, documentaries and shorts' not only about British Jewish life but also about 'the diversity of . . . Israeli life and culture'.[50] Yet when a row over its sponsorship erupted in summer 2014, the festival's organisers denied that its long-standing Israeli embassy support and dual Jewish *and Israeli* focus meant it served political propaganda purposes. Founder Judy Ironside insisted that the film festival was 'not political',[51] while its chair Stephen Margolis declared, 'We're not propagandists'. Simultaneously, however, each expressed Zionist political positions conflating Judaism with Israel. Ironside stated that since the film festival was a celebration of Jewish culture, it was therefore 'of course intrinsically connected to the State of Israel'.[52] Similarly, Margolis asserted the existence of an 'unbreakable connection between the Jewish people and the State of Israel', while also continuing to insist that the festival was 'entirely apolitical'.[53]

Since 2006, the festival had been hosted annually at the Tricycle Theatre in North London. In 2013, as calls for a cultural boycott of Israel were gathering steam, a small group of anti-Zionist Jews had protested outside the Tricycle during the film festival due to its Israeli embassy sponsorship, which they said made it part of Israel's PR campaign. The following summer, when Israel began bombing the Gaza strip intensely, the board of the Tricycle Theatre democratically decided to ask the festival to remove the Israeli embassy's logo from its promotional materials. They offered to reimburse the small amount of sponsorship money involved to ensure the festival could go ahead. The theatre's artistic director, Indhu Rubasingham, portrayed the move as an attempt to strive for political neutrality within a fraught situation, saying, 'I just didn't want to take sides in a very emotional, passionate situation.'[54]

Although the Tricycle insisted that its move was not intended as a BDS initiative, Stephen Margolis declared that it was 'in essence, a cultural boycott'.[55] Similarly, Judy Ironside accused the Tricycle of choosing 'a boycott over meaningful engagement', and the film festival's organisers refused the theatre's request to remove the embassy's logo.[56] On 5 August, the row first broke in the press with articles in the *Jewish Chronicle* and *Huffington Post*. The following day, the story was headline news in all major British press and broadcast media, including the BBC, *Telegraph*, *Daily Mail*, *Independent* and *Times*. The Tricycle alleged that these press reports contained 'misleading information', since most presented the theatre as having effectively 'banned' the film festival.[57] Indeed, much of the press coverage implied that the theatre's request was an example of anti-Semitism. An opinion piece by Hadley Freeman in the *Guardian*, for example, ended with the words, 'Watch yourself Europe, your roots are showing'.[58] Rubasingham felt obliged to state in the press that she was 'not anti-Semitic'.[59] Then on 15 August – just over a week after the story first appeared in the media – the Tricycle suddenly announced it had reversed its original decision. This change of direction had come about after many different elements of the Zionist movement had mobilised to apply pressure on the Tricyle from all sides.

One key actor was a group called Campaign Against Antisemitism, founded shortly before the Tricycle row hit the headlines. Although the organisation has been described by sociologist Keith Kahn-Harris, writing in the *Jewish Chronicle*, as one of the wave of 'grassroots' groups which emerged during the summer of 2014, 'bypassing venerable communal institutions in favour of more direct activism', Campaign Against Antisemitism enjoyed remarkable levels of *elite* support as well as proximity and access to state power.[60] For instance, several members of Parliament supportive of Conservative Friends of Israel (Bob Blackman, Matthew Offord, Eric Pickles and

Mike Freer) were originally listed as its patrons, alongside Labour Friends of Israel stalwart Lord Parry Mitchell.[61] In addition, Campaign Against Antisemitism's chair lobbied at the very highest political levels, meeting then Home Secretary Theresa May in January 2015, just six months after the Tricycle affair.[62] There is no evidence, however, to suggest that the organisation's establishment was linked to the Israeli embassy.

Kahn-Harris also notes that many of the relatively recently founded, ostensibly grassroots groups tend to 'lean to the right'. In the case of Campaign Against Antisemitism, this was certainly true. The group's chief executive, Gideon Falter, was also a vice-chair of the Jewish National Fund UK. Its founding spokesperson, Jonathan Sacerdoti, formerly worked at the Zionist Federation. Another early key figure, Mandy Blumenthal, was national director of revisionist Zionist body Herut UK and spoke at the latter's 2018 relaunch along-side her partner Mark Lewis of UK Lawyers for Israel.[63] Finally, another member, Joseph Cohen, went on to establish a small group called the Israel Advocacy Movement, after he reportedly 'decided that "anti-Semitism wasn't the problem – anti-Israel/Zionism is"'.[64] In 2019, the Israel Advocacy Movement hosted neo-Nazi Mark Collett in an online 'debate' called 'Should Zionists Support a White Ethno State?'[65] When criticised, the group claimed its intention was to 'show how evil' the far right is, yet its own material calls the Nakba a 'myth' and uses rhetoric associated with the far right, such as stating that Israel prevents Palestinian refugees from returning because they would constitute 'a fifth column' and pose a 'demographic threat'.[66]

Campaign Against Antisemitism has itself taken some troubling positions which call into question its anti-racist credentials. For example, the organisation once published a graphic called 'Profile of British Muslim Anti-Semitism', showing a figure labelled with traits such as 'male', 'in social housing', and 'first-generation immi-grant' – complete with brown skin. On another occasion, the group claimed that Black Lives Matter 'spreads hatred' after the anti-racism movement made its pro-Palestinian stance clear.[67] Campaign Against Antisemitism has also invited speakers such as the Henry Jackson Society's Douglas Murray, who denies the existence of Islamophobia, to address its rallies.[68] Moreover, it has been criti-cised by groups such as the Institute for Jewish Policy Research, the

Community Security Trust, the Jewish Leadership Council and the Board of Deputies – with the latter two bodies stating that Campaign Against Antisemitism's claims about anti-Semitism were 'exaggerated' and based on methodologically flawed polling.[69]

Nonetheless, Campaign Against Antisemitism's characterisation of the Tricycle Theatre row strongly shaped media narratives. At the heart of the group's interpretation of the affair was the idea of a 'new' anti-Semitism – which it described as 'antisemitism which masquerades as political opposition to Israel'.[70] On 7 August, the group organised a protest outside the theatre, attended by a few hundred people – among them Steven Jaffe, who'd helped the Israeli embassy set up local pro-Israel groups.[71] The crowd waved Israeli flags and held placards with slogans such as 'Boycott Divides, Culture Unites', 'Don't Punish London's Jews' and 'No to Jewish Film Festival ban'. Campaign Against Antisemitism's promotional material for the protest even claimed that the Tricycle's move 'echoes the Nazi boycott of Jewish enterprise after Hitler's election'.[72] This comparison angered British Jewish lawyer and academic Philippe Sands, a member of the Tricycle's board, who complained in correspondence obtained via freedom of information requests that it seemed 'intended to be highly provocative and offensive'. Alongside the protest, the theatre was, Sands claimed, 'inundated with abusive and wholly inappropriate phone calls and emails'.[73] Many of the callers accused the theatre of racism, in line with Campaign Against Antisemitism's representation.

The fact that British media coverage of the Tricycle saga also amounted, effectively, to an echo chamber of Campaign Against Antisemitism's perspective may have reflected the role of one of Britain's leading public relations firms, The PR Office.[74] Prior to working on behalf of the UK Jewish Film Festival during the Tricycle affair (as it had done in previous years), the company had worked for a number of pro-Israel bodies, counting among its previous clients the Jewish National Fund UK, the Jewish Leadership Council and religious Zionist group Aish UK.[75] Its founder and chairman, Shimon Cohen, ex-CEO of PR giant Bell Pottinger, had served on the Board of Deputies and as a director of UK Israel Business.[76] Cohen also appears to have been 'on message' with regard to Brand Israel since at least 2006, explicitly praising the programme in a letter to the *Jewish Chronicle* that year and calling for *hasbara* to focus on Israel's positive aspects.[77] In the Tricycle furore, The PR Office claimed responsibility for having 'secured over 250 pieces of media coverage', including 'thought pieces that meaningfully influenced the debate'.[78]

In contrast, there were barely any articles published in the press that were sympathetic to the Tricycle's position. In one of the few, an interview in the *Evening Standard* Rubasingham, she characterised moves by a clutch of private donors who sought to exercise leverage by threatening to withdraw support from the theatre as 'bullying'.[79] Tal Ofer, a pro-Israel activist involved in the Board of Deputies and Jewish Labour Movement, claims to have 'masterminded' this 'campaign to target donors' to the Tricycle.[80] On 6 August, the day after the dispute became public, he published and distributed online a list of forty-nine Tricycle donors, together with their contact details, urging people to 'call them and ask them to pull their funding'. Some patrons, including Allan Morgenthau, Celia Atkin and Trevor Chinn – the latter two also donors to pro-Israel bodies BICOM and Labour Friends of Israel, respectively – reportedly *did* withdraw their financial support from the theatre.[81]

However, contrary to speculation at the time, Brent Council – despite being accused of 'funding anti-Semitism' – did not cease financing the Tricycle.[82] Critically, nor did another public funder – the Arts Council, an arm's-length, non-departmental public body which provided the Tricycle with a basic annual grant of approximately £725,000, representing about 30 per cent of the theatre's income and making it the largest single donor. While at least one MP, Conservative Friends of Israel member and Campaign Against Antisemitism patron Mike Freer, did write to the Arts Council about the matter, there is no evidence that the Arts Council itself threatened to defund the theatre. In fact, its chief executive, Alan Davey, appears to have robustly defended its non-interventionist stance in his reply to Freer.[83]

The real threat to the theatre's funding came from Sajid Javid, Conservative secretary of state for culture, media and sport at the time. A long-standing member of Conservative Friends of Israel, Javid had visited Israel several times and praised the country for its 'warm embrace of freedom and liberty'. On 12 August 2014, senior figures in two key pro-Israel organisations wrote to Javid urging him to intervene in the matter. Jewish Leadership Council chair Mick Davis, a major donor to the Conservative Party, penned a letter jointly with Board president Vivian Wineman. The pair's missive claimed that Israeli state grants to the arts were 'apolitical' – a demonstrably false assertion given the Brand Israel campaign. Placing the incident squarely in the context of 'increasing attacks on Israeli culture in the UK', they exhorted Javid to act:

> We appreciate that artistic independence works both ways, and that there are real limits on Government's influence, even on ACE [Arts Council England]-funded institutions. However, we feel that the Tricycle's behaviour crosses the line into political activism and we are concerned that others will follow its lead. We believe it is important that Tricycle hears the message that politically-motivated boycotts are not acceptable from all parts of society, including from DCMS [Department for Culture, Media and Sport]. We hope you will find a way to make your views known to the theatre.[84]

On the same day that this letter was sent, Javid was quoted in the press criticising the Tricycle.[85] However, what even these leading supporters of Israel apparently did not yet know was that behind the scenes and away from the media furore, Javid had in fact *already* been closely personally involved in the row several days before – making what seems to have been the decisive intervention.

'Quiet and effective intervention'

A week after the denouement of the Tricycle affair, an article in the *Jewish Chronicle* made passing reference to the fact that the theatre's U-turn had come about 'after Israeli ambassador Daniel Taub and Culture Secretary Sajid Javid intervened'.[86] Remarkably, this was the only public reference to Taub's role, and the nature of his intervention, alongside Javid, was not explained. However, correspondence disclosed through freedom of information requests reveals the full extent of their behind-the-scenes activities, which went otherwise entirely unreported in the press.

Documents show that several days prior to being contacted by the Board of Deputies and Jewish Leadership Council, Javid had already made his views known in person to the Tricycle's artistic director – in no uncertain terms. In fact, the moment the scandal broke in the major national dailies, Javid's office had contacted the theatre and demanded a meeting. A press officer for the Tricycle informed a contact at the Arts Council about this unusual ministerial intervention in an email sent at 9:32 a.m. on 6 August: 'You should know that Sajid Javid has requested a meeting with Indhu which I am trying to set up for noon today.'[87] A meeting did then take place between Javid and Rubasingham. Though Javid's follow-up letter on 11 August was not disclosed, Rubasingham's short reply to the minister on 12 August read:

Dear Secretary of State,

Thank you for your letter of yesterday, and our recent conversation setting out your views in relation to the Tricycle hosting the UK Jewish Film Festival. I recognise your concerns and respect your desire that I and the Board of the Tricycle strive to secure an acceptable resolution that will enable the Festival to go ahead as planned. I would like to reassure you that we are working closely with the UK Jewish Film Festival to pursue every avenue to allow the festival to move ahead. We will keep you abreast of any key developments as a priority, and look forward to being in touch again soon. Thanks again for taking the time to meet and share your views.[88]

While we cannot know precisely what was said at the minister's face-to-face meeting with Rubasingham, accounts from both pro-Israel and pro-Palestinian sources close to the affair – as well as Javid's own subsequent public statements – are remarkably consistent.

The version offered by playwright April De Angelis, a friend of Rubasingham's and a supporter of the BDS movement, was that Javid 'threatened the theatre, he threatened Indhu's job and he threatened the theatre's funding'.[89] It would be easy to dismiss De Angelis's account as biased were it not for the fact that her claims are supported by pro-Israel sources too. Vivian Wineman, the Board president at the time and a prominent opponent of BDS, provided a very similar account, claiming: 'He [Javid] . . . said, "look if you want to keep your . . . government funding . . . you're going to have to climb down over the film festival".'[90] Indeed, these testimonies match up with the way Javid himself would represent his intervention in the Tricycle affair.

Interestingly, Javid appears to have acknowledged that interference in the Tricycle case would be inconsistent with the principle that government should not meddle with freedom of expression in the cultural sphere. However, he did so in a letter to the UK Jewish Film Festival which simultaneously confirmed that he had done just that:

> As Secretary of State, it is not for me to seek to intervene in this issue, but I want to ensure the public interest is weighed carefully in any final decision by the Tricycle. I have made clear to the Tricycle that I thought their approach to this issue was misguided.[91]

In pro-Israel circles, Javid claimed credit for the theatre's U-turn more explicitly, making clear that his involvement had gone far beyond public criticism alone. For example, in a December 2014 speech to the Union of Jewish Students, he said: 'The moment I heard about the Tricycle ban I knew I couldn't just let it go. It's completely unacceptable for a theatre to act in this way, and I didn't shy away from telling its directors that.'[92] Similarly, in March 2015, Javid told an audience from the Board: 'I intervened. I thought it was totally and utterly unacceptable and wrong. I have made it absolutely clear what might happen to their [the theatre's] funding if they try, or if anyone, tries that kind of thing again.'[93]

But Javid was not the only government official involved in the matter. Israeli state actors, specifically Ambassador Daniel Taub, had quietly been pursuing the same goals as pro-Israel civil society organisations and the British minister. Documents obtained through freedom of information requests reveal that Taub initially met privately with Tricycle board member Philippe Sands and others when attempting to resolve the dispute. Subsequently, he was part of a number of email exchanges. Significantly, Taub, like the other players mentioned, gave Sajid Javid credit for the eventual outcome of the affair. In a warm letter to Javid, Taub thanked him for his 'quiet and effective intervention', writing:

> I am writing to express my enormous appreciation for your quiet and effective intervention in the matter of the Tricycle Theatre and the UK Jewish Film Festival. Not only did your influence help bring this unfortunate incident to closure, but I think that it also constituted an important statement at a time when calls for cultural boycotts and shutting down cultural ties are regrettably gathering steam.[94]

In November 2014, Javid and Taub were pictured together at the opening night of the UK Jewish Film Festival – which, despite the Tricycle's U-turn, was nonetheless held at a different venue. Taub's letter revealed that Javid had been invited as guest of honour to the festival at his suggestion. The Tricycle subsequently rebranded itself as Kiln Theatre.

Casus belli

In a letter to the UK Jewish Film Festival's chair, Stephen Margolis, Tricycle board member Philippe Sands stated his belief that the response to the dispute had been about something much larger than just the theatre's hosting of the film festival and its relatively miniscule amount of funding from the Israeli embassy. He described it as part of a 'casus belli' – an act used to justify a war – with 'wider aims'.[95] Critically, this wider war was *not* the fight against anti-Semitism, but the fight to halt the BDS movement. While Sajid Javid would later seek to legitimise his intervention by branding cultural boycotts of Israel 'a form of the oldest hatred in the world'[96] and the Tricycle saga would be mischaracterised by the Conservative Party as 'Jewish films being banned',[97] the letter from Ambassador Taub, tellingly, did not mention anti-Semitism at all. Instead, he made it clear that the concern was 'calls for cultural boycotts [of Israel] . . . gathering steam'. In turn, Sajid Javid's words quoted earlier ('if anyone tries that kind of thing again . . .') implied that the disciplining of the Tricycle was calculated to serve as an example to deter other actors in the wider cultural arena from engaging in BDS activism.

Taub's involvement adds weight to the view that the UK Jewish Film Festival, rather than being an 'apolitical' cultural endeavour, chimed with the goals of the Brand Israel project. Javid's intervention illustrates new public diplomacy scholar Jan Melissen's point that a political leader may 'engage in public diplomacy in defence of a foreign counterpart's international reputation'.[98] Critically, Taub's and Javid's roles also serve as a reminder of the importance of state power. Although the Tricycle theatre saga involved noisy grassroots protests, donor pressure, professional PR and a maelstrom of media coverage, it appears to have been chiefly the senior British government minister's resolute determination to oppose the boycott movement and his 'quiet and effective' top-down intervention which were decisive in the outcome of the affair. Moreover, Javid had acted *well before* pro-Israel groups in civil society had urged him to do so, apparently in coordination with Taub but *not* with the Board or Jewish Leadership Council, rendering their influence on this occasion marginal.

The episode raises the question of whether Javid was acting in his capacity as a government minister or as a member of Conservative Friends of Israel. As we saw in chapter 1, the blurred boundaries of governance in the contemporary era mean that, in anthropologist Janine Wedel's words, huge potency lies 'at the nexus of official and private power', two realms which 'reinforce each other'.[99] She describes how specific actors who 'perform overlapping roles' at this nexus, straddling and manoeuvring across public and private realms, are able to enlist 'access and information available in one [sphere] to open doors or enhance cachet in another'. Such actors operate with an 'ambiguity' which 'yields not only flexibility but deniability'.[100] Seen in this light, Javid's claim to have acted in the 'public interest' is highly dubious. His moves certainly chimed with the wider agenda of the Conservative government to curb the independence of the cultural sphere.[101] Yet arguably, the critical factor was likely his role within the pro-Israel lobby. As the previous chapter discussed, a close relationship to Conservative Friends of Israel can ingratiate MPs with key party donors.[102] Given that a few years later, Javid made an unsuccessful bid to become Conservative Party leader, his intervention in the Tricycle affair – leveraging all the weight of his public office – may have been motivated, at least in part, by a desire to win their private support.

Nonetheless, the Tricycle episode illustrates not only the considerable power of pro-Israel activism but also its acute *limitations*. The Zionist movement was able to exert influence from multiple directions: civil society, state power and, to an extent, media and economic leverage. As a result, the Tricycle Theatre was humiliated and forced to backtrack. Yet, if indeed the UK Jewish Film Festival was aligned with Brand Israel, its goal of manufacturing consent for Israeli apartheid through soft power had clearly been unsuccessful. Ultimately, it was necessary to resort to the hard power of threats, coercion and bullying to achieve compliance. Moreover, the wider impacts of the Tricycle case, which became something of a cause célèbre, were ambiguous. Just a few weeks after the affair, a film festival in Bristol announced it had turned down Israeli embassy funding.[103] The episode also stimulated the creation of Artists for Palestine UK, which published a short pamphlet, *The Case for a Cultural Boycott of Israel*, and organised the cultural boycott pledge mentioned earlier in the chapter. Longer term, while the row may have helped to chill some cultural boycott initiatives, the strong-arm tactics used may equally have helped to entrench support for BDS in other quarters. Certainly by 2021, cultural boycott victories were still occurring. That year, for instance, acclaimed Irish novelist Sally Rooney refused to sell the rights to her latest book to an Israeli publisher. Despite a degree of backlash from the mainstream media, the most prominent response from other cultural figures was a letter of *support* for her position, which prompted no counter-response at all, since Culture for Coexistence had long since ceased to exist.[104]

6

Waging Lawfare

'Operation Defensive Shield' was the code name Israel gave to its largest military operation in the West Bank since it occupied the territory in 1967. It took place in the spring of 2002, during the brutal repression of the Second Intifada, a major Palestinian uprising against the Israeli occupation. Operation Defensive Shield alone saw Israel kill approximately 500 Palestinians and injure another 1,500. At least fifty-two of those people were confirmed to have been killed during a ten-day military assault on Jenin refugee camp in April 2002 – despite confusion about the death toll as a result of Israel attempting to prevent the media and UN from investigating.[1] The refugee camp, just 0.4 kilometres square, was home to 13,000 Palestinian refugees, around 4,000 of whom were left homeless by the destruction Israel's Caterpillar D-9 armoured bulldozers wrought. Around half of the dead were reportedly Palestinian militants, and twenty-three Israeli soldiers were killed too. Human rights groups also accused Israel of war crimes, documenting the deaths of some of the Palestinian civilians killed. Among them, Kamal Zghair, a fifty-seven-year-old wheelchair user, was shot and then run over by an Israeli tank, while Jamal Fayed, a thirty-seven-year-old man with quadriplegia, died under the rubble of his home after an Israeli military bulldozer operator refused to allow his family to rescue him before razing the house to the ground.[2] The man in charge of the Israeli military at the time was Shaul Mofaz, an Iranian-born stalwart of the Kadima party.

Thirteen years later, when Mofaz visited Britain, lawyers acting on behalf of Palestinian victims of these war crimes responded by calling for the police and Crown Prosecution Service to arrest him on suspicion of violating the 1957 Geneva Conventions Act. Attempts to use the law to hold Israeli officials accountable while on foreign soil were not new. So-called universal jurisdiction legislation enables those suspected of war crimes to be arrested and prosecuted anywhere in the world, regardless of where their crimes were committed. In 1998, for example, former Chilean dictator General Augusto Pinochet was famously detained in Britain, where he was held under house arrest for a year and half before being released. When, in 2005, an arrest warrant was issued by a British court for retired Israeli military general Doron Almog – based on his own role in war crimes committed in Gaza – he was forced to fly straight back to Israel without leaving his plane. Similarly, in 2009, former Israeli foreign minister Tzipi Livni was tipped off about an arrest warrant issued by a British court in relation to yet more crimes committed in Gaza and was forced to cancel her visit.

For years, the Israeli government and its friends lobbied hard for a change to universal jurisdiction law. In time, their cause won bipartisan support. By 2009, Labour foreign secretary David Miliband promised to look 'urgently' at ways to alter universal jurisdiction legislation.[3] But it was David Cameron's Conservative government that in 2011 eventually amended the law,[4] a move for which Conservative Friends of Israel said it had campaigned 'at all levels of the Conservative Party'.[5]

The changes made universal jurisdiction arrest warrants subject to the approval of the director of public prosecutions – a political appointee – thus reducing the likelihood that war criminals from nations viewed as *allies* would be held accountable. Sure enough, just weeks after the change, then director of public prosecutions Keir Starmer (today the Labour Party leader) blocked a new attempt to serve Tzipi Livni with an arrest warrant.[6] Then in 2015 – on the very same day that former Rwandan spy chief Karenzi Karake was arrested in London on suspicion of involvement in genocide – elsewhere in the city, Shaul Mofaz, in spite of the widespread calls for his arrest, enjoyed total impunity and even spoke in Parliament.[7]

The backlash begins

As we have seen, from around 2010, the crisis of Zionism intensified. Brand Israel was failing, and successive bouts of intense state violence saw Israel losing more and more support in the court of global public opinion, while simultaneously the BDS movement was growing. In response, Israel and its supporters turned increasingly towards more aggressive tactics. In particular, coercive 'lawfare' – the repressive use of the law to achieve political goals[8] – was seen as a means to retaliate against attempts to hold Israeli military and political personnel accountable for their crimes. Intimately tied not only to Israeli exceptionalism but to the US-led War on Terror and its associated erosion of international law, the embrace of lawfare also shifted the battle onto a terrain which – given the material resources usually required to access and navigate state legislatures or the legal system – tends to favour social movements from above.

Globally, pro-Israel lawfare has two main fronts. Firstly, both official and civil society actors have lobbied Israel's allies to outlaw BDS – the outcomes of which in Britain are discussed later in this chapter. Secondly, there have been increased attempts to prosecute BDS advocates in court, in order to repress the solidarity movement for Palestinian rights. This latter strategy, as chapter 2 explained, has its roots in Israeli counterterrorism and typically involves collaboration across state–private networks, a modus operandi which combines the resources and power of government with the access and flexibility of private actors, while also transferring risk away from officials and making such actions deniable. Israeli law firm Shurat HaDin, a leading actor working according to this model, quietly collaborates with the Israeli government and even takes direction on which cases to pursue. However, both funding and training have been provided by the Israeli government to many other pro-Israel lawfare actors to bring cases against BDS. As chapter 2 explained, well as working with established law firms and pre-existing pro-Israel groups, Zionist strategists have noted that manufactured civil society bodies could also be 'established in the applicable European countries . . . to hold a counter-campaign and methodically file lawsuits'.[9]

In Britain, the pro-Israel lawfare offensive has followed the global pattern of state–private networks. In February 2013, the Ministry of Foreign Affairs' Amir Saghi notably claimed that the Israeli government had 'worked in partnership' with British Zionist bodies on two BDS court cases in the space of just six months.[10] These appear to have been an employment tribunal which pro-Israel maths lecturer Ronnie Fraser brought against the University and College Union (UCU) and a case which Moty Cristal, a reserve lieutenant colonel in the Israeli army, brought against public sector union UNISON. Jeremy Newmark, then head of the Jewish Leadership Council, played a central role in both cases, as did elite corporate law firm Mishcon de Reya, which had previously worked on a number of pro-Israel and anti-BDS cases, including representing the Israeli embassy.[11]

In the first case, on which prominent pro-Israel lawyer Anthony Julius of Mischon de Reya reportedly worked pro bono, Fraser alleged that he had been subjected to anti-Semitic discrimination by the UCU when opposing academic boycott initiatives.[12] There were 'close discussions' between his team and the Israeli embassy about the case, and Israeli diplomats were reportedly 'keen to see it happen'.[13] But all claims were dismissed in March 2013, with the judge declaring the case 'devoid of any merit' and labelling it 'an impermissible attempt to achieve a political end by litigious means'. Notably, the ruling also declared that 'a belief in the Zionist project or an attachment to Israel or any similar sentiment cannot amount to a protected characteristic'.[14]

The second case, brought by Cristal – who said he aimed to 'fight the delegitimisation movement'[15] – reportedly involved 'a much closer piece of working' with the Israeli embassy and again alleged discrimination.[16] That case, which revolved around the boycott of a lecture Cristal was due to give on conflict resolution, was discontinued in May 2014 before entering the courts.[17] While both the Fraser and Cristal cases were, then, ostensibly *unsuccessful* for pro-Israel actors, the threat or reality of costly litigation, combined with the media coverage around it, was nonetheless intimidatory. Thus, as well as diverting resources away from actually implementing BDS, such lawfare initiatives still served to exert, at least to some extent, a chilling effect on boycott activism within the trade union movement.

The main target of pro-Israel lawfare in Britain, however, has been the sphere of local government. While town halls' expressions of support for the Palestinian cause were not a novel phenomenon, the 2005 BDS call gradually transformed such support from symbolic rhetoric into a more potent form of solidarity. Annual operating budgets of local councils in Britain usually total hundreds of millions of pounds, while local authority pension funds are often worth billions. Therefore, moves to exclude certain companies from procurement processes (public contracts put out to tender), or to divest pension funds from particular firms, were potentially highly commercially significant. Collectively, Britain's nationwide Local Government Pension Scheme invests around £4.4 billion in companies complicit in Israel's violations of Palestinian rights.[18] Since many such schemes also have investments in fossil fuels, tobacco companies and the arms trade, ethical divestment campaigns similar to BDS are a common feature of local government politics. Significantly, this constellation produced common corporate, pro-Israel, and British government interests in limiting local democracy.

Partly an outgrowth of solidarity activism in trade unions and other spheres, the rise in municipal boycott and divestment activism in support of Palestinian rights in Britain was slow and disparate, with flurries of boycott activity tending to occur following periods of intensified Israeli state violence. Notably, following Operation Protective Edge in summer 2014, Leicester City Council passed a motion to boycott Israeli-settlement produce – the largest local authority to take action of that nature.

Meanwhile, a flagship local authority BDS campaign took on Veolia, a French multinational company providing waste disposal to many British councils. Veolia was involved in the Jerusalem Light Rail project on occupied Palestinian territory, serviced bus routes to and from illegal settlements, and (through a subsidiary) operated the Tovlan landfill site in the occupied Jordan Valley. Due to these activities, the company became a major target for campaigners seeking to exclude it from council contracts on the grounds of its complicity in violations of international law. Over the course of several years, Veolia lost contracts worth around $20 billion dollars (around £18 billion pounds) with local authorities. In 2015, the company pulled out of Israel as a result.[19]

For the Israeli government and the Zionist movement, these BDS victories were cause for concern. While, as chapter 4 explained, the sphere of central government has been relatively insulated from pro-Palestinian sentiment in civil society, these local government BDS actions represented an alarming encroachment of the Palestinian cause into the peripheries of state power.

Lawfare would soon become the pre-eminent tactic of the Zionist movement's backlash in the local government arena, and two new organisations – UK Lawyers for Israel and Jewish Human Rights Watch – would form the vanguard of the pro-Israel lawfare offensive. There is evidence that these groups (particularly the former) emerged from networks close to the Israeli state and cooperate with Israeli government officials in a manner consistent with the pattern of public–private pro-Israel lawfare partnerships. However, attempts to rejuvenate pro-Israel activism in local councils, or at least to dampen pro-Palestinian BDS initiatives, also had a number of other facets. The Board of Deputies, for example, distributed copies of an anti-BDS report called *A Better Way than Boycotts* at a September 2015 event for local councillors in London.[20] The Jewish Leadership Council began funding trips to Israel for local councillors, mimicking tactics used by parliamentary Friends of Israel groups, and sent three delegations of councillors to the country in 2015 alone.[21] BICOM spin-off We Believe in Israel did the same: by 2019, it was running two annual trips and reported having taken sixty local councillors to Israel on nine different 'study tours'.[22]

We Believe in Israel, as chapter 5 showed, helped the Israeli embassy to manufacture hyperlocal 'grassroots' (or astroturf) pro-Israel groups across Britain. It was also behind the creation of a new network called Local Government Friends of Israel.[23] Launched at the Local Government Association conference in summer 2015, its stated aim was to 'combat attempts to boycott and delegitimise' Israel in local authorities, for example by furnishing councillors with 'advice about responding to boycott proposals'. We Believe in Israel's director, Luke Akehurst, observed that since 'a lot of councillors go on to hold national political offices', this network was also of longer-term strategic value for Israel's supporters, allowing them to build relationships with aspiring MPs 'at the start of their political careers'.[24]

By May 2019, Akehurst claimed, Local Government Friends of Israel had recruited 700 supporters from councils across the country.[25] Himself a former Labour councillor in the East London borough of Hackney, Akehurst was able to promote this private pro-Israel initiative to contacts made through his time in public office. For example, he emailed 'friends' at Hackney Council about the Local Government Friends of Israel launch event, explaining he would be attending in his 'work capacity'.[26] This was not the first time Akehurst had leveraged elected office to further Israel's cause, however, having previously done so while still serving as a councillor.

'Part of my day job'

Seven London boroughs, including Hackney, together constitute the North London Waste Authority partnership. By the winter of 2012, BDS activists living in these boroughs had been campaigning for a year against the award of a waste-disposal contract worth £4 billion over twenty-five years to Veolia. Despite the campaign, the company had been short-listed for the contract. However, councillors would get to cast the deciding votes, and pro-Palestinian activists were using every avenue they could to implore their elected officials to reject Veolia on human rights grounds.

In late 2012, a sympathetic councillor from Hackney Council had invited a local resident and boycott campaigner named Caroline Day to speak for five minutes in the council chamber to outline the case against awarding the contract to Veolia – a deputation that had been approved by the council's legal officer and was due to take place on 21 November. However, before it could happen, pro-Israel actors scuppered the initiative using low-level administrative lawfare tactics. Behind-the-scenes manoeuvring by both We Believe in Israel and UK Lawyers for Israel led to councillors overruling the legal officer's decision and blocking Day's speech, justifying the move on the grounds that it was 'inappropriate for Full Council to debate what is intrinsically an international political issue'.[27]

The motion to block Day's speech was proposed by Conservative councillor Linda Kelly. However, its success rested on the fact it was seconded by the Labour mayor of Hackney, Jules Pipe, and received near-unanimous cross-party support from other councillors after the majority Labour group's vote was whipped.[28] The first of two pro-Israel actors who had quietly intervened to influence this outcome and ensure that BDS was kept off the agenda was We Believe in Israel's Luke Akehurst, himself a serving Hackney councillor at the time. Due to the clear conflict of interest between his private role and his public position, Akehurst consulted with the council's solicitors and, as he reported it, 'erred on the side of caution' by declaring his interest and not participating in the vote. However, Akehurst did play a role as an intermediary, relaying Conservative councillor Kelly's intentions to the mayor and chief whip while, he claims, making no attempt 'to influence their or the Labour Group's response'.[29]

Yet, in his private capacity as a pro-Israel campaigner, Akehurst was far from neutral. Indeed, he openly acknowledged lobbying on the issue for We Believe in Israel, writing: 'I am entitled to campaign on the Veolia boycott issue in my work capacity, it is part of my day job to do so'.[30] Thus, while formally playing by the rules, Akehurst appears to have nonetheless been instrumental in securing the Labour vote which saw the motion passed. In the previous chapter, we saw how Sajid Javid's overlapping roles as both Conservative Friends of Israel member and secretary of state for culture led to ambiguity over the capacity in which he intervened in the Tricycle Theatre affair. In this case, anthropologist Janine Wedel's observation that players who straddle both official and private realms can enlist 'access and information available in one [sphere] to open doors or enhance cachet in another' aptly encapsulates how Akehurst leveraged the personal relationships developed in his public role as a councillor to successfully pursue his private goals as a pro-Israel campaigner.[31]

Indeed, Akehurst's role was lauded as 'fundamental' by UK Lawyers for Israel, who were also involved in the episode. The group reports having reached out to Akehurt to help achieve cross-party support, after consulting first with Councillor Linda Kelly. It describes how Akehurt's intervention 'changed the situation from one in which Linda was going to make a motion and cause a bit of a fuss, probably without achieving anything, to something that was going to work'.[32] The lawfare group's own role in the incident, and its wider networks, deserve close scrutiny.

UK Lawyers for Israel

UK Lawyers for Israel, established 2010, swiftly became the leading pro-Israel lawfare body in Britain. Founded as 'a voluntary association of lawyers',[33] reportedly offering their services pro bono, its 'eminent patrons' have included a host of pro-Israel British peers such as Lord Carlile, Baroness Deech, Lord Howard, Lord Pannick, Lady Cosgrove, Lord Trimble and Lord Young of Graffham. Alongside links to the Conservative Party, the organisation is connected via key personnel to other deeply right-wing groups, including the Zionist Federation and Henry Jackson Society.[34] Additionally, lawyer Mark Lewis – one of the organisation's original directors and leading lights, until he emigrated to Israel – helped to relaunch Herut UK, a hard-right body espousing revisionist Zionist ideas like those of Vladimir Jabotinsky and Menachim Begin.[35] In 2019, UK Lawyers for Israel hosted a speaker from the far-right, pro-settlement Israeli organisation Regavim in London. Regavim's founder, the Israeli Knesset member Bezalel Smotrich, the leader of Israel's far right Religious Zionist Party, is known for living in an illegal settlement and advocating positions such as the segregation of Jewish and Arab women in maternity wards.

The evidence suggests that, in keeping with the pattern set by Shurat HaDin and other pro-Israel lawfare actors, UK Lawyers for Israel is closely tied to state–private networks. In particular, it has – at the very least – a close informal working relationship with the Israeli Ministry of Foreign Affairs. According to a page announcing the creation of UK Lawyers for Israel on the ministry's website, the group was formed 'following the Maale HaChamisha conference'.[36] While the precise nature of this conference is not clear, it may be a reference to one of the aforementioned events run by the Israeli government or Shurat HaDin to train lawyers from overseas to counter the BDS movement using legal means.

Certainly, from its earliest days, UK Lawyers for Israel collaborated closely with Israeli government actors. In June 2012, the organisation co-hosted a two-day London seminar with the Israeli Ministry of Foreign Affairs and the Israeli embassy, and in 2013, it gave a platform to Arthur Lenk of the ministry's legal division.[37] In 2015, barrister Jonathan Turner – UK Lawyers for Israel's co-founder and chief executive – acknowledged consulting with the Israeli embassy.[38] In 2017, the group hosted the former director-general of the foreign ministry, Arthur Koll, and in 2020 during the COVID-19 pandemic its charitable arm held a webinar with former Israeli ambassador Daniel Taub.[39]

Jonathan Turner of UK Lawyers for Israel was, at one stage in 2021, also listed as a staff member of the International Legal Forum, a lawfare body which has been directly funded by Israel's Ministry of Strategic Affairs.[40] Additionally, Turner has stated that his organisation played a critical role in scuppering the 2011 flotilla of ships seeking to reach Gaza from Greece. The group advised Greek coastal police through 'a top Greek lawyer', he claimed, 'grounds on which the ships could be arrested'.[41] Israeli law firm Shurat HaDin, known to have collaborated across the state–private network with the Israeli government, also took a leading role in blocking the boats. It is reasonable to assume, then, that UK Lawyers for Israel worked with both parties on this case.

As well as involving itself in the local government sphere, UK Lawyers for Israel has made numerous interventions to repress BDS initiatives in solidarity with Palestinians in the realms of culture, academia, trade unions and the charity sector. Among the many targets of its legal harassment campaigns are the Royal Institute of British Architects, Manchester's Whitworth Gallery (a case mentioned in the previous chapter), University College London, King's College London, a host of charities (such as Interpal, War on Want, Defence for Children International and Medical Aid for Palestinians),[42] and even Middle East history textbooks used in schools.[43] Its deployment of lawfare tactics in the local government arena, in the Hackney Council case, was thus part of a much-wider campaign across many sectors of civil society.

UK Lawyers for Israel reportedly became involved in the Hackney Council-Veolia incident after being contacted by Councillor Kelly, who told a local paper that the group 'helped . . . all the way through'.[44] In fact, one week after triumphantly celebrating the blocking of the planned pro-BDS speech, UK Lawyers for Israel secretary David Lewis claimed in the *Jewish Chronicle* that the group had *itself* prepared the motion to deny the deputation.[45] Although subsequently Mayor Jules Pipe disputed this claim, UK Lawyers for Israel's role was evidently critical.[46]

However, it is important to note that although We Believe in Israel and UK Lawyers for Israel managed to prevent BDS campaigners from making their case within the Hackney Council chamber, the wider outcome of the campaign to block Veolia from the North London Waste Authority partnership was chalked up as a boycott victory. Before councillors even cast their votes to decide which company should be awarded the contract, Veolia withdrew its bid. This took place amid reports that several councillors had assured BDS campaigners they would be opposing the Veolia bid, testament to the strength of the campaign mobilised by Palestine solidarity organisers.[47] The support for Israel present in Hackney Council was outweighed by support in other boroughs for holding the country, and complicit companies, accountable through BDS. As boycott campaigner Michael Deas observed, the outcome illustrated

> the kind of power that the Israel lobby does and doesn't have . . . by the time [they] had intervened there were already major local community bodies across North London on board with the campaign, signed up to letters, signed up to statements, that had gone to all of the Councillors. So, by that point . . . that quite strong-arm approach . . . can only work in certain circumstances. It can very rarely work to overturn an actual mass body of public support within a community.[48]

Extracting a price tag

In 2010, influential Tel Aviv–based Zionist think-tank the Reut Institute called for Israel and its allies to work on extracting a 'price tag' – a phrase borrowed from the Israeli settler movement – from Palestinians and their supporters, in revenge for 'acts of delegitimis-ation', especially boycotts. Reut explained: 'Today, attacking Israel is "cheap" and convenient, but it can be turned into a more risky enterprise.'[49] Accordingly, aggressive and punitive lawfare strategies have increasingly become a key tactic used by the Zionist movement to increase the costs associated with BDS activism in solidarity with Palestinians. In 2014, the question of 'whether to file legal suits in European and North American courts' against organisations advocating boycotts or divestment was one of the issues discussed at a ministerial meeting convened by Israeli prime minister Benjamin Netanyahu to discuss the threat of the BDS movement. As we have seen, such prosecutions were not actively pursued by the government itself but by third parties, such as Shurat HaDin, with which it collaborated closely across state–private networks.

In June 2015, Israeli justice minister Ayelet Shaked announced that the ministry was 'going on the offensive against international initiatives to boycott Israel' and was 'preparing to file lawsuits against activists who call for blacklisting the Jewish state'.[50] Two months later, in August 2015, a small, recently founded British organisation launched a legal case against local councils endorsing BDS. That organisation was the aforementioned Jewish Human Rights Watch.

The case brought by Jewish Human Rights Watch primarily sought to challenge the high-profile Leicester City Council motion passed in the wake of Operation Protective Edge in summer 2014. Leicester councillors had resolved 'insofar as legal considerations allow, to boycott any produce originating from illegal Israeli settlements in the West Bank until such time as it complies with international law and withdraws from Palestinian Occupied territories'.[51] In August 2015, Jewish Human Rights Watch filed for a judicial review of this decision at the High Court. Despite the wording of the motion having emphasised the aim of holding Israel accountable for its breaches of international law, the crux of its case was the public sector equality duty set out in the 2010 Equality Act, resting on the allegation that the motion negatively impacted the local Jewish community. A Jewish Human Rights Watch spokesperson told the press that the council's policy amounted to 'a get-out-of-town order to Leicester Jews'.[52] As such, the argument had notable resonances with the concept of 'new anti-Semitism' and the International Holocaust Remembrance Alliance's definition of anti-Semitism, which conflates some forms of criticising Israel or

Zionism with anti-Jewish racism. In October 2015, Jewish Human Rights Watch lodged further claims against two Welsh councils, Swansea and Gwynedd, which had adopted similar policies in support of Palestinians. The three cases were heard together in the summer of 2016.

According to pro-Palestinian campaigner Ryvka Barnard, the complainants likely brought the case experimentally as a way of 'testing the water' to see what the courts would permit.[53] It was clearly intended to punish, if possible, the pro-BDS councils concerned, but it likely also sought to deter others from following suit. Legal advice received by Leicester City Council warned of potentially punishing costs of up to £200,000 should it contest the case and lose. Given this financial risk, the council seriously considered rescinding the motion and settling out of court, councillors later conceded. Such a move would certainly have been hailed as a lawfare victory by pro-Israel actors.[54] However, the local authorities perceived the legal case as an effort to stop councils from adopting political stances – a form of attempted censorship to which they were reluctant to bow. In the end, the case was heard – and dismissed – by the High Court in June 2016. Jewish Human Rights Watch appealed, but this, too, was dismissed.

Swansea council leader Rob Stewart described the decision as 'a victory for free speech'. The deeper underlying issue at stake, however, was democracy itself and the fundamentally anti-democratic potential of lawfare – what American philosopher Judith Butler, writing about Trump's failed lawsuit attempting to overturn the 2020 US presidential election result, calls 'the power of litigation to destroy democratic norms'.[55] As Leicester's mayor, Peter Soulsby, noted, the outcome reinforced the right of councillors to 'discuss issues of concern to their electorate'.[56] Yet while, like Trump, Jewish Human Rights Watch failed in its lawfare exercise and did not secure the anti-BDS legal precedent it sought, the case nonetheless may have served a wider disciplinary purpose by exerting a chilling effect.

Despite technically losing its 2018 appeal, Jewish Human Rights Watch claimed victory, arguing that the ruling constituted 'a vital change in the law to the way in which councils can propose and discuss these controversial boycott motions'.[57] Thus, as well as tying up several local authorities supportive of boycotts in lengthy, time-consuming and potentially costly court cases, the affair generated significant media controversy – with newspaper headlines conveying the highly intimidating message that councils could and would be sued for supporting BDS. At least one council subsequently dropped a similar motion after the Board of Deputies and Jewish Leadership Council 'wrote to warn of the legal implications of such a move'.[58] Jewish Human Rights Watch's wider aim of preventing a domino effect in local authorities was, in this way, substantially achieved.

However, while the group portrayed itself as fighting anti-Semitic discrimination, this characterisation was rebuffed in court. Importantly, the judge rejected the claim that Jewish Human Rights Watch had 'consulted widely among the Jewish community' before bringing the case, saying this assertion was 'not supported by any evidence'.[59] Whose interests, then, did Jewish Human Rights Watch actually represent?

Jewish Human Rights Watch

Jewish Human Rights Watch was, like UK Lawyers for Israel, part of the post-2010 wave of new pro-Israel groups which, according to sociologist Keith Kahn-Harris, 'bypassed' established pro-Israel organisations and often worked in 'opaque' ways.[60] Founded in February 2015, the group states that it was set up to combat 'the anti-Jewish boycott movement's action'.[61] Again like UK Lawyers for Israel, it has strong right-wing connections, as well as links to both British and Israeli state actors, and its targets have included academia and the charity sector.[62]

According to a report in the *Jewish Chronicle*, American businessman Emmanuel 'Manny' Weiss was the founder of Jewish Human Rights Watch.[63] Though the organisation's finances are opaque, Weiss was likely also its primary funder. Weiss's political views are deeply conservative. As a young man, he worked for US senator Henry Jackson, a Democrat known as a Cold Warrior stridently opposed to détente.[64] In subsequent years, Weiss helped to establish and was a 'generous supporter' to the Henry Jackson Society think-tank – named after the late politician and, as chapter

3 explained, a key outpost of neoconservatism in Britain.[65] Senior Conservative minister Michael Gove, himself a strong supporter of neoconservatism and Israel, counts Weiss among his 'great friends'.[66] Having originally made his millions in commodities trading, Weiss has donated to Gove's office and to that of Israeli prime minister Benjamin Netanyahu.[67] His brother, Moshe Weiss, previously served as an Israeli government advisor.[68] The man behind Jewish Human Rights Watch, then, had not only considerable wealth but significant ties to right-wing political elites in Britain, Israel and, to an extent, the US.

Similarly, the staff of Jewish Human Rights Watch also have deeply right-wing associations. Manchester-based insolvency lawyer Robert Henry Festenstein, quoted in the press as a spokesperson for Jewish Human Rights Watch, appeared in a video with far-right activist Stephen Yaxley-Lennon, widely known as 'Tommy Robinson' in 2017. Festenstein later denied that the anti-Islam agitator was a client of his law firm.[69] Previously, Festenstein was also listed as a member of North West Friends of Israel, the supposedly 'grassroots' group which, as the previous chapter discussed, was singled out for praise by senior Israeli government ministers including Benjamin Netanyahu and Gilad Erdan.[70] In 2021, when Festenstein's Jewish Human Rights Watch colleague Jonathan Neumann stood for election as president of the Board of Deputies, a rival faction branded Neumann 'far right'.[71] In addition, right-wing pro-Israel activist and blogger David Collier was in 2019 commissioned by Jewish Human Rights Watch to write a report attacking human rights group Amnesty International.[72] Collier has criticised a pro-Palestinian Jewish activist for marrying a Muslim, and has shared a platform with right-wing journalist Melanie Phillips, who has denied that Islamophobia exists. He also had ties to state–private networks, having conducted 'advocacy training' at the Israeli embassy in 2016 and spoken at an Israeli government conference a few years later.[73]

It is important to place Jewish Human Rights Watch connections and activities in the context of the established global pattern of covert outsourcing and deniable state–private networks involved in pro-Israel lawfare cases, both in Britain and worldwide, explored respectively in this chapter and chapter 2. As the latter explained, public–private lawfare partnerships may be, according to legal scholar Orde Kittrie, 'at their most effective, from the perspective of the government, when the instigating government's hand is relatively hidden'.[74] It also noted that Strategic Affairs Minister Erdan has declared that most of his ministry's actions 'are not of the ministry, but through bodies around the world who do not want to expose their connection with the state'.[75] Given all this, and even if its collaboration with the Israeli government is less clear than that of UK Lawyers for Israel, it is conceivable – perhaps even likely – that the cases Jewish Human Rights Watch brought against pro-BDS councils in Britain were at least tacitly granted approval by Israeli officials.

Banning boycotts in Britain?

While lawfare in Hackney by UK Lawyers For Israel and We Believe in Israel blocked discussion of Palestine and BDS on the grounds that it was an 'international political issue', Jewish Human Rights Watch's lawfare saw councils' right to discuss issues of international politics upheld. However, a third type of lawfare strategy pursued by pro-Israel actors in Britain has seen the central government seek to restrict local authorities' right to *act* on the basis of their concerns.

As chapter 2 explained, the Israeli government and Zionist movement began considering a strategy of outlawing BDS around 2010, viewing legislative arenas as a more favourable turf on which to confront the boycott movement as opposed to university campuses or civil society. In early 2016, the Ministry of Strategic Affairs announced that it had stepped up its own efforts to secure anti-BDS legislation in other jurisdictions, while pro-Israel groups in civil society lobbied on a parallel track for the same thing. This two-pronged strategy proved highly effective, with many allied nations – and numerous US states – passing new measures to prohibit anti-Israel boycotts.

The strategy pursued in Britain was the same: seeking to harness state power to proscribe pro-Palestinian BDS initiatives and create an environment conducive to litigation should they occur. The

Israeli government and the Zionist movement both lobbied British ministers for the introduction of new laws which would restrict the BDS movement by shrinking the space in which it could emerge and flourish. According to Israeli paper *Yedioth Ahronoth*, Israel's London embassy carried out a diplomatic campaign to convince the British government 'to pass a directive prohibiting municipalities and public bodies from taking decisions to boycott Israel'.[76] The paper characterised this campaign as 'quiet and effective' – precisely the words with which Ambassador Taub praised Sajid Javid's intervention in the Tricycle Theatre case.

Simultaneously, a range of pro-Israel civil society groups also lobbied the British government. In January 2016, for example, then prime minister David Cameron held a meeting to discuss 'the government's approach to the Middle East conflict'. Billed as a meeting with representatives of the Jewish community (including the Board of Deputies, the Union of Jewish Students, the Community Security Trust and the Jewish Leadership Council), exclusively *pro-Israel* groups such as BICOM were also present, represented by hedge fund manager and Conservative Party donor Edward Misrahi.[77] The Jewish Leadership Council's representative at the meeting, Mick Davis, was also a Conservative donor and just a few weeks later would be appointed co-treasurer of the party.

Separately, that same month, records show that Jewish Human Rights Watch lobbied Cabinet Minister Matthew Hancock on 'foreign policy'.[78] Though we do not have minutes of either meeting, in a *Jewish Chronicle* article published during a visit to Israel, Hancock would later praise Jewish Human Rights Watch as well as the Board of Deputies and Community Security Trust for keeping the issue of BDS on the government's agenda.[79] Soon after that, Jewish Human Rights Watch founder Manny Weiss's close friend Michael Gove declared that 'a campaign led by the pioneering organisation, Jewish Human Rights Watch, which I wish to salute today' had prompted new government moves intended to communicate 'that local authorities and public bodies cannot adopt BDS policies aimed at Israel'.[80]

The British government's first concrete statement that it would seek to outlaw BDS came in the form of a press release from the Conservative Party head office, released on the eve of its October

2015 party conference. Declaring that the government would take firm action to stop 'divisive' town hall boycotts and sanctions, the press release mentioned two measures to prevent BDS. Firstly, the 2009 Local Government Pension Scheme regulations would be amended to stipulate that divestment should only be pursued 'where formal legal sanctions, embargoes and restrictions' have been imposed by central government. They would also give the secretary of state for communities and local government a 'power of intervention' to veto locally made investment decisions. Secondly, a 'revised Procurement Policy Note' would be issued, which would similarly tell local councils 'that boycotts in procurement policy are inappropriate' except where put in place centrally first.

In November 2015, proposed changes to local authority pension regulations were indeed announced, with some media fanfare. Then, in February 2016, Hancock travelled to Israel and, at a press conference in Jerusalem alongside Benjamin Netanyahu, he made an announcement about a procurement policy note which the Cabinet Office issued the same day.[81] Reportedly, Conservative ministers had shoehorned pro-Israel measures into a pre-existing local authority reform agenda in a top-down fashion with very little notice, to the surprise of even senior civil servants within the Department for Communities and Local Government.[82]

Whereas the landmark pro-Israel lawfare campaign which won changes to the implementation of universal jurisdiction, described at the start of this chapter, received support from both Labour and the Conservatives, measures to repress the BDS movement – at least in their early iterations, advanced while Jeremy Corbyn was leader of the Labour Party – had a distinctly more partisan flavour. As one commentator observed, the fault-lines broadly took the shape of 'an ideological battle between the UK [central] government – run by the Conservative Party, and local government – mostly controlled by Labour administrations'.[83] Conservative ministers lined up to condemn the BDS movement and make clear their support for Israel's campaign against it, demarcating themselves in the process from Corbyn's Labour. Hancock declared that the government was determined to prevent 'playground politics undermining our international security', while Secretary of State for Communities and Local Government Greg Clark claimed that local government pro-Palestine activism would 'undermine good community relations and harm the economic security of families by pushing up council tax'. The aforementioned Conservative Party press release was laden with references to Corbyn, his ally and shadow chancellor John McDonnell and 'hard-left campaigns' by 'Labour-affiliated trade unions'.[84] Thus, the issue of combating BDS became something of a political football in Britain, as it had in Israel.

Critically, as well as name-checking Leicester City Council's BDS motion and Jewish Human Rights Watch's judicial review against it, alongside the Tricycle Theatre affair (mischaracterised as 'Jewish films being banned'), the Conservative press release also mentioned the need to protect the arms industry. It alleged that 'British defence companies' must be shielded from boycotts in order to preserve both geopolitical security and the economy. As well as hindering 'joint working with Israel to protect Britain from foreign cyber-attacks and terrorism', it cited 'Britain's £10 billion export trade' in arms and painted local authority activism as 'destroying British jobs'. For, alongside pro-Palestine activism, anti-militarism campaigners had been seeking to undermine arms companies via local councils. Similarly, climate activists had been calling for divestment from the fossil fuels industry, and public health activists had been discouraging investment in tobacco. These overlapping campaigns had created a considerable convergence of interests between corporate, Zionist and Conservative actors in limiting economic activism in local authorities. Similarly, in the US context, it emerged in 2022 that the American Legislative Exchange Council, a corporate lobbying group, had used anti-BDS legislation as a blueprint for legal efforts to blacklist companies that boycott the oil industry.[85]

While, then, the Israeli government and Israel lobby were key drivers of change in the effort to limit local government ethical divestments and boycotts, their success rested in part on the fact that their aims coincided with the wider agenda of other powerful actors, not least the neoliberal British government. The government did not want politically active pension funds and contentious local authorities any more than it wanted agitating trade unions, politicised charities or independent and vocal cultural organisations – sectors whose political voice it had also sought to curb.[86] Indeed, government efforts to outlaw BDS were just one part of a wave of authoritarian legislation – including the Police, Crime, Sentencing and Courts Act and the Nationality and Borders Act – which restricted human rights, expanded police powers and repressed protest.[87]

In fact, the British government's moves contained strong echoes of a previous Conservative administration's repression of local boycott activism targeting a different apartheid state. As economic geographer David Harvey notes, Margaret Thatcher's neoliberal reforms in Britain had involved 'attacking all forms of social solidarity that hindered competitive flexibility', including 'those expressed through municipal governance'.[88] Specifically, in 1988, Thatcher's government introduced a policy intended to limit the actions local councils could take to end British complicity in the South African apartheid regime, which her Conservative Party remained loath to sanction in any significant way.[89] Yet, as scholars Davina Cooper and Didi Herman have observed, local authority BDS activism now, as then, constitutes 'a refusal on the part of municipal government to be fully governed by the concerns of the local or by the international agendas of the nation-state'.[90] Similarly, in defiance of the Conservative-run British government's stance, both the Labour-run Welsh government and Scottish National Party–run Scottish government also sought to discourage trade with illegal Israeli settlements.[91]

Despite grandiose rhetoric from ministers and newspaper headlines warning of a 'ban' on boycotts,[92] for many years the Conservative government actually produced little of substance in its effort to outlaw BDS. The Cabinet Office's procurement policy note, some analysts observed, in large part merely reiterated existing guidance.[93] Meanwhile, the government's changes to pension regulations were successfully challenged – and in June 2017 deemed 'unlawful' in the High Court – following a long-running legal campaign by the Palestine Solidarity Campaign.[94] That decision was temporarily overruled in the Court of Appeal, only for the Supreme Court, in turn, to once more uphold the principle of local government autonomy in an April 2020 verdict celebrated by BDS campaigners.[95]

Yet senior Conservatives continue to reiterate the government's 2019 manifesto pledge to 'ban public bodies from imposing their own boycotts, disinvestment or sanctions campaigns'.[96] The measures were mentioned in the queen's speech in May 2022, which suggested a bill to effectively nullify the Supreme Court's ruling could be tabled soon, and in December that year Prime Minister Rishi Sunak repeated the pledge.[97] Power, however, produces resistance. In anticipation of primary legislation potentially being introduced, Palestine solidarity bodies, climate justice groups, peace campaigners and a broad coalition of other civil society organisations issued a joint 'Protect the Right to Boycott' statement.[98] Meanwhile, pro-Palestinian 'legal mobilisation' – which legal scholar Jeff Handmaker distinguishes from lawfare because it serves liberatory ends (as opposed to the repressive ends of states or corporations) – has begun to emerge.[99] A body called Palestine Legal, founded in 2012, led the way in the US, while the European Legal Support Centre was established in 2019, followed soon after in Britain by an outfit called the International Centre of Justice for Palestinians. These developments suggest that the British state and pro-Israel lawfare actors will struggle to snuff out the threat of local authority boycott and divestment activism. Some supporters of Israel even fear that the resort to coercive lawfare tactics to crush BDS could backfire and instead – as one *Haaretz* report frets – end up 'breathing new life into the boycott Israel camp'.[100]

7

Battling Academic Boycott

In 2013, the University of Sussex created a new academic post called the Yossi Harel Chair in Modern Israel Studies. Born Yosef Hamburger, Yossi Harel is chiefly remembered today as the commander of the *Exodus*, a steamship which set sail for mandatory Palestine from Europe in 1947 with around 4,500 Jewish refugees, mostly Holocaust survivors, on board. In response, the British imperial authorities ruling Palestine at the time – during this period restricting Jewish immigration – ordered naval vessels to intercept the ship using force, killing at least three people. Later, despite a hunger strike protest, the British promptly deported the ship's passengers back to Europe, where many ended up in displaced-persons camps in Germany.

The affair galvanised global public sympathy and influenced international diplomatic support for the creation of Israel. By 1960, the American filmmaker Otto Preminger had produced a film named after the ship, often credited with increasing support for Zionism in the US. In it, Hollywood star Paul Newman played 'Ari Ben Canaan', a character loosely based on Yossi Harel. Yet there was also a darker side to Harel's Zionist activities, quite different to the heroic exploits depicted in the film.

Several historical sources document how, years prior to commanding the *Exodus*, Harel helped to terrorise Palestinian villages. Even a fawning biography, *Commander of the Exodus*, describes how Yitzhak Sadeh, the commander of the Palmach Zionist militia (and later a founder of the Israel Defense Forces), led Harel and others on night raids he referred to as 'putting the lights out in Arab villages', advising his fighters that 'instead of their coming to you,

you go to them', taking advantage of 'the element of surprise, stealth and the darkness of night'.[1] Sadeh was 'loved', 'admired' and seen as a father figure by Harel, according to the latter's biographer, who also documents an incident in which Harel and two other Sadeh protégés, after hearing of the murder of several Jews near Jerusalem's Old City, set off for the area 'intent on revenge'. Upon finding British soldiers patrolling, they instead randomly targeted Palestinians elsewhere: they 'hurled some grenades into a coffee-house [in which] a handful of Arabs were sitting' in Abu Ghosh, then proceeded to Qalunya ('Colonia'), a Palestinian village west of Jerusalem, where they 'shot indiscriminately at some harvesters in a field'. Reportedly, 'no-one was killed' in the coffeehouse, but the account says nothing about the outcome of the second attack.[2]

Later, fighters from Sadeh's field companies, including Yossi Harel, deployed the same tactics with the Haganah Zionist para-military force as part of the so-called Special Night Squads led by British military commander Orde Wingate. A passionate Christian Zionist, Wingate is notorious for his extreme and sadistic violence against Palestinians. Harel's biographer concedes that 'more than once' Wingate lined up Palestinian 'rioters' in a row 'and shot them in cold blood' but also states that Harel 'loved' and 'mourned' Wingate when he later died.[3] Meanwhile, historian Anita Shapira documents Harel's participation in an attack on the Palestinian village of Lubya, the purpose of which was reportedly 'to strike at a house in the heart of the village' in order 'to make an example of it'.[4] The Zionist attackers, including Palmach commander Yigal Allon, arrived at midnight under cover of darkness. There, at least one innocent Palestinian man, unfortunate enough to emerge from his house at the wrong moment, was shot by Harel using a sub-machine gun, who may – or may not (Shapira equivocates) – have then released several further rounds into the house.[5]

The village of Lubya was completely ethnically cleansed during the Nakba. Palestinian historian Walid Khalidi records how the debris of its destroyed homes are today buried under the Lavi pine forest, planted by the Jewish National Fund.[6] Yossi Harel went on to become a leading figure in Israeli military intelligence. When he died in 2008, an obituary in the *Guardian* noted euphemistically that he had once been 'involved in . . . inter-communal violence between Arabs and Jews'.[7] More accurately, these accounts appear to describe extrajudicial executions. Yet in 2013, when the University of Sussex received a large donation from a consortium of pro-Israel donors, including venture capitalist and Labour Friends of Israel supporter Ronald Cohen – the husband of Yossi Harel's daughter, Sharon – the Yossi Harel Chair in Modern Israel Studies was born.[8]

'Delegitimisation' and academia

Academia has long been a critical arena of concern for the Zionist movement. Many of the key North American and European nodes in the so-called delegitimisation (anti-Zionist) network challenging the legitimacy of Israeli apartheid – as mapped out by Israeli think-tank the Reut Institute – were universities. Similarly, US-based lobby group The David Project called universities 'the leading venue for anti-Israel activity'.[9] The principal reason that higher education holds this status as an arena of delegitimisation par excellence is the academic boycott campaign. A key plank of the wider BDS movement, some advocates argue that academic boycott could play as pivotal a role in the struggle to end Israeli apartheid as the sports boycott did, in previous decades, in the campaign against South African apartheid.[10]

As in other arenas, the pattern of political sympathies within universities tends to map on to power relations consistent with this book's characterisation of the pro-Israel and pro-Palestinian solidarity movements as social movements from above and below, respectively. Thus, as Peretz Lavie of Israel's Association of University Heads has remarked, the boycott movement 'gains support at the "ground level" from student unions and academic associations', while in contrast, 'relations between Israeli and American universities remain strong at the institutional and leadership levels'.[11]

In 2014, for example, a group of US university presidents responded to students and faculty support for academic boycott by issuing a joint condemnation of BDS, constituting what political theorist Corey Robin observed was 'a very elite backlash'.[12] Despite this strong support from the top, Zionist movement strategists recognised that they could not afford to be complacent. Pro-Israel group StandWithUs lamented that the 'leaders of tomorrow' were being educated in environments hostile to Israel.[13] Similarly, The David Project argued that 'campus often serves as an incubator' and trends in the academy frequently portend the future direction of wider society because 'the thinking of America's future political leadership is molded' while at university.[14]

In Britain, some friends of Israel dismissed the threat of academic boycott with jovial confidence. For example, Boris Johnson – mayor of London at the time – declared in typically flamboyant language that supporters of BDS in universities consisted merely of 'corduroy-jacketed, snaggle-toothed academics' with 'no real standing in the matter', who were 'unlikely to be influential'.[15] However, recognising that universities represent 'a microcosm of wider political argument over the Middle East', others saw the trajectory of British universities as deeply concerning.[16]

Indeed, if the academic boycott is the leading campaign within the wider BDS movement, then British universities have often been placed at the vanguard of this vanguard. For instance, the Reut Institute identified London specifically as the 'hub of hubs' of the global 'delegitimisation network', particularly singling out the capital's university campuses. Legal scholar Lesley Klaff, a member of UK Lawyers for Israel, similarly argued that 'British universities have become key conduits in the global assault on Israel's legitimacy', while Harold Brackman of the pro-Israel Simon Wiesenthal Centre wrote sardonically that British universities had earned the 'academic [boycott] honours'.[17]

How did Britain's universities gain this reputation? As early as 2002, during the Second Intifada – even before Palestinian civil society issued its official collective call for BDS – UK-based scholars had made calls for boycotts of Israeli universities.[18] Five years later, at its inaugural May 2007 conference, Britain's University and College Union (UCU) saw lecturers again call for an academic boycott of Israeli universities on the grounds of their deep complicity in the apartheid system.[19] This was the first time BDS had reached such a large and mainstream audience in Britain. A fierce backlash – including condemnations from the British and US governments – combined with legal advice, saw the drive for boycott within the UCU stalled and the threat kept at bay.[20] Yet the episode was a huge scare for the Zionist movement and was seminal in eliciting new initiatives intended to foreclose the possibility of future academic boycotts of Israel.

Almost immediately, the saga triggered a visit to Israel by a delegation of British government officials and university vice-chancellors, whose October 2007 trip was a clear sign of elite intent to fortify academic links between the two countries in response to the grassroots threat of BDS. Meanwhile, BICOM funder Poju Zabludowicz pledged to create a £300,000 'anti-BDS fighting fund', while the Board of Deputies promised that £1 million would be spent fighting boycotts and 'delegitimisation'.[21] In the longer term, the UCU controversy stimulated two projects examined in this chapter: firstly, the fostering and expansion of 'Israel studies' as an academic subject by pro-Israel donors and, secondly, the creation of 'BIRAX' – a multimillion pound partnership between British and Israeli universities established with the support of both countries' governments and, once again, private pro-Israel philanthropists. Both projects inherently function to undermine the academic boycott and are part of an effort to effectively 'relegitimise' Israel on campus.

As we will see, this effort to reshape the academic landscape in a manner favourable to Israel had limited efficacy. The trajectory of the UCU was not unique, and soon the student movement followed suit. In the wake of Operation Cast Lead in 2008–9, when Israel killed over 1,400 Palestinians in Gaza, students across at least sixteen British universities protested by staging an unprecedented wave of sit-in occupations – part of a broader global upsurge of solidarity activism with Palestinians, a trend which continued in the ensuing years.[22] In 2008, the leadership of the National Union of Students – a body representing 7 million UK-based students – had condemned BDS; but by 2015, its members voted to officially endorse the boycott movement, prompting a condemnation from Israeli prime minister Benjamin Netanyahu.[23] In the context of this uptick in Palestine solidarity activism, the Zionist movement has increasingly relied upon a second, more visible and more noticeable strategy: attempts to censor, marginalise and silence ideas deemed to surpass the acceptable in their criticism of Israel. These efforts are examined later in this chapter.

These two prongs of the Zionist movement's response to BDS – the attempt to shape the parameters of legitimate knowledge through Israel studies and BIRAX, and simultaneously to police the boundaries of legitimate debate through censorship – both take place in the context of university privatisation and neoliberal governance, an important contextual factor which enables significant donor influence. And both strategies, as we will see, are chiefly pursued through top-down, undemocratic methods via channels largely protected from public scrutiny.

Understanding 'Israel studies'

To understand the rise of 'Israel studies' in Britain, it is useful to trace its roots back to contestation within the Israeli academy. There, the work of the 'new historians', who challenged the foundational Zionist myths of the Israeli state – pointing to evidence of deliberate and systematic ethnic cleansing of Palestinians during the 1948 Nakba – was central to the so-called post-Zionist turn of the 1990s. One such historian, Ilan Pappé, argues that this hopeful current was effectively defeated by the 'triumph of neo-Zionism', the more 'nationalistic, racist and dogmatic' brand of Zionism prevalent in Israeli politics today.[24]

This political schism also expressed itself within Israeli sociology in the last decade of the twentieth century. What Uri Ram calls 'critical sociology', an approach informed by post-Zionism, adopted a 'colonization perspective' by taking 'the Israeli-Arab binational set of relations as its vantage point'. This approach argued, in effect, that Israel could only be understood by way of reference to the Palestinians, so intrinsic was the settler-colonial encounter in shaping the country. In contrast, what Ram dubs 'national sociology' took a 'dualist approach', viewing Israel and the Palestinians as separable entities and drawing 'the boundaries of "'Israeli society'"' around the territorial and ethnic Jewish presence'.[25] When we look at the way the Association for Israel Studies defines Israel studies – as 'the study of Israel, the Zionist movement, or the pre-state Jewish community in Palestine'[26] – we can see that this framing, privileging Jewishness and marginalising Palestinians entirely, clearly fits within the latter, orthodox Zionist approach.[27]

Given its framing, the field of Israel studies is entirely consonant with the Israeli government's Brand Israel project, which aimed to 'broaden the conversation' so that Israel's image would move 'beyond the conflict', rather than be viewed through the lens of state violence towards Palestinians.[28] Although the first Israel studies course, established in the US in 1998, predates this official propaganda programme (launched in 2005), the two nonetheless neatly dovetail.[29] Advocates of Israel studies describe it in very similar terms, complaining, for example, that Israel is 'almost exclusively studied through the prism of the conflict' and stressing the importance of 'broadening [the] scope' of Israel-related courses 'beyond the conflict'.[30]

Due to this compatibility, pro-Israel strategists have articulated the idea of exploiting Israel studies as a tool in the struggle against 'delegitimisation' on campus. For instance, Mitchell Bard, formerly of the US lobby group AIPAC and later a key figure in the expansion of Israel studies in North America, noted in 2009 that 'chairs and centers of Israel studies are being created in the US and, more recently, the UK' and called this phenomenon 'critical to countering present campus-based efforts to delegitimize Israel', recommending 'encouraging more Israel Studies on campus as part of a broader rebranding'.[31] Similarly, the Reut Institute asserted that 'in the context of Reut's current work on how to fight the delegitimacy of Israel, the suggestion to create chairs of Israel Studies in leading UK universities could act as an important component of Israel's strategy'.[32]

Critically, as some scholars have noted, in the US context the expansion of Israel studies courses and posts has been 'a response to supply' rather than demand.[33] In other words – in sharp contrast to student and faculty calls for more public funding of subjects like Black Studies – the growth of Israel Studies has been fostered via a 'top down process with private funding' from external donors.[34] Many, if not all, of the philanthropists funding the rise of Israel studies have political motivations. Some have been explicit about this, such as Fred Lafer (of the Taub Foundation, which funded Israel studies at New York University), who declared that he wanted to counter the 'Arabic point of view'.[35] In short, according to the Israel on Campus Coalition, the scholarly framing of Israel 'in terms of the conflict' is 'exactly' what donors to Israel studies in the US are 'fighting against'.[36]

In some cases, the ideological commitments and political motivations of Israel studies donors are somewhat more obscure but can be inferred from their other philanthropic activities – principally contributions to Zionist advocacy bodies. For example, the Charles and Lynn Schusterman Family Foundation, which funds Israel studies at three US universities (Brandeis, the University of Oklahoma and the University of Texas at Austin), also financially supports the Reut Institute, the Israel on Campus Coalition and the American Israel Education Foundation, a charity channelling funds to AIPAC.[37] Sometimes, donors' views come into play only when certain lines are crossed. For instance, in February 2022, the University of Washington was forced to return an Israel studies gift of $5 million (£4.7 million) after the donor, Becky Benaroya, objected to the postholder, Liora Halperin, signing a statement condemning Israel's 'unjust, enduring, and unsustainable systems of Jewish supremacy, ethnonational segregation, discrimination, and violence against Palestinians' and defending the right to respond through boycott.[38] Halperin was stripped of the endowed chair.

Elite attempts to instrumentalise academia to bolster state power are neither new nor unique to the Zionist movement. In the contemporary era, large Middle East–related donations to British universities are not unusual and include considerable support from the Saudi royal family for the University of Oxford and others.[39] As chapter 1 explained, in the latter half of the twentieth century, the 'Big Three' American foundations – Ford, Carnegie and Rockefeller – funded universities in ways that sought to preserve US hegemony during the Cold War. Domestically, they played a fundamental role in the rise of international relations as an academic subject, while overseas they helped establish 'networks of pro-American universities' – activities which scholar Inderjeet Parmar explains were 'rarely, if ever . . . [conducted] without the input and advice of US state agencies'.[40] The foundations also targeted certain countries perceived as particularly prone to anti-Americanism. As we will see, Zionist philanthropic foundations in Britain have taken a similarly targeted approach, and their efforts should be understood analogously.

Building Israel studies in Britain

All Israel studies posts in British universities were established after the turn of the millennium, when the crisis of Israel's legitimacy crystallised. As in the US, the emergence and proliferation of Israel studies was driven by the top-down supply of private funding, rather than demand from students. All of the philanthropic foundations funding Israel studies have close links to the Zionist movement, mapped in figure 7.1, which shows known Israel studies posts and the connections (both past and present) of the donors' endowing the subject at each institution. (As the introduction to this book explained, some organisations which are Jewish communal bodies rather than explicitly Zionist advocacy groups – such as the Jewish Leadership Council, Board of Deputies and Community Security Trust – are included because of strong empirical evidence of pro-Israel campaigning activities, including explicit declarations by the heads of some of these organisations that they proudly lobby for Israel.)

Trevor Pears and Michael Lewis, two of the three men once described as 'the driving force' behind both Conservative Friends of Israel and BICOM, are also among the donors to Israel studies.[41] Indeed, the Pears Foundation is the most significant player in the field, having contributed to every single Israel studies post in Britain. Its eponymous chief executive, Trevor Pears, is a property investor and Conservative donor who was knighted in 2017 and has served on the boards of BICOM and Conservative Friends of Israel, as well as donating to the New Israel Fund.[42] Meanwhile, the most substantial gift – a £3 million donation to the University of Oxford in 2011 – was made by the Stanley and Zea Lewis Family Foundation, named after the parents of businessman and Conservative donor Michael Lewis. A past donor to BICOM, the United Jewish Israel Appeal and Conservative Friends of Israel, Lewis has also served on the Conservative Friends of Israel board.

The consortium of donors to Israel studies at the University of Sussex, meanwhile, was led by publishing magnate George Weidenfeld. A cross-bench life peer in the House of Lords until his death in 2016, the late Lord Weidenfeld – to whom Benjamin Netanyahu

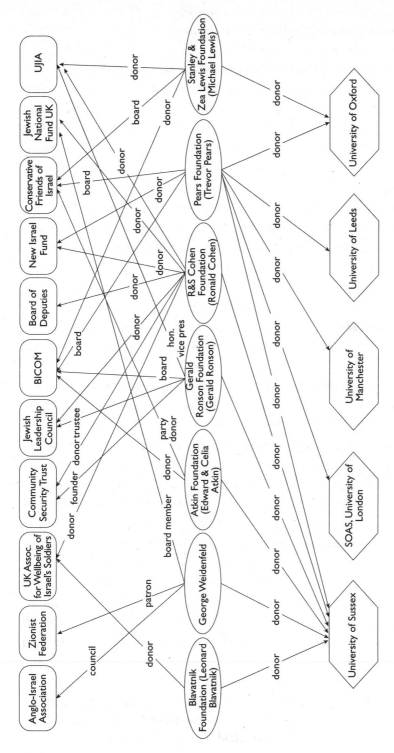

Figure 7.1. Pro-Israel advocacy links of donors to Israel studies posts at British universities[43]

paid tribute after his death – was a lifelong Zionist and a former advisor to Israel's first president, Chaim Weizmann,[44] with ties to the Anglo-Israel Association, Zionist Federation and Jewish National Fund UK. The Sussex consortium also included Leonard Blavatnik, the owner of Warner Music. Named Britain's richest man in 2015 and knighted in 2017, Blavatnik has previously financially supported the UK Friends of the Association for the Wellbeing of Israel's Soldiers.[45] Joining Weidenfeld and Blavantink was business tycoon Gerald Ronson, founder of the Community Security Trust and previously a board member of a number of other pro-Israel bodies. Both Blavatnik and Ronson also contributed to Israeli prime minister Benjamin Netanyahu's election campaigns.[46] Finally, the consortium brought together Conservative Party donors like the late businessman Edward Atkin and his wife Celia Atkin (trustees of the Atkin Foundation) with a significant contributor to the Labour Party, Ronald Cohen – the private equity pioneer and son-in-law of Yossi Harel. As figure 7.1 shows, Cohen has been either a donor, director or board member of at least seven pro-Israel groups.

Many of these British donors, like their counterparts in the US, appear to see Israel studies as a weapon in an ideological war to push back against 'delegitimisation' of Israel at universities and in wider society. Several have been fairly explicit about their political motivations. Most brazenly, Lord Weidenfeld welcomed the chair of Israel studies at Oxford University by calling the subject 'vital in the fight against anti-Zionism' and 'conducive to fighting the boycott'.[47] He even articulated the conscious political strategy guiding the process, stressing the importance of establishing Israel studies in key universities, particularly 'those with an anti-Israel' presence – likely a reference to universities like Sussex, Manchester and the School of Oriental and African Studies (SOAS), well known in Britain as hubs of left-wing politics, including Palestine solidarity activism.[48] Meanwhile, the Pears Foundation has made clear that it seeks to 'support Israel' (albeit 'by being a critical friend').[49] And although the original benefactor to Israel studies at Oxford (prior to the Lewis Foundation) remained anonymous, the university's former Israel studies fellow Emanuele Ottolenghi has said that the unnamed donor had a firm 'commitment to Israel'.[50]

In addition to every donor having direct links to the Zionist movement, the group are considerably internally cohesive. For instance, Michael Lewis served as chair of Weidenfeld's Institute for Strategic Dialogue think-tank, and the ISD held joint events with Ronald Cohen's non-profit body the Portland Trust.[51] Weidenfeld's publishing house also produced a book commissioned by Trevor Pears, *Israel in the World*, which showcased Israel's scientific achievements and was considered such a powerful PR weapon that hundreds of copies were distributed by Israeli embassies around the world.[52] This consistency in affiliation makes it reasonable to assume that all the donors shared broadly similar aims in funding the expansion of Israel studies in Britain.

Because donors' activities and connections to the Zionist movement were suggestive of a pro-Israel agenda, staff and students from some of the universities in question resisted the establishment of Israel studies. In response, the universities offered assurances that Israel studies donors had no influence on the appointment process for the posts they endowed. Even if this were true, according to the argument made by former London School of Economics professor Harold Laski – incidentally an ardent Zionist – in an essay entitled 'Foundations, Universities, and Research', this would not prevent donor influence. Donors do not need to exert 'the slightest control . . . or interference', he claimed, for 'it is merely the fact that a fund is within reach which permeates everything'.[53] Here, Laski may actually have painted an overly deterministic picture of the donor–recipient relationship. As it turns out, internal correspondence obtained via freedom of information requests shows that some Israel studies donors *did* in fact seek to influence university appointment processes.

Most notably, in 2011 Lord Weidenfeld sent a list of names he explicitly suggested could be candidates for the Israel studies post he was co-funding at Sussex to the university's vice-chancellor, Michael Farthing – who then chaired the appointment panel. Because of redactions, we do not know if the successful candidate was one of his suggestions. But the considerable influence of donors was also illustrated by the decision to name the post after Yossi Harel.[54] Initially, vice-chancellor Farthing advised the donors that the university's policy was only to name posts after donors themselves. However, after a professor at the university assured his colleagues that only a 'staunch and ideological anti-Zionist' would object to a post named after the Haganah fighter, the name 'Yossi Harel Chair in Modern Israel Studies' was agreed.[55]

At the University of Leeds in June 2011, Vice-Chancellor Michael Arthur was asked by staff to suspend the appointment process for an Israel studies chair funded by the Pears Foundation, pending wider consultation. However, staff dissent was briskly swept aside by the university chief in favour of accepting the large financial endowment. Despite clear evidence of Pears's pro-Israel politics, Arthur dismissed the concerns raised, claiming that the case for the Pears Foundation being a 'pro-Zionist' organization was 'flimsy' and 'indirect'.[56] In doing so, he bore out another observation of Harold Laski's, expressed in the latter's aforementioned essay:

> A university principal who wants his institution to expand has no alternative except to see it expand in the directions of which one or other of the foundations happens to approve. There may be doubt, or even dissent among the teachers in the institution, but what possible chance has doubt or dissent against a possible gift of, say, a hundred thousand dollars?[57]

While Laski wrote his essay in 1930, his observation is more pertinent than ever in the contemporary neoliberal era, in which privatisation at universities has intensified. Universities' reliance on donor fundraising was evident, for example, in the economic arguments made by staff in favour of the new Israel studies posts. At SOAS, Professor Colin Shindler wrote to the vice-chancellor, describing Israel/Palestine as 'a "hot" subject' which 'brings in lots of students', meaning it 'therefore brings in fees and is financially viable'.[58] At Sussex, Professor Christian Wiese expressed support for the Israel studies proposal to the vice-chancellor by declaring: 'I am convinced this is a golden opportunity which goes well beyond this single chair. Sussex is now on the radar of very potent donors.'[59] In both cases, financial incentives won the day.

Importantly, none of this evidence necessarily dents the scholarly credentials of the individual academics occupying the posts concerned. Moreover Israel studies courses themselves are certainly not mere propaganda. However, Israel studies as an academic subject can never be completely separated from the political networks and agendas of its funders. At the institutional level, especially given the commercial environment discussed, the philanthropic foundations promoting Israel studies as a subject have clearly had considerable impact, enabling certain ideas to become more prominent, making specific research areas more employable and, in the process, helping to marginalise other ideas. Thus, they help shape and define the parameters of 'legitimate and illegitimate knowledge' which ultimately filters into the public sphere.[60]

Meanwhile, the charter of the European Association of Israel Studies – based at SOAS and funded by the Pears Foundation – states that it will 'encourage' links with Israeli universities.[61] In this sense, funding Israel studies is also a *practical* way to undermine the academic boycott movement in universities. The same can be said of the International Centre for the Study of Radicalisation at King's College London – partnered with Israel's Interdisciplinary Centre Herzliya and explicitly conceived by its key funder, Henry Sweetbaum, as a response to the BDS movement[62] – and of an important project called BIRAX.

BIRAX: Academic 'facts on the ground'

The Britain Israel Research and Academic Exchange Partnership (BIRAX) scheme is, like Israel studies, part of a long-term strategy for reshaping the academic landscape in Israel's favour. Like Israel studies, BIRAX was engineered from the top down and structurally impeded the BDS movement in British universities by establishing academic 'facts on the ground' (a phrase used in the Israel/Palestine context to describe how settlement construction, by altering material and demographic realities, aims to obtain more land for Israel). Facilitated by the British Council, to date BIRAX has provided over £12 million worth of funding for scientific research collaborations between British and Israeli universities, mostly in the form of three-year projects. While British–Israeli academic collaborations were far from new, BIRAX represented a significant step-change in terms of the levels of financing provided. This reflected the project's status as the flagship initiative in a wider effort to strengthen institutional links between the two countries' universities.

BIRAX grew out of the aforementioned 2007 trip to Israel by a delegation of officials from the British government and several university vice-chancellors, itself triggered by the UCU boycott debate that same year. In 2008, BIRAX was launched with a joint statement by then prime ministers of Israel and Britain, Ehud Olmert and Gordon Brown.[63] State support for the project was based on the fact that BIRAX represented a neat convergence of interests. Universities are vital to each country's economy, so preserving collaboration was seen by both as essential. Indeed, David Quarrey, then British ambassador to Israel, declared that 'science diplomacy' was at 'the heart of the UK's relationship with Israel'.[64] To this end, the two governments signed a memorandum of understanding on scientific cooperation in 2013.

This bilateral agenda also chimed with the Israeli government's Brand Israel strategy, which, as chapter 2 noted, sought to highlight among other things Israel's scientific and technological achievements. The other advantage of the exact sciences was that these disciplines were deemed less pervaded by 'delegitimisation' and boycott supporters than humanities and social sciences; pro-Israel group The David Project claimed, for example, that while so-called anti-Israelism was rife in the latter, by contrast 'the hard sciences point to new opportunities to promote Israel to receptive audiences'.[65]

BIRAX was lauded by its supporters as a 'unique model', one that Israeli minister of science and technology Danny Danon was 'keen to replicate' in other European countries.[66] Embodying neoliberal ideals, it operated as a public–private partnership. Initial bilateral seed funding from the public purse underwrote the project, including early pledges of support by Britain's Foreign Office and Department for Innovation, Universities and Skills and Israel's Ministry of Foreign Affairs and Ministry of Science and Technology.[67] This state sponsorship was more than matched by a network of private donors. Indeed, the 'business case' for BIRAX boasted that it had 'successfully responded to genuine market demand'. Just as with Israel studies, this demand was not coming from universities themselves but primarily from Zionist philanthropists.

Among the philanthropists supporting the BIRAX project, at least two – the Pears Foundation and the Atkin Foundation – also funded Israel studies. Indeed, the original proposal for BIRAX, produced by the British Council, was addressed to the Pears Foundation, suggesting that this body was as critical to BIRAX as it was to the funding of Israel studies. Meanwhile, the United Jewish Israel Appeal was involved both as an 'intermediary' in the initial Pears Foundation donation to Israel studies at the University of Manchester and as a contributor to BIRAX. Other BIRAX donors had close ties to the Zionist movement too. Poju Zabludowicz, a key supporter of both BICOM and Conservative Friends of Israel, supported BIRAX via the Zabludowicz Trust's sponsorship of the UK-Israel Science Council.[68] Another major Conservative donor and former party treasurer, ex–hedge fund manager Stanley Fink – who we encountered in chapter 5 via his support for the anti-BDS initiative Culture for Coexistence – also donated to BIRAX.

In addition, billionaire Nathan Kirsh, named Britain's seventeenth-richest person in 2015, gave at least £176,000 to BIRAX.[69] At one point, Kirsh was the biggest shareholder in Magal Security Systems – a company heavily involved in Israel's apartheid wall, declared illegal by the International Court of Justice.[70] In addition, two branches of the Wolfson family supported BIRAX. The first, the Wolfson Family Charitable Trust, counts Lord Leslie Turnberg, a Labour peer and Labour Friends of Israel supporter, among its trustees. The second, the Charles Wolfson Charitable Trust, boasts businessman and Conservative peer Lord David Wolfson, a former chief of staff to ex–prime minister Margaret Thatcher, as a trustee and has also funded bodies like the Israel-Diaspora Trust and Anglo-Israel Association.[71] Finally, Yad Hanadiv, the charitable foundation of the Rothschild family – an important Zionist dynasty which helped to fund early Jewish settlements in Palestine – also contributed to BIRAX. In recent years, Ronald Cohen, the Labour Friends of Israel stalwart and Israel studies donor, has served on Yad Hanadiv's board,[72] and the former Israeli ambassador to Britain, Daniel Taub – who was central to the Tricycle Theatre saga chronicled in chapter 5 – became its director of strategy in 2016.[73]

On all of these accounts, the money behind BIRAX was suggestive of a clear political agenda. As we will see, however, the project's *explicitly* anti-BDS purpose was kept deliberately obscure.

'An eloquent answer to calls for boycotts'

The BIRAX project was facilitated by the British Council, a quasi-autonomous non-governmental organisation (or 'quango'). Publicly, the British Council claims to be a 'non-political' body. It explicitly described itself as such, for example, in 2012 after the Palestine Festival of Literature – which the British Council sponsored – showed support for BDS, prompting the latter to hastily issue a statement condemning the move.[74] Yet the impression of political neutrality which the British Council sought to cultivate was merely a public performance. Originally established in 1934 under the auspices of the Foreign Office for the purpose of supporting foreign policy goals through culture and educational means, the British Council is among the reasons Britain is widely considered a world leader in soft power.[75] Historically, its staff were vetted by MI5.[76] As a quango, the British Council remains accountable to Parliament but is no longer fully funded by the Foreign Office. Today, required to raise most of its revenue from private sources, it has become, through BIRAX, an enthusiastic partner to the Zionist movement and wider British government apparatus in actively countering the BDS movement.

The British Council's public statements about BIRAX intentionally obfuscated its political genesis. Presented as being, in the Council's words, 'principally about great science',[77] the project was in fact *explicitly conceived* as a top-down response to the pro-Palestinian boycott movement emerging from below. The British Council's original May 2008 proposal for the project, addressed to the Pears Foundation, called BIRAX a 'practical response' to 'calls in the UK for an academic boycott of Israel'. The document was crystal clear that the project's key raison d'être was to 'deepen institutional links' between British and Israeli universities.[78] In addition, there was no mention at all in the original proposal of regenerative medicine. This specialism, on which BIRAX would eventually focus, was only announced in 2011, three years after the project was initiated, underlining the fact that the fundamental driving force of the project was political, not scientific.[79]

Although few of the earliest donors to BIRAX had a record of funding medical research, major health specialists such as the British Heart Foundation did later become involved – showing that the project had genuine medical merits. However, documents obtained through freedom of information requests provide further evidence of decidedly political (as opposed to scientific) rationale for elements of the BIRAX programme. For example, in its early years, a travel fellowship formed an integral part of the project. In correspondence with the British Council, the Atkin Foundation expressed a desire for these fellowships to go to individuals 'who ideally have not visited Israel previously'.[80] Similarly, a donor whose name was redacted before documents were disclosed declared unambiguously that fellowships were 'a good way of introducing scientists to the real Israel as opposed to British media & therefore countering academic boycott movements'.[81]

In private, British Council staff themselves were just as candid about the counter-boycott aims of BIRAX. In internal emails, disclosed partially redacted, employees discussed pitching BIRAX to potential donors as an 'anti-BDS' project. One read:

> Here is some general background about [REDACTED] – that I mentioned yesterday, as a possible patron for BIRAX. Here is some recent info about his interest in supporting anti-BDS activities . . . [REDACTED] asked that we send him a couple of paras on the pitch we'd like him to make to individuals around BIRAX and BIRAX/BDS.[82]

Similarly, in March 2014, the British Council sought 'commercial investment' in the project at an international fundraising conference in Miami. Its pitch for BIRAX in an email about the conference – 'How does British govt respond to the boycott movement?' – was unequivocal. In another message that same year, a British Council staffer described the BIRAX programme as 'an eloquent answer to those calling for boycotts'.[83]

Indeed, the British Council's Israel office sought to counter the BDS movement at universities not solely via BIRAX but through other means as well.[84] Internal correspondence shows that, behind the scenes, staff closely monitored developments in the boycott movement on British university campuses and strategically intervened to undermine it when they could. For instance, just a day after the National Union of Students endorsed the boycott of Israel in June 2015, British Council staff sent emails with the subject 'BDS', outlining possible responses and planning collaboration with the British embassy in Israel.[85] They also reacted immediately to an academic-boycott pledge issued by 300 UK-based scholars in October 2015 and saw fit to circulate an anti-boycott statement in response. Staff even asked leaders within the Union of Jewish Students, via email, to be kept abreast of 'what's happening re the boycott on campuses' and offered to support that organisation's work combating BDS.[86]

The Union of Jewish Students (UJS) was founded in 1973, in part, according to sociologist Keith Kahn-Harris, as a response to anti-Zionist activism on British campuses.[87] It is funded by the United Jewish Israel Appeal, Jewish Leadership Council and others – including, according to the 2017 account of one prominent student activist from the group, the Israeli embassy.[88] UJS does considerable positive work supporting Jewish student life – but it also fosters support for Israeli apartheid. Notably, the union's constitution states that its objectives include encouraging students 'to make an enduring commitment' to Israel.[89] To this end, it facilitates trips to Israel, including on highly subsidised tours organised by the Zionist group Birthright. According to former BICOM and Labour Friends of Israel researcher Toby Greene, these trips can make a lasting impact on students in their formative years. 'In a number of cases', Greene notes, 'rising Blairites had their first contact with Israel . . . from travelling to Israel on a trip sponsored by the Union of Jewish Students' and 'went on to become MPs active in LFI'.[90] Illustrating the centrality of Israel to the work of the UJS, in 2019 the organisation appointed Arieh Miller, a former head of the Zionist Federation, to be its chief executive.[91] To promote engagement with Israel, UJS also hosts several *shlichim* (emissaries) from the Jewish Agency.

Contrary to the admonitions of one prominent anti-Zionist professor, these affiliations do not make Jewish students 'pawns' of the Israeli government.[92] Moreover, it is important to note that some Jewish students disagree strongly with their representative body's pro-Israel stance. For two consecutive years in 2016 and 2017, explicitly non-Zionist Jewish students ran in elections for the presidency of the organisation. One, Annie Cohen, pledged to 'review UJS finances in order to divert funding away from Israel tours to student welfare services and hardship grants'.[93] The other, Israeli anti-Zionist Eran Cohen, was abused as a 'traitor', 'kapo' and a 'self-hating Jew' for his pro-BDS stance.[94] Neither came close to victory, however, and the UJS actively campaigns against the BDS movement to this day. In 2016, the organisation launched a campaign called 'Bridges Not Boycotts' in collaboration with the Board of Deputies, and it held a conference of the same name the following year with speakers such as We Believe in Israel's Luke Akehurst.[95]

The British Council's offer of support for UJS's counter-boycott work confirms that BIRAX, while a flagship anti-BDS project, was just one element of the quango's efforts to hinder the boycott movement. Together with Israel studies, then, the establishment of BIRAX was undeniably part of a multidimensional top-down effort to institutionally defeat the academic boycott movement targeting Israeli apartheid, dovetailing with the Israeli government's official propaganda aims.

Censorship and silencing

The other side of the coin to projects like Israel studies and BIRAX, which are focused on altering the academic landscape to defend Israel, are more readily observable and highly conflictual efforts to censor and silence criticism of Israel or Zionism. These activities go hand in hand with repressive attempts to suppress scholarship and activism in support of, and by, Palestinians. They have been pursued by several of the same pro-Israel groups involved in promoting and funding Israel studies and BIRAX.

To understand the role that censorship plays in the project to defend Israel's legitimacy, it is instructive to consider Colin Leys' observation that 'for an ideology to be hegemonic, it is not necessary that it be loved. It is merely necessary that it have no serious rival.'[96] In other words, if enthusiastic support for Zionism could not be generated, merely preventing any viable alternative to Zionism – such as the counter-hegemonic vision advanced by the BDS movement – from gaining widespread legitimacy might be sufficient to preserve Israeli apartheid. In recent years, as Israel's apartheid nature has become increasingly clear and soft power projects like Brand Israel have failed to manufacture support, aggressive tactics, including censorship of critics, have become a more and more appealing backlash strategy for the Zionist movement.

Within Israel/Palestine, censorship and violent repression have been imposed on Palestinian universities for decades. In the post-2000 period, pockets of 'post-Zionist' dissent within Israeli universities also increasingly became targets for silencing. Notably, a so-called ethical code for academics, commissioned in 2017 by the far-right education minister Naftali Bennett (later Israel's prime minister), sought to ban scholars in Israeli universities from supporting BDS.[97] Simultaneously, private Zionist bodies like Im Tirtzu have long worked to police dissent in Israeli universities, pre-empting similar efforts in the US by blacklisting bodies like Canary Mission. In the past three years alone in North America, wealthy supporters of Israel appeared to have applied financial pressure on Canada's University of Toronto and Harvard University in the US to deny employment and tenure, respectively, to Israel-critical scholars Valentina Azarova and Cornel West.[98]

Such controversies have taken place within the global context of a toxic debate around 'cancel culture' and 'free speech' on university campuses, predominently driven by culture warriors committed to white supremacy and transphobia. In Britain, one recent report found that academic freedom in universities was among the most weakly protected in Europe – and in decline.[99] While the so-called 'Palestine exception to free speech' is long-standing and worldwide, other contemporary phenomena have exacerbated the situation in Britain.[100] The growing influence of market forces and accompanying corporate-governance practices have helped foster a culture of risk aversion at the top of universities, among a managerial class hyper-sensitive to media criticism. Lower down the ranks, where employment precarity is now pervasive, a climate of self-censorship has become ingrained.

Britain's toxic racial politics has also intensified the silencing of Palestinians and their allies. On the one hand, the government's pre-crime 'counter-extremism' Prevent programme has, under the tenuous guise of national security and countering terrorism, obligated publicly funded bodies, including university staff, to watch for and report signs of so-called extremism – defined in racialised and hopelessly vague terms. As well as impinging on the free exchange of ideas in academia in general, Prevent has disproportionately impacted people of colour, particularly Muslims. Those engaged in Palestine-solidarity activism, criticism of the 'War on Terror', or indeed many other forms of activism and dissent, risk being reported as potential 'extremists' and ending up with their name on a police database – despite never having committed a crime. In this way, as well as institutionalising Islamophobia in public life, British state racism in the form of Prevent helps silence and censor opposition to Israeli state racism.

Simultaneously, this fertile climate for pro-Israel censorship was stoked by the British political elite's embrace of the International Holocaust Remembrance Alliance definition, which as chapter 2 discussed, sought to widen the meaning of anti-Semitism to include some criticisms of Israel. In September 2020, just twenty-nine of Britain's 133 higher education institutions had adopted the IHRA definition, given widespread concern about its impact on academic freedom.[101] However, after Conservative education minister Gavin Williamson threatened to cut the funding of universities which refused to adopt the definition, that number rocketed.[102] By November 2021, almost a hundred universities had adopted the IHRA document.[103] Thus, as pro-Palestinian academic and campaigner Sai Englert observed, 'while claiming to defend free speech from a supposedly censure-obsessed left, the [British] government . . . repeatedly tried to shut down political debate and criminalise activism'.[104] This happened despite considerable dissent from Jewish scholars of anti-Semitism such as David Feldman and Seth Anziska, the latter as part of a University College London working group whose report pointed out that the IHRA text 'obfuscates rather than clarifies the meaning of anti-Semitism', making it a counterproductive tool in the fight against anti-Jewish racism.[105]

Finally, various pro-Israel actors sought to influence the debate on British campuses to further shrink the space for pro-Palestine speech and activism. In Al Jazeera's 2017 undercover documentary *The Lobby*, pro-Israel student activists stated that 'the Israeli embassy in the UK gives money' to supportive student groups – including, as noted, the UJS.[106] It also revealed that US-based group AIPAC provided funding for pro-Israel activists Adam Schapira and Elliott Miller to establish a campus-based Zionist-advocacy group called the Pinsker Centre – which claimed to be 'vibrant and grassroots'.[107] Miller, once a member of a secret Facebook group in which pro-Israel students discussed how to 'attack BDS' with 'smear campaigns',[108] had previously worked for the Israeli government and for 'Student Rights', a side-project of neoconservative think-tank the Henry Jackson Society. In 2016, he was caught on camera being violent and racially abusive towards pro-Palestinian students in London.[109] All these phenomena have made speaking out for Palestinians on British university campuses a hyper-visible and risky endeavour.

'Surpassing the acceptable'

The combined dynamics of university privatisation and toxic racial politics have been the backdrop for a plethora of instances of, or attempts at, top-down silencing by pro-Israel actors. Certain ideas – specifically, strong criticism of Israel or Zionism – were deemed beyond the pale. And certain people – student activists, in particular women of colour, including Palestinians – were frequent targets. Very often, allegations of both 'extremism' and anti-Semitism were involved.

In April 2015, an academic conference called 'International Law and the State of Israel: Legitimacy, Exceptionalism and Responsibility' was due to take place at the University of Southampton. At the event, a number of legal scholars highly critical of Israel were billed to speak. The pro-Israel response epitomised the extent of top-down external political pressure that the Zionist movement could mobilise and was reminiscent of the Tricycle Theatre saga of the previous year. Once again, opposition came both from state actors and civil society groups. Britain's ambassador to Israel, Matthew Gould, wrote to the university vice-chancellor expressing concerns and was involved in meetings about the conference with the sector-wide body Universities UK.[110] Four members of Parliament from Conservative Friends of Israel also intervened, either by writing to the university vice-chancellor or by letting their disapproval be known via the press.[111] External donors applied pressure too: the press reported that 'at least two major patrons' of the university were 'considering withdrawing their financial support'. Lawyer Mark Lewis, a prominent figure in UK Lawyers for Israel, told the press he would look 'unfavourably' on job applications from Southampton University graduates.[112] Notorious Islamophobe Douglas Murray of the neoconservative Henry Jackson Society described the proposed conference as evidence that universities were 'hotbeds of extremism'.[113] Finally, the Board of Deputies, Jewish Leadership Council and Union of Jewish Students wrote a joint letter to the university claiming the topic of the conference would 'surpass the acceptable'.[114] The cumulative pressure of lobbying, intense media coverage, and apparently fraying donor relations saw the conference called off.

Later that same year, however, the University of Exeter resisted pressure from BICOM, the Board and the Jewish Leadership Council to cancel a conference on 'Settler Colonialism in Palestine'.[115] Organisers of the cancelled Southampton conference eventually staged the event two years later, after relocating to University College Cork in Ireland.

Equally if not *more* unacceptable to Israel's supporters were the annual Israeli Apartheid Week events that have taken place at university campuses across the world since 2005. Groups such as the Israel Britain Alliance, a side-project of the Zionist Federation founded in 2016, stated openly that they would seek to use the IHRA redefinition of anti-Semitism to try to shut down Israeli Apartheid Week events.[116] Sure enough, soon after the Conservative government adopted the IHRA definition in late 2016, an immediate chilling effect was clear: several Israeli Apartheid Week events due to take place on British campuses in February 2017 were shut down.[117] Since then, students have continued to face challenges organising events highlighting Israeli apartheid – despite major reports from human rights groups Amnesty International and Human Rights Watch confirming that Israel's practices meet the international legal definition of the crime of apartheid.

The demonisation of student activism is far from exclusive to the issue of Palestine solidarity. For decades, students protesting against higher education cuts and fees have been characterised as 'mobs' or 'yobs'. Indeed, authoritarian repression of all forms of protest in Britain reached new heights in 2022 with the passage of the draconian Police, Crime, Sentencing and Courts Act. Nonetheless, student Palestine solidarity activism has repeatedly proven particularly easy to stigmatise. As early as 2010, in response to large student demonstrations against a speech at the University of Manchester by Israel's deputy ambassador, her embassy colleague Ron Prosor declared that 'extremism' was 'not just running through these places of education – it is galloping'.[118] On the day, police were called and, subsequently, one young activist was placed on a 'de-radicalisation' scheme, part of the aforementioned Prevent programme, as a result of his participation in the protest.[119]

Since then, a host of official and unofficial representatives of Israel have spoken at British universities. In recent years in London alone, these have included former Shin Bet head Ami Ayalon, ex-soldier Hen Mazzig, former Israeli ambassador Mark Regev and his far-right successor Tzipi Hotovely, respectively at King's College London, University College London, SOAS and the London School of Economics. In each case, the lively student protests provoked by the appearance of advocates for Israeli apartheid have been demonised in the national press as either 'anti-Semitic', 'extremist', or both. Some even resulted in disciplinary proceedings against pro-Palestinian students by their own universities.[120] Astoundingly, Home Secretary Priti Patel – whose deep involvement in Conservative Friends of Israel was discussed in chapter 4 – called for a police investigation into one such non-violent student protest.[121]

Individual students have been targeted too – as previously mentioned, disproportionately women of colour. They have included leading Palestinian scholar-activists Malaka Shwaikh and Shahd Abusalama, doctoral students at university in Exeter and Sheffield, respectively.[122] In the US, such complaints about young female doctoral research students teaching on Palestine have on occasion been lodged by Israeli diplomats themselves.[123] In Britain, both women were the subject of complaints initiated by Campaign Against Antisemitism, a group which, as chapter 5 explained, had very dubious anti-racism credentials.[124] Supported by allies such as the European Legal Support Centre, both successfully defended themselves against administrative proceedings.[125]

Certain institutions, especially those considered part of the Russell Group of prestigious universities, have faced repeated complaints from pro-Israel actors. In 2021, the University of Glasgow caved to pressure to disown a research paper by doctoral student Jane Jackman on the topic of the pro-Israel lobby in Britain.[126] Although peer reviewed at the time of its publication in 2017, it later generated complaints from supporters of Israel. Prominent among them was David Collier – as chapter 6 explained, a right-wing Zionist blogger who had worked with the Israeli embassy and Jewish Human Rights Watch – who was mentioned by name in Jackman's paper.[127] Rather than censoring the piece outright, the university decided to add, as a preface, a statement impugning the scholarship of the article and saying that it promoted 'what some would regard as an unfounded anti-Semitic theory', though following a counter-protest from pro-Palestinian scholars, the word 'anti-Semitic' was later removed.[128] That same year, citing the IHRA definition and counterterror legislation, Glasgow University took the highly unusual step of asking Somdeep Sen, author of the book *Decolonizing Palestine*, to share a transcript of his planned talk in advance – prompting him to cancel his appearance in protest.[129]

At the University of Bristol in 2017, Islamic studies professor Rebecca Gould was the subject of anti-Semitism allegations, again emanating from Campaign Against Antisemitism and again related to a text written several years earlier. After investigating, the university found that her article was 'not anti-Semitic and does not breach the proper bounds of freedom of speech'.[130] In 2021, Bristol spent six months investigating sociology professor David Miller after a long-standing campaign which included Campaign Against Antisemitism launching legal proceedings against the university. It concluded that Miller's controversial comments 'did not constitute unlawful speech' but fired him anyway, stating that he 'did not meet the standards of behaviour we expect from our staff'.[131] Meanwhile, the University of Manchester forced a Jewish Holocaust survivor critical of Israel's treatment of Palestinians to change the title of her talk, which drew parallels with her own harrowing experiences. This intervention happened in 2017, after the Israeli embassy complained that such comparisons were inherently anti-Semitic, citing the IHRA definition.[132] In 2022, as chapter 5 noted, the Whitworth Gallery (part of Manchester University) forced out its own director following a row the previous year involving UK Lawyers for Israel.[133]

Universities will continue to be a major battlefield for Palestine solidarity – and for pro-Israel actors' attempts to quash the Boycott, Divestment and Sanctions movement. Despite projects like Israel studies and BIRAX successfully altering the academic landscape, they have *not* been particularly effective at suppressing BDS activism, as shown by the need to escalate censorship efforts in recent years. These pro-Israel efforts to police the boundaries of debate have, meanwhile, evidently had significant impact, with senior management echelons of British universities demonstrating considerable willingness to undermine academic freedom in order to avoid criticism. Moreover, as anthropologists Lara Deeb and Jessica Winegar point out, each widely publicised censorship controversy helps create a febrile atmosphere in which subtler practices of self-censorship become commonplace.[134] That said, rising censorship is also a sign of rising *insecurity* on the part of Israel's supporters as the country's apartheid nature – and the acronym 'BDS' – are increasingly recognised within the mainstream. Despite the costs associated with speaking out in solidarity with Palestinians at British universities, the threat from below remains.

8

Influencing the Media

One evening in January 2009, Izzeddin Wahid Mousa was sitting with his wife, Samira, and their children in the yard of their home in the densely built-up Sabra district of Gaza City. Once again, Israel was bombing the besieged Gaza Strip – this time, as part of the campaign code-named Operation Cast Lead. Fathiya, one of the couple's daughters, describes what happened that night:

> It was 8.30pm on 14 January; the area was quiet except of course there was always the noise of F-16s, Apaches, drones. There was no electricity. All the family were in the yard or the house listening to the news, negotiations in Egypt, martyrs, etc. The missile hit. Four were dead at once; my brother's body was all in pieces.[1]

Six members of the Mousa family were killed that night. Seven more, including Fathiya, were injured but survived. Fathiya told Amnesty International:

> We are neither Hamas nor Fatah. We are all civilians . . . Until now we don't understand why . . . we want to know why me and my sisters have been orphaned. Why did they kill our parents, our family? Who will take care of us?

During its three-week operation, Israel used white phosphorus munitions illegally and indiscriminately, caused massive destruction to infrastructure, and killed 1,471 Palestinians.

Later that month in Britain, a coalition of charities called the Disasters Emergency Committee launched an appeal for Gaza, seeking to raise funds for humanitarian support for the devastated coastal enclave. Normally, when the organisation mobilised to support communities around the world stricken by war and other disasters, it could expect the major British broadcasters to promote its work. But not on this occasion. While ITV and Channel 4 screened the appeal, Sky and the BBC refused to air it. The latter's director-general, Mark Thompson, claimed that to broadcast the Gaza appeal would risk 'reducing public confidence in the BBC's impartiality'.[2]

The decision provoked public outcry, leaving the BBC in the uncomfortable position of having to report on a controversy about itself. It led to a memorable moment in British television history when Tony Benn, a veteran Labour MP and pro-Palestinian cam-paigner – a former BBC employee himself – was invited into television studios during the evening news to comment on the head-line story. His hands shaking with outrage, Benn denounced the BBC's decision, before promptly proceeding – live on air – to read out the Gaza appeal from a small scrap of paper, so that viewers could donate nonetheless. In horror, he told the news anchor: 'People will die because of the BBC's decision . . . it has capitulated to Israeli pressure, that's the truth.'[3] The appeal raised just half the expected amount.[4]

Media matters

Analysis of *why* stark and systemic anti-Palestinian bias exists in the British media, especially in relation to pro-Israel pressure, must be conducted carefully and with awareness of the fact that conspiracy theories about 'Jewish control' of the media have a long, dark history. These anti-Semitic themes remain very much alive today, sometimes appearing in relation to Israel/Palestine.[5] For example, a tiny fraction of the considerable criticism BBC direc-tor-general Mark Thompson received for his decision not to air the Gaza appeal involved anti-Semitic abuse referring to the fact that his wife was Jewish. Some years earlier, in 2002, the left-liberal *New Statesman* magazine ran a cover article about pro-Israel media influence which linked this influence to Judaism. The article, enti-tled 'A Kosher Conspiracy', was accompanied by a front-cover image of the Jewish Star of David piercing a Union Jack flag.[6] It is imperative that such anti-Semitic tropes, insinuations and ideas are forcefully rejected.

The truth is that the media is a hotly contested field in which many actors – including pro-Israel actors – do of course seek to exert influence. It is not hard to comprehend the reasons why. The power of the moving image and the written word is such that the media plays a critically important role in framing how Israel/Palestine is understood. Moreover, media representations not only help to shape *public* perception and mould the boundaries of legitimate debate, but also set the parameters of *government* accountability. As a paper called 'Winning the Battle of Narrative', presented at Israel's premier strategic gathering, the Herzliya conference, once observed:

> Whilst foreign policy decision-making includes a closed circle of people, usually consistent of the very elite of each society (politicians, advisors and renowned academics included), public opinion and atmosphere still matter . . . the public's mood and the media's coverage (especially in the UK) determine the government's leeway to pursue a pro-Israeli foreign policy agenda.[7]

As noted in chapter 4, the Zionist movement is acutely aware of the need to insulate British legislators from the increasingly pro-Palestinian sympathies of the British public. That a supportive or hostile media plays a vital mediating role here – either granting social licence or holding to account – is a reality by no means unique to policy on Israel. Media management and spin are crucial components of modern-day statecraft in all areas.[8] To see this, one need only think of the way the intelligence dossier on 'weapons of mass destruction' in Iraq was used by British government spin doctors to make the case for the 2003 invasion and sell it to the public, via the media, as a necessary war.

As an arena of ideological struggle, the British media specifically is of *global* importance. Not least because of the worldwide reach of the BBC, London is a focal point for media-management efforts by a range of corporations and nation-states. In summer 2011, for example, when Channel 4 broadcast a documentary called *Sri Lanka's Killing Fields* documenting allegations of war crimes, a demonstration was organised outside the company's London head-quarters. This protest, the channel's head of news Dorothy Byrne later told a House of Lords communications committee, had been organised by the Sri Lankan ministry of defence.[9]

Similarly, the Israeli embassy and the Zionist movement's media advocacy efforts are long standing. The embassy's press secretary once boasted:

> London is a world centre of media and the embassy here works night and day to influence that media. And, in many subtle ways, I think we don't do a half bad job . . . We have newspapers that write consistently in a manner that supports and understands Israel's situation and its challenges. And we have had influence on the BBC as well.[10]

But should we take this claim at face value? To what extent do Israel's friends really influence British media outlets? And what other factors, besides organised pro-Israel activism, contribute to the media mostly failing to reflect Palestinians' reality? This chapter surveys the British media landscape and offers an overview of key pro-Israel pressure groups and their tactics, paying special attention to groups which exemplify divergent 'carrot' and 'stick' strategies. It then analyses how these forces play out with regard to the BBC and the press, arguing that pro-Israel actors operate in an already largely hospitable media climate, command considerable resources and make a significant impact. Importantly, however, it also echoes and evidences the point that it is precisely the lobby's *lack* of 'control' that necessitates it working so hard to monitor and influence the media.[11]

Factors shaping British media output include deeply embedded prejudices rooted in Britain's colonial history. As well as blatant forms of racism, especially virulent anti-immigrant xenophobia and anti-Traveller sentiments in the press, more subtle forms of racism – including orientalist anti-Arab stereotypes as well as anti-Semitism – also find voice in the British media. These underlying cultural values frame both domestic and foreign news content, and the Middle East is no exception. They also impact audience reception. In their systematic 2011 study *More Bad News from Israel*, sociologists Greg Philo and Mike Berry found that Israelis were more likely to be presented and seen by British media consumers as 'people like us'. This 'Western' cultural identification with Israel's Ashkenazi-dominated society, and the racialised notion of a shared 'Judeo-Christian' heritage, was strengthened by media references to Israel as an 'island of democracy'. In contrast, some participants in their study confessed to perceiving aspects of the (predominantly Muslim) Palestinian culture as 'strange and difficult'. However, while identification and alienation can profoundly shape our ability to empathise – rendering some lives more grievable than others[12] – Philo and Berry also emphasised that people *were* overwhelmingly able to relate, across differences, to fundamental human suffering and oppression.[13]

For this reason, all governments try to influence media output, especially to shape how victims of their own state violence are represented. In 2012 for instance, a study by the Ministry of Defence, obtained by the *Guardian* under freedom of information laws, argued that since the British public were 'casualty averse', involvement in future wars must be made more palatable by reducing the public profile of repatriation ceremonies for those killed in combat.[14] Meanwhile, the British government is able to censor newspaper outlets via the Defence and Security Media Advisory Committee (or 'D-Notice'), run by the same ministry. While this body's advisories are not technically legally binding, media representatives who sit on the committee alongside government representatives tend to comply voluntarily when an issue is flagged as too sensitive, in national security terms, to be reported in the press. As we will see, the British state has also long exercised both formal and informal influence on the BBC – including via its regulatory body, the BBC Board.

Meanwhile in Israel, the government has also been known to intervene in and censor the domestic media, and has even purchased positive coverage in friendly newspapers such as the *Jerusalem Post*.[15] Elsewhere, the Israeli state wields the blunt but effective tool of physically restricting media access to the Palestinian areas which it militarily occupies. For example, it has repeatedly banned foreign journalists from entering Gaza in an attempt to hide the war crimes it commits there. Israel's military also has a long-standing practice of intimidating and targeting journalists, especially those it deems too critical – patterns documented by both Reporters Sans Frontières and the Foreign Press Association.[16] In May 2021, during another intense bombardment of Gaza code-named Operation Guardian of the Walls, Israel killed over 250 Palestinians and directly attacked reporters, dropping missiles which destroyed the offices of Al Jazeera and the Associated Press. One year later, Israeli soldiers killed veteran Palestinian journalist Shireen Abu Akleh – while she was reporting from Jenin wearing a 'press' vest – a murder which Israeli authorities then tried to blame on Palestinian militants.[17]

Alongside state powers, corporations wield considerable influence on the media. While lazy critiques of the corporate 'MSM' (mainstream media) can oversimplify the way commercial forces shape the news we consume, the fundamental need to compete for advertisers, readers and viewers has wide-ranging effects, especially in the digital age. Nor is the primarily taxpayer-funded BBC immune to such influence. Investigative journalist Nick Davies argues that commercial imperatives constitute 'the greatest obstacle to truth-telling journalism'.[18] Financial pressures on the media industries, Davies explains, are increasingly leading to journalists having to write more column inches in fewer hours. This fosters a media culture he calls 'churnalism', since such conditions provide ample opportunities for lobbyists and PR operatives to insert their version of events into newsroom narratives spewed out 24/7 in a constant stream of coverage. After all, as Philo and Berry note, 'it is easier for journalists to accept the routine supply of information than to undertake the difficult, expensive and sometimes dangerous path of generating independent material'.[19] As we will see, individual media owners and their personal political agendas also play a role; while no proprietor ever has complete control, the owners of more than one British media outlet have been accused of either directly or indirectly silencing criticism of Israel.

It is not the case, then, that pro-Israel media pressure groups somehow nefariously impose their will on reporters who would *otherwise* be sympathetic to Palestinians and fearlessly hold Israel to account. The journalists staffing most leading British newspapers and broadcasters tend to be drawn from upper-middle-class backgrounds and rarely rise through the ranks by being critical of existing power structures. The aforementioned cultural, political and commercial forces help create media institutions in which self-censorship is a sad reality. In the case of the BBC, for instance, upon joining the newsroom, reporters are immersed in a journalistic culture characterised by sociologist Tom Mills as ultimately loyal to 'the political institutions of the British state'. Moreover, Mills points out, there is a notable 'revolving door' between the media, Westminster and lobbying worlds, indicative of the cosy and cooperative (rather than conflictual) relationships which often exist across these supposedly distinct spheres.[20] For instance, Terence Prittie, the former *Guardian* journalist we met in chapter 3, went on to work in Israel advocacy, as have numerous other media personnel. When such actors seek to lobby their former colleagues in the media, they are of course intimately familiar with the demands, priorities and constraints of the job – and know precisely how to delicately exert influence. This does not, however, mean that all pressure groups are routinely effective, nor even that they favour the same tactics.

Carrots and sticks

The ecosystem of Zionist groups seeking to influence representations of Israel in broadcast media and the British press has evolved over several decades. However, their strategies and tactics can consistently be grouped into two broad categories: the 'carrot' and the 'stick'. The former describes influence using softer means such as incentives and rewards, while the latter indicates attempts to induce or prevent certain behaviours using disincentives or the prospect of potential punishment.

The Zionist movement's most tried-and-tested 'stick' strategy is what scholars Noam Chomsky and Edward Herman, in their famous propaganda model of media biases and filters, call 'flak'. This they define as 'a means of disciplining the media' through 'negative responses' to media output – such as accusations of bias – which can include letters, phone calls or petitions, and may or may not be centrally organised.[21] As writer Antony Lerman observes, bias is often 'in the eye of the beholder'.[22] However, when allegations of bias are strategically mobilised in this way, they are intended, over the long term, to push media outlets in a desired direction. Journalists themselves often understand this very well. For instance, the BBC's former director of news, Helen Boaden, commented in 2011 that 'sometimes, when people complain about a lack of impartiality, they are simply trying to impose their version of the truth on us'.[23] Despite this awareness, when significant numbers of volunteers can be coordinated to file orchestrated complaints (or, indeed, require no coordination), flak campaigns can nonetheless be highly effective, both in single instances and cumulatively over time.

As the *Observer* newspaper noted in June 2001, 'For many years, pro-Israel organisations have organised letter-writing campaigns to protest against articles and programmes they dislike' – campaigns which have become quicker and easier since the advent of the internet and email.[24] One relatively early example comes from 1977, when the British-Israel Public Affairs Committee (BIPAC), the Zionist Federation and the Board of Deputies jointly published 'Israkit', an 'information tool kit' for Israel advocates which detailed the importance of complaining to the media.[25] In subsequent years, considerable monitoring of the British media was actually conducted by pro-Israel flak groups across the Atlantic. For instance, the US-based Committee for Accuracy in Middle East Reporting in America (CAMERA), formed in 1982 in response to media criticism of Israel following its invasion of Lebanon, infamously encouraged its volunteers to edit *Wikipedia* pages to reflect better on Israel.[26] It also ran an attack blog called *CiF Watch* dedicated to monitoring the *Guardian*'s 'Comment is Free' opinion site. Another body, Jerusalem-based HonestReporting, was mentioned in chapter 2 as an example of a group founded (in 2000) with the support of Israeli government actors. In the US, HonestReporting has coordinated mass email complaint campaigns against CNN and others, and assisted in the production and dissemination of the notorious Islamophobic film *Obsession*. In Britain, the organisation's targets have included the *Guardian, Independent* and even the *British Medical Journal* after it dared to publish an article about Palestinian health under Israeli occupation.[27]

From around 2002, British solicitor Trevor Asserson pioneered a similarly confrontational approach to that of CAMERA and HonestReporting in Britain via an organisation called BBC Watch.[28] When Asserson moved to Israel, this outfit lay dormant for some years, but it was resurrected in 2012 and more recently rebranded as CAMERA UK. In the intervening years (around 2008–2011), a body called Just Journalism sought to fill the void. Just Journalism also adopted a belligerent approach, seeking to 'name and shame' reporters and newspapers it deemed insufficiently sympathetic to Israel. The story of its brief existence provides an instructive case study in the limitations of the flak approach.

Operating from the offices of the neoconservative Henry Jackson Society think-tank, Just Journalism's self-declared aim was to 'promote accurate and responsible media coverage of Israel'. Former Middle East correspondent Adel Darwish, who became the organisation's first director, claims he was offered 'big money' to join the Britain Israel Communications and Research Centre (BICOM) but turned it down because he saw the latter as a lobbying group. Just Journalism, by contrast, he declared at its launch event, was 'in no way a lobby group to push Israel's political agenda'. It is noteworthy, however, that Darwish also says he would 'frequently' converse with then Israeli ambassador Ron Prosor. Moreover, within months of joining Just Journalism, his position had changed. In January 2009, Darwish resigned, issuing a statement criticising founder Dana Brass for 'putting pressure on researchers' to reach as many journalists as possible to be 'ticked off or . . . told that their work did not meet the criteria'. He warned that the organisation's modus operandi risked becoming 'a McCarthyist witch hunt of fellow journalists'.[29] Whether Just Journalism had 'become a "Zionist propaganda organisation" or not', Darwish concluded obliquely, 'is a matter for the organisation's board of directors to address'. His own view was implied.

Just Journalism continued to operate, publishing lengthy critiques of outlets such as the *Independent, Financial Times, Guardian* and BBC, but subsequent directors' terms were also short lived. Its closure in September 2011, reportedly due to a lack of funds, was surprising given the largess of some of its 'loyal donors' – among them Stanley Fink, the multimillionaire former hedge fund manager who, as we have previously seen, also supported Conservative Friends of Israel, Culture for Coexistence and BIRAX.[30] It may be that donors withdrew support due to a strategic realisation that, in Britain at least, Just Journalism's haranguing style was far inferior to the more positive approach exemplified by BICOM, by far the most important media-focused pro-Israel organisation in Britain today.

The turn of the millennium, as sociologist Keith Kahn-Harris notes, precipitated a 'wave of institution building in support of Israel' in response to what I have described as the crisis of Zionism.[31] BICOM was established in this period with the intention of filling the void left by the closure of BIPAC, the pro-Israel body modelled on US group AIPAC, which operated between 1976 and 1999. BICOM emerged in 2001 from a 'crisis room' reportedly convened with support at the 'highest level' of the Israeli foreign ministry.[32]

The *Jewish Chronicle* reports that a day after the outbreak of the Second Intifada, Israeli ambassador Dror Zeigerman sought the help of wealthy pro-Israel businessmen to fund a new lobbying and PR outfit.[33] Property billionaire Poju Zabludowicz – who inherited his wealth from his arms-trader father, Shlomo (who sold weapons to some of the world's most repressive regimes)[34] – was the first to contribute and is thought to remain BICOM's main funder today. Zabludowicz was a friend and erstwhile donor to Israeli prime minister Benjamin Netanyahu and an associate of Gideon Meir, the Israeli diplomat who first introduced Michael Levy to Tony Blair.[35] Thus, critically, the organisation grew directly from state–private networks and collaboration between the Israeli embassy and wealthy pro-Israel elites. Some of BICOM's earliest senior figures, such as Daniel Shek, were former Israeli diplomats, and today the organisation often fundraises via business delegations to Israel offering access to leading politicians, indicating a continuing close relationship with the Israeli government.

BICOM recruits PR professionals, former MPs and ex-journalists. Though, in its early days, the organisation's website made references to shifting 'public opinion', the outfit very quickly narrowed its target audience to 'journalists, politicians and other senior opinion formers'.[36] This was because BICOM's senior personnel had concluded that public opinion 'does not influence foreign policy in Britain'[37] and, therefore, that the Zionist movement should seek to 'create barriers to delegitimisation, insulating policy-making environments' – namely politicians and the media.[38] To this end, while supporting deeply right-wing Zionist positions – including Nakba denial – BICOM maintains a façade as a reasonable and even intellectual organisation, embodying a more sophisticated approach to influencing the news than Just Journalism.

BICOM was not the first to seek to foster positive relationships with journalists. Indeed, at least as far back as the 1980s, the Zionist Federation and BIPAC were organising Israel trips for media professionals and running competitions for British journalistic writing on Israel with thousand-pound prizes, sponsored by the World Zionist Organization.[39] However, BICOM took such an approach to unprecedented levels. Although its earliest incarnation had included a 'rebuttal desk' to correct perceived errors in media reports, its strategists had soon decided that 'harassing the media is a counter-productive tactic, which limits dialogue', and adopted a very different approach.[40]

In place of the hectoring style of bodies like Just Journalism, BICOM took a long-term, strategic approach to communication, couching its Israeli-exceptionalist stances in language based on detailed public opinion surveys. From its earliest years, it hired PR professionals (such as Luke Akehurst and Lee Petar from lobbying firm Weber Shandwick) alongside former journalists (like Mark Berg and Dermot Kehoe from the BBC) to deliver these messages. These staff worked to develop cooperative, reciprocal relationships with key media personnel, guided by the philosophy expounded in Robert Cialdini's well-known book *Influence: The Psychology of Persuasion*. The approach soon paid off, with the *Jewish Chronicle* reporting in 2006 that BICOM had achieved 'unprecedented access to the BBC to brief the corporation's staff', including for flagship programmes such as *Hardtalk* and *Newsnight*.[41]

One of the key 'carrot' mechanisms BICOM uses to build relationships of influence with journalists and editors is by offering them free trips to Israel. As part of its regular group delegations,

BICOM typically hosts twenty to thirty journalists per year, from leading outlets like *The Times*, *Sun*, *Independent* and *Sky News*. Even some left-leaning bloggers have attended such trips. One such blogger wrote a revealing account of his 2017 trip with BICOM for *Vice* magazine, describing how the group were taken to visit the Golan Heights without being informed that they were in Israeli-occupied Syrian territory:

> One day we headed to Mount Bental to look out over the border to Syria. From the top we could see the Syrian town of Old Qunietra. It's been a ghost town since the 1973 Yom Kippur War. A 1974 UN report notes Qunietra's 'deliberate and total devastation' was in violation of the Geneva Convention, but that didn't get a mention . . . As it turns out – also not mentioned – we were actually in Syria under international law . . . When we'd come down from the mountain we went to a fancy winery and tasted delicious Israeli wine from sovereign Syrian territory while listening to lounge music.[42]

Despite the occasional critical article like this, in general these junkets enable BICOM to develop and maintain a network of friendly contacts in the media. These relationships with journalists are key strategic assets. During episodes of intense Israeli state violence, BICOM goes into crisis communications mode to defend the indefensible, distributing daily briefings, pitching stories on unfolding news items, offering 'talking heads' and, above all, pressing reporters to adopt what a leaked email once paradoxically referred to as 'the most objectively favourable line' on Israel.[43]

Bias at the BBC?

Most people in Britain get their world news primarily from watching television and, thanks to its global reach, the BBC is of paramount importance in the broadcasting arena. Assessing the impact that various pro-Israel pressure groups have had on BBC output requires proper contextualisation.

As sociologist Tom Mills explains in his book *The BBC: Myth of a Public Service*, the broadcaster has never been meaningfully independent from the British state. Members of the BBC Board, the organisation's regulatory body (formerly known as the BBC Trust) are appointed 'by the crown on the advice of the prime minister' – and are hence often 'highly politicised'. Moreover, Mills notes that the secret vetting of many BBC employees by the security services, which began in the 1930s, only ended in 1985. And the ongoing close relationship between the BBC and political elites continues to shape news output today, creating a tendency to defer to power in the BBC's reporting. This has been exacerbated by processes of neo-liberalisation from the 1980s onwards, which deepened the centralisation of editorial authority within the corporation. On issues ranging from Ireland and the Troubles to the 1984–85 miners' strike, the BBC – very much part of the establishment itself – consistently exhibits systematic anti-union and pro-state bias. Ultimately, the BBC's 'ethic of political neutrality' understands 'balance' and 'objectivity' in a manner which privileges powerful interests.[44]

Despite this environment, the BBC has long been accused of left-wing bias by the organised right – a claim which has constituted, Mills argues, 'part of a broader mobilising narrative adopted by the conservative movement'. Politicians such as Winston Churchill in the late 1940s, Norman Tebbit in the 1980s, and more recently Julian Lewis all ran media monitoring projects from within the Conservative Party – projects which Mills characterises as attempts at '"policing" public space' to marginalise left-wing actors and ideas.[45] In recent years, right-wing influence at the BBC has seen the corporation ban its journalists from so-called 'virtue signalling' on social media[46] and withdraw from LGBTQ+ charity Stonewall's diversity scheme, known for its uncompromising stance on transgender equality.[47]

Attempts to influence the BBC by both Israeli state actors and pro-Israel civil society groups build on these long-standing right-wing flak initiatives. According to Ben Bradshaw, a former BBC reporter who later served as culture secretary in a Labour government, the Israeli authorities have a 'reputation' for 'bullying the BBC'.[48] Greg Philo and Mike Berry suggest the same thing, quoting an anonymous senior BBC editor describing how executives 'wait in fear for the phone call from the Israelis' after a potentially controversial item is broadcast.[49] Israeli embassy press officers have even been known to convince producers on BBC Radio 4's flagship *Today* programme to run items against the advice of the corporation's own correspondents in Israel.[50] An important example of direct Israeli government intervention occurred in March 2003 – shortly before the US and Britain invaded Iraq on the false grounds that the country had undisclosed weapons of mass destruction – when BBC World screened *Israel's Secret Weapon*, a documentary about Israel's very real nuclear weapons capabilities, which had become an open secret in global affairs. The Israeli government reacted by restricting BBC journalists' visas and, when Israeli prime minister Ariel Sharon visited London in July 2003, the BBC found itself banned from attending the press conference.[51] In doing so, Israel joined a small band of highly repressive countries effectively (albeit briefly) boycotting the BBC, including North Korea and Zimbabwe under Robert Mugabe.[52]

Civil society pro-Israel actors have also wielded influence. Before the BBC's controversial 2009 decision not to screen the Disasters Emergency Committee appeal for Gaza, cumulative pressure had been building on the corporation for some time. Alongside CAMERA, Jonathan Turner – then of the Zionist Federation (and subsequently of UK Lawyers for Israel) – had filed a series of escalating complaints into reports by Middle East editor Jeremy Bowen, dating from 2007. The aforementioned BBC Watch group provided additional weight to the campaign against Bowen, whose offending radio and online journalism had discussed the fortieth anniversary of the onset of Israel's military occupation. In April 2009, just a few months after the refusal to screen the Gaza appeal, the BBC Trust ruled that Bowen had breached accuracy and impartiality guidelines – a ruling on which the Israel lobby seized. Zionist Federation chair Andrew Balcombe declared Bowen's position 'untenable' and wrote to the BBC demanding his sacking.[53] Perversely, it was claimed that Bowen's judgement was skewed because the Israeli army had killed his former cameraman – and therefore he should lose his job, as well as his colleague.[54] Although this did not happen, former BBC news editor Charlie Beckett described 'extraordinary pressure' on the corporation and claimed the ruling 'struck a chill' through the newsroom, signalling to BBC journalists that 'they were under assault'.[55]

Some of the Zionist movement's complaints have been entirely legitimate. In 2012, for example, StandWithUs criticised BBC correspondent Jon Donnison for tweeting a picture of an injured Syrian child which had been inaccurately captioned as an image from Gaza. However, attempts to extrapolate such instances to call the BBC 'anti-Israel' can be met with a host of counter-examples from the pro-Palestinian side. Some blatant examples of censorship have occurred: for instance, rapper Mic Righteous's attempt to say 'Free Palestine' was overdubbed by BBC Radio 1Xtra in 2010; violinist Nigel Kennedy's attempt to criticise Israeli 'apartheid' during coverage of the BBC Proms a few years later was edited out of the audio; and in 2021, in response to a complaint from UK Lawyers for Israel, the BBC even removed a series of educational videos intended to teach GCSE-age schoolchildren the historical facts surrounding the origins of the Israel/Palestine situation.[56]

The fact that both 'sides' can point to instances of bias does not mean the BBC is essentially fair. Indeed, any credible study of the broadcaster's relative bias must go beyond anecdotal accounts to assess its reporting on a systemic level. One such internal study was the 2004 Balen Report, commissioned by the BBC's head of news following persistent complaints from pro-Israel groups and the Israeli government's aforementioned boycott. Yet subsequently, the BBC spent hundreds of thousands of pounds on legal fees to defend its refusal to release the report, sparking a long-running court case.[57] However, Balen's recommendations – which remain a mystery to this day – were reportedly implemented. Israel advocates view this saga as evidence of an attempt on the part of the BBC to hide its purported anti-Israel bias. However, the subsequent 2006 Thomas Report – commissioned by the board of governors and produced by an independent panel – found evidence of precisely the opposite.

As well as noting that there was 'little reporting of the difficulties facing Palestinians in their daily lives', the Thomas Report found that 'the BBC's concern with balance gave an impression of equality between the two sides which was fundamentally, if unintentionally, misleading'. It concluded that this constituted a 'failure to convey adequately the disparity in the Israeli and Palestinian experience, reflecting the fact that one side is in control and the other lives under occupation'.[58] Former BBC Middle East correspondent Tim Llewellyn calls this 'the tyranny of spurious equivalence'.[59]

Rigorous academic studies conducted at the universities of Loughborough, Goldsmiths and Glasgow all support the conclusion that Israel's perspective dominates overall patterns of coverage.[60] This manifests itself in a plethora of ways: the presentation of history (or lack thereof) to contextualise the situation; the language used; the headlines chosen; the extent to which Palestinian casualties and fatalities are considered newsworthy compared to Israelis; and the number of appearances and 'talk time' given to each. Philo and Berry's study recorded just seventeen lines of historical information from a total of 3,500 transcribed from TV news. Israeli interviewees had twice as much time to speak compared to Palestinians, and headlines tended to 'highlight Israeli statements, actions or perspectives'.[61] Moreover, different language was often used to describe deaths and casualties, with Israeli soldiers beaten 'savagely' and killed 'barbarically' by a 'frenzied mob . . . baying for blood', but with the killing of Palestinians by Israelis never described using such emotionally loaded words. In their sample, Israeli security concerns consistently had strong prominence. And, while new bouts of intense violence made headline news, little attention was paid to the underlying slow violence of military occupation which Palestinians endure on a daily basis.[62]

A cat called Herzl

The BBC's choice of so-called Middle East experts is a notably problematic area. Right-wing and pro-Israel voices tend to dominate its coverage, and there are glaring examples of failures to accurately label think-tanks. In November 2012, for instance, Israel was once again bombing Gaza, in a campaign called Operation Pillar of Defense. Its military killed 150 Palestinians over eight days. During this period, BBC producers chose to invite a man called Raheem Kassam on television as an expert commentator. Kassam was introduced by the corporation as if he was a neutral analyst. Counter to its own guidelines, the BBC neglected to mention that the Henry Jackson Society think-tank he was representing had stridently right-wing, pro-Israel politics. Moreover, Kassam was given this BBC platform despite the fact that his Henry Jackson Society side project 'Student Rights' had previously been the source of a wholly inaccurate claim that Zionist Federation activist Jonathan Hoffman had been subjected to 'anti-Semitic jeering' at a 2009 pro-Palestinian event in London. At the time, the BBC uncritically regurgitated this allegation before swiftly correcting the story when video evidence showed it to be false.[63] After his 2012 appearance, Kassam bragged online about having – again inaccurately – referred to Jerusalem as 'Israel's capital' live on air.[64] He would go on to work for alt-right political strategist Steve Bannon's *Breitbart* website and subsequently as an aide to UK Independence Party leader Nigel Farage before standing unsuccessfully for the party leadership himself.

Another prominent guest during the same period was Jonathan Sacerdoti, who, in the space of two days in November 2012, appeared unchallenged four times on various BBC television news programmes. Sacerdoti was introduced as a director of the 'Institute for Middle Eastern Democracy', a neutral-sounding organisation but one which had no track record in the field. The early archives of its website – created not long before its director's appearance on the news and defunct soon after it – show that the 'institute' began life as an explicitly pro-Israel advocacy body but soon adjusted its output to appear more academic and balanced.[65]

Sacerdoti himself was, in fact, very far from an objective commentator. Just two years before, he had been a spokesperson for the Zionist Federation and had even appeared on the BBC in that capacity.[66] Indeed, evidence of his pro-Israel affiliations was plastered all over the internet. Even a cursory online search by a producer would have returned Sacerdoti's LinkedIn page – which proudly advertised his attendance at an Israeli foreign ministry–run Israel-advocacy course – and photos of him at a London rally draped in an Israeli flag. If any doubts could still remain as to Sacerdoti's stance on Israel, his Facebook profile even featured a picture of his pet cat, together with a caption displaying its name – 'Herzl', after the Zionist movement's primary ideologue.[67]

BBC producers had failed spectacularly to ensure impartiality. Following long-running complaints, the corporation eventually acknowledged that Sacerdoti's pro-Israel standpoint should have been made clear to viewers and that the failure to do so constituted a breach of impartiality.[68] By that point, however, the damage was done.

The BBC's problem with biased talking heads is pervasive across a range of topics and far from exclusive to the Middle East. An eyebrow-raising recent example was the platform the BBC gave to Alan Dershowitz, the ex-lawyer of US financier and convicted sex offender Jeffrey Epstein, following the sex-trafficking conviction of Epstein's partner, Ghislaine Maxwell. Shockingly, Dershowitz (incidentally, also a long-standing pro-Israel activist) was introduced by the BBC merely as 'a constitutional lawyer'. He used the opportunity to attempt to impugn the credibility of Maxwell's victim, Virginia Giuffre, who it just so happened had also accused Dershowitz himself of sexual abuse.[69] Again, the BBC later conceded its journalism had egregiously breached its own editorial standards.

Cases like this are an important reminder not to attribute all individual instances of pro-Israel bias, and the broader patterns they constitute, to the organised activities of the Zionist movement while ignoring institutional factors. That said, BBC journalists report, according to Oborne and Jones, that 'rarely a week goes by without having to deal with [pro-Israel] complaints about their coverage of the Middle East'. This considerable pressure instils significant anxiety inside BBC circles and does appear to have at least *some* impact on editorial decisions. Ex-BBC news editor Charlie Beckett, for instance, attributes the BBC's refusal to screen the humanitarian Gaza appeal to 'pressure from an extraordinarily active, sophisticated, and persuasive lobby sticking up for the Israeli viewpoint'.[70]

It is a long-standing reality, meanwhile, that pro-Palestinian counter-attempts to monitor and influence the media have never carried even remotely comparable weight. Indeed, in 1974, BBC editor James Norris wrote to the pro-Palestinian Council for the Advancement of Arab–British Understanding (CAABU) that

> one must acknowledge that journalists doing an honest job in this country have to take account of the fact that Israeli or Zionist public relations activities are conducted with a degree of sophistication which those on the other side have rarely matched, and that

supporters of Israel in this country represent a much more vocal and powerful minority than supporters of the Arab cause. In other words, an accurate reflection of publicly expressed attitudes on the issue may well inevitably reveal at times a preponderance of sympathy for the Israeli side.[71]

This remarkable statement suggests that, as far back as the mid-1970s, some senior executives simply accepted that BBC coverage would – and perhaps even *should* – reflect a pro-Israel position, simply by virtue of the superior strength of its lobby.

It is worth remembering, though, that the BBC's pro-Israel slant is not *all* the result of pro-Israel lobbyists' work. Sometimes, journalists *themselves* are already ideologically sympathetic to the Zionist cause. In these cases, the lobby is very much pushing at an open door. A case in point is Danny Cohen, former BBC director of television, who shortly before leaving the corporation in 2016 signed an open letter opposing a cultural boycott of Israel.[72] Perhaps a more consequential example is veteran *Panorama* journalist John Ware, who in 2015 accepted an award from the Women's International Zionist Organization[73] and in 2021 became a trustee of the same body.[74] Among Ware's programmes, and perhaps his most influential intervention, was the *Panorama* episode 'Is Labour Anti-Semitic?', which was broadcast five months before the 2019 general election and was accused of bias by critics who unsuccessfully sought to challenge communications regulator Ofcom's decision not to investigate complaints.

Meanwhile, Ware's fellow *Panorama* journalist Jane Corbin was behind 'Death in the Med', a programme on the 2010 Israeli military attack on the Gaza Freedom Flotilla which provoked over 2,000 complaints. According to the Palestine Solidarity Campaign, the account in the programme portrayed the nine Turkish activists killed during the Israeli commandos' raid on the *Mavi Marmara* 'as violent terrorists'. The BBC Trust, by contrast, concluded it was 'accurate and impartial' overall. Notably, Corbin's late husband, ex-member of Parliament John Maples, was a former president of Conservative Friends of Israel. In addition, she has written openly and admiringly about being a descendent of Leo Amery, one of the British imperial politicians who drafted the

Balfour Declaration.[75] Thus, Britain's historic role in the injustice done to Palestinians continues to haunt the present day. It would be difficult, if not impossible, to find a senior BBC journalist with comparable links to the Palestinian cause.

Policing the press

The BBC's news agenda closely follows that set by the British press. And whereas broadcasters have a statutory duty of fairness, the press – albeit less influential – is more flagrantly partisan. In general, the British press has echoed the 'narrow views of the foreign policy establishment'.[76] Moreover, the press landscape has become increasingly conservative over time. As Tom Mills notes:

> In 1950, newspapers supporting the Conservative and Labour parties were split evenly in terms of circulation. By 1974, political support for the Conservatives and Labour had split 71–32 per cent respectively – and by 1983 it was 78–22 per cent. This had the effect of shifting political culture in the UK to the right.[77]

Subsequently, the 1986 Wapping dispute – a failed strike by the print workers responsible for producing Rupert Murdoch's News International (now News UK) titles – shifted the political economy of the media industry further to the right.[78]

It is in this environment that BICOM builds relationships with broadsheet and tabloid journalists, just as avidly as it does with television reporters. Yet its influence is largely invisible. The briefings and free trips to Israel which it provides are rarely mentioned in the coverage which results. For example, a 2009 post–Cast Lead delegation, during which British reporters were briefed by Israeli defence strategists, produced articles in the *News of the World*, the *Mirror* and the *Sunday Times*, but only the latter made any reference to BICOM. Similarly, a 2011 *Financial Times* editorial which argued that Palestinian refugees should be paid off in return for 'not exercising the right to return' made no mention of BICOM – but a leaked email revealed that BICOM's Lorna Fitzsimons had 'briefed' leader writer Jonathan Ford the previous day.[79]

Britain's leading liberal broadsheet, the *Guardian*, has had a complicated relationship with Israel and the Palestinians. In its early incarnation as the *Manchester Guardian*, it supported Zionism more fervently than any other outlet, in large part thanks to the leadership of then owner and editor C. P. Scott. Famously, it was Scott – a Liberal member of Parliament and supporter of Zionism – who in the early years of the twentieth century introduced the future Israeli president Chaim Weizmann to David Lloyd George and other senior members of the British government. As such, he made a significant personal contribution to the eventual Balfour Declaration, which paved the way for the creation of Israel.

Soon after 1948, historian Natan Aridan notes, Marcus Sieff – a leading Zionist – was reportedly encouraged by Israel's finance ministry to suggest a news item to his friend at the *Observer*, the *Guardian*'s Sunday sister paper. The front-page story about Israel's impending 'financial collapse' was intended to encourage Britain to give Israel a loan – but this plan backfired. Nonetheless, the episode illustrates the Zionist movement's early ability to influence liberal press coverage in Britain.[80]

Over the years, however, the *Guardian*'s attitude towards Israel began to shift. Israel's occupation of the West Bank, Gaza and Golan Heights in 1967 marked the beginning of what author Daphna Baram calls the newspaper's 'disenchantment' with Israel, but the early 1980s were perhaps a more significant turning point.[81] A May 1981 *Guardian Weekly* leader which criticised the 'almost total Judaisation of the occupied territories' and called for Britain to support the Palestinians provoked a letter of complaint from the Zionist Federation.[82] While change was by no means linear, by the time the Second Intifada erupted, relations between the *Guardian* and Israel were at an unprecedented low. The Israeli government's press director, Danny Seaman, claimed in 2002 that the country had 'boycotted' the newspaper and forced it to relocate Middle East correspondent Suzanne Goldenberg to Washington – a claim which *Guardian* editor Alan Rusbridger disputed.[83]

In 2006, the Zionist movement mobilised against the *Guardian* in response to the publication of an article by journalist Chris McGreal. The piece drew parallels between Israel's system of control and South African apartheid – a controversial comparison in Britain at that time, though today a framework applied by major human rights bodies. The Israeli embassy played a 'coordinating' role in this backlash, according to journalists Peter Oborne and James Jones, with an 'emergency meeting' called at the Israeli ambassador's residence attended by representatives of BICOM, Labour Friends of Israel, the Board of Deputies and the Community Security Trust. The latter two organisations then paid Alan Rusbridger a visit to express their outrage, but he reportedly refused to accept Community Security Trust chairman Gerald Ronson's claim that, by publishing the offending article, the *Guardian* was responsible for anti-Semitic attacks. Although CAMERA lodged a complaint with the Press Complaints Commission, it was not upheld.[84]

In the contemporary era, the *Guardian* has published Palestinian voices like Arwa Mahdawi and, on occasion, BDS movement co-founder Omar Barghouti. But it has also provided a platform for writers like Hadley Freeman to imply that boycotting Israel is anti-Semitic.[85] More importantly, the paper's editorials have frequently been penned by opinion editor Jonathan Freedland. As pro-Palestinian journalist Ben White observes, Freedland – a leading light of British liberal Zionism – has long been, effectively, an apologist for the ethnic cleansing of the Nakba as a 'moral necessity'.[86] For instance, White notes that Freedland has written that Israel should 'admit the reality of 1948 – and . . . defend it all the same', while elsewhere acknowledging that this reality involved 'four hundred [Palestinian] villages' being 'emptied'. In 2011, Freedland was also among the 'eminent speakers' at an Israel-advocacy conference organised by BICOM spin-off We Believe in Israel.[87]

While left-winger Jeremy Corbyn was leader of Labour, the paper's attacks, in common with much of the media, were relentless (despite Corbyn's appointment of former *Guardian* journalist Seamus Milne – a rare champion of the Palestinian cause to have once had a mainstream media platform – as his communications manager).[88] In November 2021, the *Guardian* even censored an image by its own long-standing political cartoonist Steve Bell, saying it felt 'uncomfortable' with the cartoon strip which depicted Corbyn being forced to apologise 'for not being a right wing

Zionist'.[89] As with the Labour Party, the issue of Palestine evidently continues to be a deep fault-line within the *Guardian* newsroom.

Today, the *Jewish Chronicle* is perhaps the most consistently pro-Israel British newspaper. However, this was not always the case. As historian David Cesarani explains, under Asher Myers in the 1900s, the paper was editorially anti-Zionist and was frequently criticised at meetings of the Zionist Federation. Indeed, prior to 1948, in collaboration with the Jewish Agency, the Zionist Federation sought to buy a major stake in the company which owned the *Jewish Chronicle* in order to alter this situation.[90] Since the creation of Israel, however, the newspaper has been a vocal supporter of Zionism and Israel, and plays an important contemporary role in suppressing Palestine solidarity initiatives emerging from within the Jewish community.

When in 2018, for example, a group of young British Jews gathered to recite a Kaddish (traditional Jewish prayer often used in mourning rituals) for Palestinian victims of Israeli state violence, they were targeted by the newspaper, sparking off a wave of online abuse.[91] That same year, together with the *Jewish News* and *Jewish Telegraph*, the paper published a joint front page attacking the Labour leadership's resistance to the International Holocaust Remembrance Alliance's definition of anti-Semitism and calling Corbyn an 'existential threat' to Jewish communities.[92]

In 2020, following financial difficulties exacerbated by the COVID-19 pandemic, the *Jewish Chronicle* was taken over by a coalition of largely anonymous donors characterised by leftist Jewish website *Vashti* as a 'shadowy consortium'.[93] As well as former Labour Friends of Israel chair John Woodcock and Henry Jackson Society supporter William Shawcross, other individuals known to be involved in the takeover included journalist John Ware and talking-head-for-hire Jonathan Sacerdoti, both discussed earlier in the chapter.[94]

'Don't mention the dead kid'

As C. P. Scott's *Guardian* and the struggle over the *Jewish Chronicle* show, ownership has always been, and remains, a critical factor influencing output. The positions which key titles adopt on Israel/

Palestine can be explained at least partly by the ideologies and interests of the media moguls behind them. There has never been a British newspaper owner who could be characterised as pro-Palestinian. In contrast, while none have been quite as explicit about their politics as German publishing house Axel Springer – which lists 'the right of existence of the State of Israel' as one of five key values and in 2021 bought the newsletter *Politico* promising to enforce this pro-Israel policy – there are several prominent examples of avowedly pro-Israel British media owners.[95]

The right-wing *Daily Telegraph*, for example, was formerly controlled by conservative Canadian businessman Conrad Black, who owned media company Hollinger, the proprietor of Israel's *Jerusalem Post*, and was later convicted of fraud in the US. Black and his wife, Barbara Amiel – who once accused the BBC of 'relentless anti-Israel' bias – were vehemently pro-Israel. In 2001, three high-profile *Telegraph* contributors wrote to the *Spectator* alleging that any possibility of the Palestinian perspective being voiced was being stifled.[96] One of the three, William Dalrymple, implied Black had made it clear 'that certain areas are off-limits to legitimate enquiry, and that careers will suffer if those limits are crossed'.[97] Such abuse of power, we should recall, is not unique to the issue of Israel. Notably, after the multimillionaire Barclay Brothers subsequently purchased the *Telegraph*, veteran journalist Peter Oborne quit dramatically in 2015, claiming that the paper had suppressed stories about banking giant HSBC in order to preserve a lucrative advertising contract.[98]

Nor indeed was Black's approach unique. Media tycoon Rupert Murdoch's pro-Israel politics are well known. In addition to significant business interests in Israel and a friendship with the country's former prime minister Ariel Sharon, Murdoch has accepted prizes from a number of pro-Israel organisations. He also contributed a foreword to the book *Israel in the World*, copies of which were distributed for propaganda purposes by Israeli embassies worldwide.[99] And while investigative journalist Nick Davies paints Murdoch as a media baron willing to allow his titles 'a flexible range of ideological activities so long as they produce the right reward', others who worked closely with him paint a different picture.[100]

Andrew Neil, former editor of the *Sunday Times* – a jewel in the crown of Murdoch's News UK empire, alongside Britain's leading centre-right broadsheet *The Times* and the bestselling tabloid the *Sun* – describes Murdoch as 'an interventionist proprietor who expected to get his way'.[101] Yet again, this was true not only with regard to coverage of Israel. Murdoch's interests also influenced coverage of other foreign policy issues; in 1997, for instance, *The Times'* China correspondent Jonathan Mirsky resigned 'in protest at the repeated restrictions imposed on his attempts to write about the suppression of dissent in China' – restrictions Davies attributes to Murdoch's desire to 'win the favour of autocrats in Beijing'.[102] In relation to Israel, however, there is a fairly consistent pattern.

Prior to Murdoch taking over in 1981, *The Times* was not remotely a 'pro-Palestinian' outlet. In fact, as early as 1969, its broadly pro-Israel position was spelled out explicitly. That year, *The Times* published a long article discussing the challenging realities of life for Palestinians in the West Bank, two years into what was at the time viewed as a temporary military occupation. The piece provoked criticism in the House of Commons from pro-Israel Labour MP Manny Shinwell (the great-uncle of a contemporary supporter of Israel, former Labour MP Luciana Berger). In a telling response, the editor penned a November 1969 leader in defence of the newspaper, stating that 'in the great war between Israel and the Arabs, *The Times* has been basically sympathetic to Israel'.[103] This was indeed true. Yet for some years after this, Robert Fisk's critical reporting on the Palestinian plight still found space in the pages of *The Times*, upsetting Britain's Zionist movement and the Israeli ambassador repeatedly – to the extent that the Zionist Federation organised a protest outside the newspaper's offices in 1980.[104] However, when Murdoch took over the following year, the paper's leeway for criticising Israel began to shrink even more sharply.

In the late 1980s, Fisk quit as Middle East correspondent. He later claimed that, although Murdoch didn't intervene directly, he 'didn't need to', because he had 'turned *The Times* into a tame, pro-Tory, pro-Israeli paper shorn of all editorial independence'.[105] A brief look at some of the personnel who played leading roles at *The Times* under Murdoch offers some support for this view. They include Michael Gove, a Henry Jackson Society supporter who was awarded a prize by the Zionist Federation in 2008 for his lifelong support for Israel, and later became a senior Conservative minister;[106] and Daniel Finkelstein, a Tory peer who formerly sat on the board of Islamophobic US think-tank the Gatestone Institute and has a strong relationship with Conservative Friends of Israel.[107] As a counter-example, one could certainly point to the *Sunday Times'* 1986 exposé of Israel's nuclear weapons, based on the account of whistle-blower Mordechai Vanunu (later abducted by Mossad and imprisoned in Israel), which even a pro-Israel, interventionist pro-prietor like Murdoch did not, or could not, suppress.[108] However, there are enough cases of apparent pro-Israel censorship to make the overarching dynamic clear.

Some years after Fisk's departure a second journalist, Sam Kiley, quit *The Times* voicing similar complaints about a culture of pro-Israel censorship, enforced by executives terrified of irritating Murdoch. In August 2001, Kiley wrote in the *Evening Standard* that editors and managers at *The Times* 'flew into hysterical terror every time a pro-Israel lobbying group wrote in with a quibble or complaint and then usually took their side against their own corre-spondent'. Kiley also alleged that he was told not to refer to 'assassinations', 'extra-judicial killings' or 'executions' when Pal-estinians were the victims and Israeli forces the perpetrators. The final straw came, he wrote, when he was asked to file a story on the Israeli army unit which infamously killed Muhammed al-Durrah – a twelve-year-old Palestinian boy whose death was caught on camera and became symbolic of the Second Intifada – 'without mentioning the dead kid'. 'After that conversation', Kiley wrote, 'I was left wordless, so I quit.'[109]

On rare occasions, Murdoch has been known to directly inter-fere. A notable example occurred when the *Sunday Times* published a caricature of Israeli prime minister Benjamin Netanyahu fol-lowing his election victory in January 2013. Long-standing cartoonist Gerald Scarfe was known for his consistently grotesque, gory, blood-spattered depictions of politicians – and his presenta-tion of Netanyahu was no different. However, Israel's ambassador and the Board of Deputies expressed outrage, the latter stating that the cartoon was 'shockingly reminiscent of the blood libel imagery more usually found in parts of the virulently anti-Semitic Arab press'.[110] Despite having previously been to Israel on a BICOM trip, the paper's recently appointed acting editor, Martin Ivens, initially defended the image.[111] It was, he said, 'a typically robust cartoon by Gerald Scarfe . . . aimed squarely at Mr Netanyahu and his policies, not at Israel, let alone at Jewish people'.[112] However, soon after this, his boss Rupert Murdoch tweeted, 'We owe major apology for grotesque, offensive cartoon.' Ivens then met with officials from BICOM, the Board, the Jewish Leadership Council and the Community Security Trust. Subsequently, he apologised 'unreservedly' on behalf of the publication for the 'terrible mistake', stating that Scarfe had 'crossed a line'. Notably, his statement also stressed that 'the paper has long written strongly in defence of Israel and its security concerns, as have I as a columnist'.[113]

Following this episode, Ivens was appointed as permanent editor. Today, the Murdoch press frequently – and without ever apologising – propagates bigotry against a range of minority groups, from Muslims to transgender people to Gypsy, Roma and Traveller communities.

'Telegenically dead'

Even though polished, professional pro-Israel spokespeople, delivering well-rehearsed soundbites, continue to dominate mainstream news platforms today, the reality of Israel's entrenched oppression of Palestinians is becoming harder to hide. The fragmentation and proliferation of the media landscape in the internet era means that footage captured on a camera phone of an Israeli soldier blindfolding a child, or executing an unarmed Palestinian at point-blank range, can – and indeed does – circulate around the world in minutes, providing a disturbing visual counter-narrative to official versions of events. Such moments, in which the brutality of Israeli apartheid is laid bare, have evoked some disturbing responses.

Elements of the Zionist movement, and sometimes the Israeli government itself, have for some time (long before the phrase 'fake news' was made infamous by former US president Donald Trump) been habitually disputing the authenticity of any media output which documents Israeli state violence against Palestinians. Tired of repeatedly being forced to adopt a defensive posture, they turn instead to outright, and sometimes elaborate, denial. The killing of Muhammed al-Durrah in 2000, over which Sam Kiley quit *The Times,* is a quintessential example. A long-running legal case, which only ended in 2013, eventually definitively rejected claims by a pro-Israel activist, Philippe Karsenty, that footage of the murder was faked. Indeed, Karsenty was convicted of defamation. Despite this, the Israeli government backed his claims in an official report, with one minister calling it 'a modern-day blood libel against the State of Israel'.[114]

Deploying the term 'Pallywood', sections of the Zionist movement frequently mock and deny the very reality of Palestinian injuries and fatalities, implying that casualties are merely play-acting for the camera.[115] Similarly, Benjamin Netanyahu has described Palestinian victims of Israeli state violence as 'telegenically dead'.[116] Disturbingly, the real horror of their deaths, in his eyes, is the damage done to *Israel's image* by the ensuing media coverage. This racist and dehumanising logic, which refuses to even acknowledge the suffering of others, arguably also animated the BBC's refusal to screen the humanitarian appeal for Gaza. Yet the tactic is not unique to Israel. Throughout much of its 2022 invasion of Ukraine, Vladimir Putin's Russian government trotted out similar lies, notably labelling images from towns like Bucha 'fakes' in a vain attempt to cast doubt on the acts of state violence they evidenced.[117]

The majority of media management work, though, is far more subtle than such flat-out denialism. Israel's case in the British media may be made most effectively by BICOM, but its work is supplemented by an array of other, often more outwardly hard-line, pressure groups. Meanwhile, though pro-Palestine efforts to monitor and influence the media (such as the Palestine Solidarity Campaign's volunteer-dependent 'Fair News' initiative) have been made, it is very clear that the pro-Palestinian movement does not have a comparably organised, sophisticated and well resourced PR network. There is nothing surprising or sinister about this; it is simply the case that the military power asymmetries between Israel and the Palestinians are mirrored in the communications arena.

Due to this imbalance, pro-Israel actors' carrot-and-stick tactics – combined with the many other factors outlined above – produce systemic bias slanted in Israel's favour. This does not, however, absolve British journalists and editors of responsibility. Indeed, the longer they allow Israeli apartheid to be presented in a less-than-truthful light, the more complicit they become in Israel's crimes and Palestinians' oppression.

Conclusion:
The Threat of Democracy

The reality of Israeli apartheid's daily colonial violence against Palestinians is impossible to deny. It is also becoming harder for Israel's Western allies to ignore. With each fresh act of racialised state violence, Israel's legitimacy fades further. After Israel's intense air strikes on Gaza in May 2021, the country's 'favourability' ratings dropped from an already-low benchmark in Britain and across Europe.[1] That same year, a quarter of US Jewish voters surveyed agreed with the statement that 'Israel is an apartheid state',[2] and two polls suggested loyalty was wavering even among evangelical Christians – one of the country's last bastions of support.[3] Yet Israel's leaders refuse to accept the simple truth that the country's legitimacy crisis will end only when its oppression and dispossession of Palestinians ends. Meanwhile, the leaders of major Western powers like Britain continue to support and grant impunity to Israeli apartheid while paying hypocritical lip service to human rights.

Yet as co-founder of the BDS movement Omar Barghouti writes, 'despite decades of ruthless Israeli ethnic cleansing and settler-colonial brutality enabled mostly by the West', Palestinians 'have not given up' but continue to struggle for freedom, justice and equality.[4] While Western governments are unwilling to hold Israel accountable, Palestinians have taken matters into their own hands, and their call for solidarity through Boycott, Divestment and Sanctions has been answered by people of conscience and civil society bodies around the world in growing numbers – including in Britain.

This book has exposed the ways that other British actors prop up Israeli apartheid, in particular through an organised backlash against that solidarity activism in support of the Palestinian liberation movement's struggle to decolonise Israel/Palestine. It has shown that Israel's supporters in Britain are consciously strategising and strenuously working to undermine pro-Palestinian solidarity and demobilise BDS initiatives, including through repressive legislation and lawfare.

On the basis that we cannot afford to be complacent about anti-Semitism, given its persistence in Britain and around the world, I have grounded the analysis presented here in anti-racist politics and clearly delineated support for Zionist ethnonationalism from Judaism.[5] In fact, although bodies like the Board of Deputies and the Jewish Leadership Council, as we have seen, do often play a role in contemporary pro-Israel activism, former leaders of both these bodies, Vivian Wineman and Mick Davis respectively, have spoken out in highly critical terms since leaving their posts.[6] In 2020, for example, Davis – a major Conservative donor by no means sympathetic to the left – wrote that Israeli politics 'violates the values' of Jewish communities and predicted that support for Zionism would continue to 'dwindle, leaving the case for Israel solely in the hands of hard right cheerleaders'.[7]

In fact, this is already happening. Notably, most of the key pro-Israel actors in this book are *not* representative Jewish communal groups. Instead, they include politicians affiliated with Conservative Friends of Israel and Labour Friends of Israel, Zionist lawfare groups like UK Lawyers for Israel, a small number of wealthy pro-Israel philanthropists (who don't represent Jewish communities), and manufactured astroturf groups with a significant evangelical Christian support base. Notably, Luke Akehurst of BICOM-spin off group We Believe in Israel has said of his organisation: 'One of the most important things we're trying to do is to recreate a campaigning culture that previously existed in the UK Jewish community . . . There were huge demonstrations, petitions and letter writing, but somehow that tradition has atrophied.'[8] Thus, the reality is that Akehurst (a non-Jewish Zionist activist), by seeking to restore a bygone era of popular support for Israel among British Jewish communities, is effectively telling Jews how they should act.

I have argued that the 'Israel lobby' is better understood and described as the Zionist movement, since it is transnational rather than solely domestic and engages in a wide range of activities beyond traditional Westminster lobbying alone. The Zionist movement deserves to be scrutinised and opposed because of its role defending Israeli apartheid. Yet within this movement, I have highlighted rivalries and tensions which mean Israel's support networks should not be seen as a homogeneous bloc. However, I have also shown that there is a long-standing pattern of different Zionist organisations uniting at critical junctures to work together towards common goals – such as opposing boycotts targeting Israel.

In particular, the book has explored the centrality of state–private networks to the backlash against Palestine solidarity. While journalist Alex Kane has dubbed the co-operation between civil society actors and the Israeli government a 'new front', the historical context traced here shows that, in fact, such relationships are an established trait of the Zionist movement.[9] I have argued, however, that in the era of (civil society–led) BDS, the Israeli government is *increasingly* reliant on, and attempting to strategically coordinate, local civil society Zionist bodies.

State–private networks, as advocated by new public diplomacy theorists, distribute labour across the state/private divide and take advantage of not only the access, flexibility and credibility of civil society groups but also the resources of government, which acts largely as a catalyst and coordinator, and sometimes a funder. As Sima Vaknin-Gil, formerly director-general of Israel's Ministry of Strategic Affairs, has pointed out, 'the Israeli government can look at the bigger picture, create cooperation and coordination', and 'fill the gaps' in pro-Israel networks.

We have seen that this modus operandi means the Israeli government has avidly pursued public–private partnerships and has sought to manufacture civil society groups, both to wage lawfare and to create the impression of spontaneous 'grassroots' support for Israel which is in large part superficial. Indeed, despite transferring responsibility for the war against BDS from the Ministry of Strategic Affairs back to the Ministry of Foreign Affairs, the Israeli government has retained its 'Concert' project in order to indirectly offer funding to pro-Israel civil society groups. However, even its attempts to mobilise the Zionist movement this way have struggled, with fewer and fewer actors willing to be co-opted into offering uncompromising support to an apartheid state.

Importantly, this book has shown that such practices are not unique to Israel. In particular, just as the BDS movement models itself on the anti-apartheid movement that helped end white rule in South Africa, the tactics Israel employs in its efforts to crush the boycott movement through a combination of repression and third-party support strongly echo those of the South African apartheid regime.

State–private networks help us to understand that Zionist civil society bodies do not in themselves possess particularly significant or mysterious power but instead wield what power they do have through collective action and in relation to their ability to complement Israeli state power. Critically, though, I have argued against interpreting the empirical reality of these state–private networks using a 'foreign influence' narrative. When applied to Israel, such narratives seek to mimic the conclusions of the Intelligence and Security Committee's 2020 Russia report, which claimed: 'lawyers, accountants, estate agents and PR professionals have played a role, wittingly or unwittingly, in the extension of Russian influence which is often linked to promoting the nefarious interests of the Russian state'.[10] Deconstructing perspectives such as this, we can see that they not only remain state-centric but are also a complete dead end for supporters of justice for Palestinians. This lesson should be clear from Israel itself, where accusations of 'foreign funding' have been used by the government to attack left-leaning human rights groups it dislikes. Likewise, in Russia, Vladimir Putin has cracked down on journalists his regime dislikes, using 'foreign agent' designations.[11]

The sole function of this narrative is to empower the state to attack its enemies. Little wonder, then, that the neoconservative Henry Jackson Society has pushed for new legislation on this issue in Britain – despite itself having accepted Japanese government money to promote anti-China propaganda.[12] Nor should it come as a surprise that former Home Secretary Priti Patel sought to implement new laws in Britain around lobbying and influence by what she referred to as 'hostile' states.[13] Such a law will not help Palestinians. Nor will it end the British government's double standards, which, as pro-Palestine campaigner Ryvka Barnard points out, extend to advocacy for boycott and divestment tactics in the case of Russia over its invasion of Ukraine, but rejection of these tactics in the case of its ally Israel.[14]

Above all, a 'foreign influence' narrative incorrectly externalises an issue which is, and always has been, about Britain too. This book has argued that the story of the Zionist movement in Britain is part of the history of British racism, and specifically part of the long and ignominious history of British support for Israeli apartheid. This is a history that, despite our tendencies towards colonial amnesia, we can ill afford to forget. As a social movement from above, the Zionist movement certainly exploits the democratic deficit in Britain, which is particularly acute with regards to foreign policy, often mobilising in top-down ways. But it certainly does not *cause* it. Studying its activities provides a window into Britain's deeply unequal and unjust power relations, but any attempt to blame a nefarious lobby for Britain's acute political crisis would be absurd. Indeed, the problem is far broader, as power in Britain today is exercised in fundamentally undemocratic ways in a range of institutions.

Within Westminster, transparency requirements and electoral laws are weak and marred by loopholes and soft enforcement. Official lobbying registers capture only a tiny proportion of influence work. In 2010, then Prime Minister David Cameron dubbed political lobbying 'the next big scandal waiting to happen'. By 2021, having left office following the Brexit vote five years earlier, he was himself exposed as having lobbied for finance company Greensill Capital, providing a typical example of the privileged access enjoyed by many corporate interests and leading the *Guardian* newspaper to declare lobbying 'no longer a scandal waiting to happen but one that is happening here, now, and at the very top of British government'.[15]

Israel is far from the only oppressive nation-state implicated. For instance, Conservative MP Daniel Kawczynski was exposed recently boasting to a fixer, in an effort to secure lucrative work in order to pay private school fees for his children, that the Saudi Arabian crown prince Mohammed bin Salman 'has stated that Saudi has no better friend in [the] UK than me'.[16] In a separate incident, his fellow Conservative MP Bob Blackman bragged about lobbying the British government on behalf of 'our good friends in Azerbaijan'.[17] As scholar-activist Amrit Wilson has noted, Blackman also helped right-wing Hindu networks supportive of Narendra Modi's Indian government to successfully undermine efforts to outlaw caste discrimination in Britain (for instance, against Dalits) under the Equality Act.[18]

Beyond Westminster, we've seen how British state racism and authoritarianism, in addition to our crisis of democracy, provide the wider context in which the Zionist movement's lobbying can thrive. The profound lack of democracy in the governance of our academic institutions and media organisations, which enable donors and lobby groups to exert influence, has prompted calls for universities to be required to disclose the identities of their donors and for democratic ownership of media institutions.[19] We've seen how state actors encroach on the cultural sphere, eroding the autonomy of cultural institutions by threatening their funding. Likewise, we've observed how the government's desire to protect the arms industry and other corporate actors, as well as oppressive allies like Israel, has seen it attempt to discipline, through central government edicts, independent-minded local authorities which dare to express views on foreign policy reflecting local democracy. In the bigger picture, such measures are just one part of a raft of repressive legislation undermining human rights and dissent. Finally, we've seen how today, in the wider context of Britain's toxic racial politics, leading Israel advocates like Michael Gove and Priti Patel promote anti-immigration 'hostile environment' policies, Islamophobic counterterrorism strategies and racially disproportionate policing tactics like stop-and-search, while simultaneously claiming to be taking a stand against racism by endorsing the International Holocaust Remembrance Alliance's definition of anti-Semitism.

Seen in this light, it is unsurprising that a lot of the Zionist movement's influence work is actually cooperative. The British establishment is a *partner* to the Israeli government and the Zionist movement in repressing opposition to Israeli apartheid, just as it repressed the anti-apartheid movement in solidarity with Black South Africans. The British government has this in common with other oppressive state powers and its actions are an example of a larger global phenomenon in which numerous authoritarian countries seek to repress political dissent by restricting civil society.[20]

The slow encroachment of state power into shrinking 'civic space' – arenas in which civil society organisations, social movements and ordinary citizens can organise – is a trend which suggests that the real fault-lines today are not between different nation-states, but between nation-states and civil society.[21] If Israel is, as one BDS campaigner suggests, 'the model coercive state', it has also considerably aided repression by other state powers worldwide, not least through authorising the export of the spyware technology Pegasus, made by the NSO Group, to at least fifteen human rights–abusing governments.[22] Moreover, the criminalisation of boycotts by pro-Israel governments, as Palestinian-American legal advocate Amira Mattar observes, is merely part of a 'broader right-wing assault on social justice movements as a whole'.[23]

Compared to the power of nation states, the Zionist movement is a relatively marginal player. However, it does play an important disciplinary role – one with theoretical implications that are worth spelling out. Civil society and social movements should not be viewed exclusively as benign, progressive actors who challenge the status quo and state power, since they can in some cases, in sociologist Narzanin Massoumi's words, be 'utilised for the purposes of advancing state capacity'.[24] Too little work pays attention to civil society bodies which support state power and contribute to the political repression of other, more antagonistic civil society groups. In the case at hand, the duality of civil society is pronounced, since Israel is, in effect, seeking to enlist some civil society bodies in support of state power while at the same time repressing others which challenge its power.

What are the implications of this book's narrative for Palestine solidarity activism? Firstly, we must have hope. The intensity of the backlash against Palestine solidarity illustrates precisely the credible challenge it poses to Israeli apartheid and is testament to the importance and effectiveness of collective action. Critically, as even supporters of the BDS campaign point out, boycott is a solidarity tactic which 'cannot "free Palestine"' and is 'not a substitute for a Palestinian national movement'.[25] But, as Omar Barghouti observes, 'hope that emanates from effective popular resistance, organically coupled with principled international solidarity, is resilient and contagious'.[26] After all, even Israel's supporters privately admit that BDS is working – while their efforts to stop it are not.[27]

The goal of pro-Israel repression is to demobilise people, making them afraid to speak or act in solidarity with Palestinians by creating a culture of silence, disengagement and passivity. This book, in contrast, aims not to deter and intimidate but to inform and empower action. The prospects for solidarity with Palestinians in Britain depend not only on the consolidation and growth of the movement itself but also on its resilience to intensifying attacks. This, in turn, requires clarity about the movement's strengths, weaknesses, strategies and goals – and those of its opponents.

Secondly, the Palestine solidarity movement must not be drawn into endless toxic debates about anti-Semitism but must retain a strong and principled anti-racist stance, opposing both Israeli apartheid and anti-Semitism. As US social democrat Bernie Sanders observes, 'The forces fomenting anti-Semitism are the forces arrayed against oppressed people around the world, including Palestinians; the struggle against anti-Semitism is also the struggle for Palestinian freedom.'

Thirdly, despite the appealing simplicity of a blinkered single-issue focus on Palestine, it is also vital that the solidarity movement builds on the basis of collective liberation politics. This is not only the right thing to do, but is also strategic. While the acronym PEP ('progressive except for Palestine') has been used to criticise liberals with a blind spot when it comes to Israel, there are also elements of the solidarity movement in Britain who are jokingly referred to as POOP ('progressive only on Palestine') by some Palestinian activists. These elements fail to take an intersectional approach to activism and end up isolated from the wider left – precisely the goal of the Israeli government and Zionist movement.

Instead, the Palestine solidarity movement must remain strongly integrated with other racial and social justice movements, from Black Lives Matter to abolitionist organising, and groups opposing Islamophobia, fracking, the arms trade and fossil fuels. This is not only because these movements have common enemies but because resistance to this top-down repressive backlash will rely on coalition building. As British Palestinian scholar-activist Yara Hawari puts it, 'Only in broad, intersectional alliances can social justice activists effectively repel state-led repression.'[28]

Due to the democratic deficit around foreign policy in Britain, the Zionist movement's strategy of principally targeting a small decision-making elite has worked relatively well for a considerable amount of time. As a result, attempts have been made to build pro-Palestinian initiatives which can rival this top-down institutional power. For example, the Palestine Solidarity Campaign has for some years been organising an annual lobby of Parliament, to counter that organised each year by the Zionist Federation and Christian Friends of Israel. Similarly, Medical Aid for Palestinians and the Council for the Advancement of Arab–British Understanding organise trips for members of Parliament, effectively as rivals to Labour Friends of Israel and Conservative Friends of Israel, though on a much smaller scale. This strategy is extremely unlikely to be effective, given the superior resources and access of social movements from above.

The Palestine solidarity movement should recall celebrated activist and writer Audre Lorde's warning that 'the master's tools will never dismantle the master's house'. The situation in Palestine is, in the last analysis, a symptom of the entrenched power inequalities of our world – a status quo which we should not legitimise through our activism. We need to do things differently. Besides, as Margaret Thatcher's resistance to sanctions against South Africa reminds us, political leaders will be the very last to shift (and this is why the Zionist movement today focuses on *downward repression* as much, if not more than, *upwards influence*). Similarly, in the US, policy on apartheid South Africa finally changed only when Republicans realised that President Ronald Reagan's 'constructive engagement' stance had become a significant partisan issue contributing to domestic unpopularity.[29] Change will not come from Westminster but from civil society.

The BDS movement looks to civil society instead of governments, as an agent of change, and implicitly puts its faith in a broader democratisation project which insists upon translating popular will into political influence, without taking shortcuts. While the Zionist movement resorts to the manufacture of astroturf civil society support, the Palestinian cause can draw 200,000 people onto the streets of Britain in solidarity. This people power is the movement's strength – and precisely what both British and Israeli governments fear.[30] Lasting change will come by building from the bottom up. This is a long game, but we are already seeing encouraging trends – not least the shrinking of Israeli apartheid's support base to older, more right-wing and often evangelically minded groups. Meanwhile, younger generations, especially on the left, are increasingly axiomatic in their embrace of a pro-Palestinian stance, giving cause for hope of a more liberated future.

Acknowledgements

It's not often that a trans person has a public platform, let alone one to speak about something other than being trans. Naturally, I chose to spend years researching and writing about the only subject equally, or perhaps even more prone to polarisation and toxicity. And writing this book, especially as a trans nonbinary person of colour, has sometimes felt like asking for trouble. The movements opposing trans liberation and Palestinian liberation appear to me to have quite a lot in common. Both use repressive legal tactics and misrepresent the truth. I won't go into that now. I will say that while I have often doubted myself, I have never doubted the justness of the Palestinian cause.

The time I spent in the West Bank had a profound effect on me. I witnessed first-hand the courage, dignity and steadfastness of Palestinians (and their allies) resisting the brutal colonial oppression of Israeli apartheid. It is to all those who continue to assert their humanity and struggle for a future based on freedom, justice and equality that I would like to dedicate this book. Khalil Gibran apparently once wrote that 'work is love made visible'. I'm unsure how true that is under capitalism, but it has the ring of emotional truth to me in this case. So, in the words of Nina Simone, please don't let me be misunderstood!

Huge thanks to my editor at Verso, Rosie Warren, for incredible patience and extremely helpful feedback. Thanks also to the Society of Authors and the Authors' Foundation for awarding me the John C. Laurence award which helped me finish the book. Much of the material in the universities chapter is based on one already published in the book *Enforcing Silence: Academic Freedom, Palestine and the Criticism of Israel* (Zed Books, 2020), and the rest of the book is based in part on my PhD dissertation, although my thinking has developed a fair bit since then. Thanks to those who helped me on that journey, and in in my research and writing since then, including Jason Hart, Ronit Lentin, Charlotte Heath-Kelly, Tarek Younis, Tom Mills, Alex Doherty, Jamie Stern-Weiner, Ilan Pappé, Tom Griffin, Narzanin Massoumi, Neve Gordon, David Landy, Mel Jones, Sharri Plonski, Will Dinan, Eveline Lubbers, Yara Hawari, Mandy Turner, Feryal Awan, Elian Weizman and others I've probably forgotten. Thanks to those who read draft chapters of this book, including Michael Bueckert, Adi Kuntsman, Neil Rogall, Louis Bayman, Elaine Bradley, Zainab, Anya, Rosa, Asa, Ronit, Becky, and Rowan. Thanks to everyone who was interviewed for the research behind this book. Comrades who've provided advice, ideas, inspiration and encouragement include Hussein, Sarona, Samir, Akram, Ryvka, Alia, Kareem and Michael.

Finally, love and thanks to my family, friends, cherished community and miscellaneous others: Sheila, Nick, Jo, Dan, Sophie, Evie, niece #2 on the way, Mike, Caroline, Kate and Ella, Helena, Chris, Caighli, Adam, Andrea, James, Clare Q., Ewa, Clare W., Leila, Dan, Rosa, Reem, Bianca, Sumayah, Naiara, Ali, Laurie, Joe, Shadin, Michael, Gordon, Dexter, Robin, Simo, TJ, Rosie, Sarch, Ben, Maggie, Bea, Len, Natalie, Flora, Anya, Mika, Arrate, Anna, Bobby, Igi and the rest. I promise you will never again hear me say, 'I have so nearly finished my book!'

Glossary of key organisations

AIPAC (American Israel Public Affairs Committee) – Major US lobby group founded in 1951. Cultivates support for Israel in Washington.

Board of Deputies of British Jews ('the Board') – Britain's oldest democratic Jewish political organisation, founded in 1760. Historically anti-Zionist, today actively supports Israel.

Boycott, Divestment and Sanctions (BDS) – Palestinian-led global solidarity campaign founded in 2005, applying pressure on Israel to comply with international law.

BICOM (Britain Israel Communications and Research Centre) – the most important British pro-Israel lobby group focusing on influencing the media, founded in 2001.

Campaign Against Antisemitism – British organisation founded in 2014, with strong ties to the right wing of the Zionist movement.

Conservative Friends of Israel (CFI) – Conservative Party pro-Israel group founded by former MP Michael Fidler in 1974 and today one of the most influential networks in Westminster.

Henry Jackson Society – British neoconservative think tank founded in 2005. Hosts Israeli political figures in Westminster and lobbies for draconian counter-terrorism measures.

Israel Advocacy Forum – Founded in 2006 as the Fair Play Campaign Group. Network bringing together various pro-Israel groups to oppose anti-Zionist activity and boycotts of Israel.

Jewish Agency for Israel – One of the early Zionist bodies known as Israel's 'national institutions', established in 1929. Principally concerned with facilitating Jewish immigration to Palestine.

Jewish Human Rights Watch – Small British 'lawfare' organisation founded in 2015. Brought an unsuccessful legal case against three local councils endorsing aspects of BDS.

Jewish Labour Movement – Labour Party–affiliated group whose aims include promoting 'Labour or Socialist Zionism'. Grew out of Poale Zion (Great Britain).

Jewish Leadership Council – Umbrella body established in 2003, with a combination of Jewish groups and Israel-advocacy groups among its thirty affiliated members. Some of its work involves fundraising for Jewish charities and schools but it also actively supports Israel.

Jewish National Fund – one of the Zionist movement's 'national institutions', founded in 1901, supported by a British affiliate. Central to the historic and ongoing colonisation of Palestine.

Keren HaYesod – Another of Israel's 'national institutions', also known as the United Israel Appeal. Set up in 1920, primarily as a fundraising body for the Zionist movement and Israel.

Labour Friends of Israel (LFI) – Labour Party pro-Israel group founded in 1957 during the heyday of left-wing support for Israel. Thought to communicate closely with the Israeli embassy.

Ministry of Strategic Affairs – Secretive Israeli government ministry which spearheaded the repressive backlash against the BDS movement between 2015 and 2021.

StandWithUs – Hard-line US-headquartered pro-Israel body founded in 2001, believed to coordinate closely with the Israeli government. British branch founded in 2010.

United Jewish Israel Appeal (UJIA) – British affiliate of Keren HaYesod. Primarily a fundraising body but also works to encourage young British Jews to support Zionism and Israel.

Union of Jewish Students (UJS) – Founded in 1973, UJS supports Jewish student life in Britain. It also works to foster support for Israel, including by facilitating highly subsidised trips.

UK Lawyers for Israel – Pro-Israel 'lawfare' group established in 2010 with close ties to a range of bodies on the right wing of the Zionist movement. Appears to collaborate closely with the Israeli government across state-private networks.

World Zionist Organization – The original umbrella body of the Zionist movement, founded in 1897 at the First Zionist Congress by Theodor Herzl.

We Believe in Israel – BICOM spin-off organisation with a majority Christian support base, founded in 2011 and involved in establishing other pro-Israel groups.

Zionist Federation (of Great Britain and Ireland) – British affiliate of the World Zionist Organization, formed in 1899. Famously received the seminal Balfour Declaration in 1917.

Notes

Preface

1. Rafeef Ziadah, 'Israel has been described as an "apartheid regime" – this will not come as news to ordinary Palestinians', *Independent*, 12 January 2021.
2. Michael Sfard, *The Occupation of the West Bank and the Crime of Apartheid: Legal Opinion*, Yesh Din, June 2020; *A Regime of Jewish Supremacy from the Jordan River to the Mediterranean Sea: This Is Apartheid*, B'Tselem, 12 January 2021, btselem.org; *A Threshold Crossed: Israeli Authorities and the Crimes of Apartheid and Persecution*, Human Rights Watch, 27 April 2021, hrw. org; *Israel's Apartheid against Palestinians: A Cruel System of Domination and a Crime against Humanity*, Amnesty International, 1 February 2022, amnesty.org.

Introduction

1. See, for example, Edward Said, 'America's Last Taboo', *New Left Review* 6 (November–December 2000); Walter Russell Mead, 'Jerusalem Syndrome – Decoding the Israel Lobby', *Foreign Affairs* 86 (November–December 2007): 161; John Mearsheimer and Stephen Walt, 'The Blind Man and the Elephant in the Room: Robert Lieberman and the Israel Lobby', *Perspectives on Politics* 7, no. 2 (2009): 260.

2. All-Party Parliamentary Group against Antisemitism, *Report of the All-Party Parliamentary Inquiry into Antisemitism* (London: All-Party Parliamentary Group against Antisemitism, 2006), 28.

3. Peter Beinart, *The Crisis of Zionism* (New York: Times Books, 2012), 181.

4. See, for example, Brian Wood, 'The Second Annual CUFI Conference, July 2007: The Christian Zionist Coalition Hits Its stride', *Journal of Palestine Studies* 37, no. 1 (2007): 79–87; Faydra Shapiro, '"Thank you Israel, for Supporting America": The Transnational Flow of Christian Zionist Resources', *Identities* 19, no. 5 (2012): 616–31; Nathan Lean, 'Of Politics and Prophecy: The Alliance of the Pro-Israel Right', in *The Islamophobia Industry: How the Right Manufactures Fear of Muslims* (London: Pluto, 2012), 119–36; Elvira King, *The Pro-Israel Lobby in Europe: The Politics of Religion and Christian Zionism in the European Union* (London: I. B. Tauris, 2016).

5. Pierre Guerlain, 'The Israel Lobby, American Democracy and Foreign Perceptions of the USA', *Journal of Public Affairs* 11, no. 4 (2011): 376.

6. Joel Kovel, *Overcoming Zionism: Creating a Single Democratic State in Israel/Palestine* (London: Pluto Press, 2007), 40.

7. Edgar Lane, 'Group Politics and the Disclosure Idea', *Western Political Quarterly* 17, no. 2 (1964): 200.

8. See, for instance, Jewish Agency, 'Herzl Creates the Zionist Movement', 3 July 2007, jewishagency.org.

9. Yasmeen Abu-Laban and Abigail Bakan, *Israel, Palestine and the Politics of Race: Exploring Identity and Power in a Global Context* (London: Bloomsbury, 2019).

10. Ibid., 13.

11. Omran Shroufi, 'The Gates of Jerusalem: European Revisionism and the Populist Radical Right', *Race and Class* 57, no. 2 (2015): 24–42.

12. Paul Gross, 'Modi, Orban, Bolsonaro: Israel Doesn't Need to Pander to Netanyahu's Autocratic Pals Any More', *Haaretz*, 29 July 2021, haaretz.com.

13. Brian Klug, 'The Collective Jew: Israel and the New Antisemitism', *Patterns of Prejudice* 37, no. 2 (2003): 122.

14. Keith Kahn-Harris, *Turbulent Times: The British Jewish Community Today* (London: Continuum, 2010), 138–9.

15. Klug, 'The Collective Jew', 124.

16. Antony Lerman, 'Sense on Anti-Semitism', *Prospect*, 20 August 2002, prospectmagazine.co.uk.

17. Brian Klug, 'Interrogating "New" Anti-Semitism', *Ethnic and Racial Studies* 36, no. 3 (2013): 473-475, 470.

18. Abigail Bakan and Yasmeen Abu-Laban, 'Palestinian Resistance and International Solidarity: The BDS Campaign', *Race and Class* 51, no. 1 (2009): 32–3.

19. Abu-Laban and Bakan, *Politics of Race*, 13.

20. Antony Lerman, 'The Farcical Attack on the UCU For Voting against Use of the EUMC "Working Definition" of Antisemitism', antonylerman.com, 2 June 2011.

21. 'About Us', International Holocaust Remembrance Alliance, holocaustremembrance.com.

22. Dan Freeman-Maloy, 'Israeli State Power and Its Liberal Alibis', *Race and Class* 52, no. 3 (2011): 61.

23. Jamie Stern-Weiner, *The Politics of a Definition: How the IHRA Working Definition of Antisemitism Is Being Misrepresented*, Free Speech on Israel, April 2021, freespeechonisrael.org.uk; Antony Lerman, 'Labour Should Ditch the IHRA Working Definition of Antisemitism Altogether', *OpenDemocracy,* 4 September 2018, opendemocracy.net.

24. Klug, 'The Collective Jew', 124.

25. Andrew Feinberg, 'Trump Accused of "Classic" Antisemitism after Claiming Israel "Had Absolute Power Over Congress"', *Independent*, 7 December 2021, independent.co.uk.

26. Christopher Williams, *Researching Power, Elites and Leadership* (London: Sage, 2012), 124.

27. 'Bill Calling to Keep Strategic Affairs Ministry's Efforts to Combat Delegitimization Secret Passes First Reading', Knesset press release, 18 July 2017, knesset.gov.il.

28. Jeffrey Goldberg, 'Real Insiders', *New Yorker*, 4 July 2005, newyorker.com.

29. Fredric Jameson, 'Cognitive Mapping', in *Marxism and the Interpretation of Culture*, Cary Nelson and Lawrence Grossberg, eds (Chicago: University of Illinois Press), 356.

30. Joan Cassell, 'The Relationship of Observer to Observed when Studying Up', in *Studies in Qualitative Methodology*, vol. 1, Robert G. Burgess, ed. (London: Jai Press, 1988), 91.

31. Kevin Walby and Mike Larsen, 'Access to Information and Freedom of Information requests: Neglected Means of Data Production in the Social Sciences', *Qualitative Inquiry* 18, no. 1 (2012): 31–42.

32. John Scott, *Matter of Record: Documentary Sources in Social Research* (Cambridge, UK: Polity Press, 1990), 10.

33. Robert Lieberman, 'Rejoinder to Mearsheimer and Walt', *Perspectives on Politics* 7, no. 2 (2009): 280.

34. Arno Rosenfeld, '"Against a wall": Boston's Jewish Leftists Conflicted by BDS Map', *Forward*, 21 June 2022, forward.com.

I. Understanding the 'Israel Lobby'

1. 'The Discriminatory Laws Database', Adalah, adalah.org.

2. Yara Hawari, 'Defying Fragmentation and the Significance of Unity: A New Palestinian Uprising', al-Shabaka, 29 June 2021, al-shabaka.org.

3. Mohammed el-Kurd, 'Here in Jerusalem, We Palestinians Are Still Fighting for Our Homes', *Guardian*, 28 July 2021, theguardian.com.

4. UKLFI Charitable Trust, '2021 05 15 Sky', YouTube video, 15 May 2021, youtube.com.

5. Email from We Believe in Israel, 11 May 2021.

6. Ilan Pappé, *The Ethnic Cleansing of Palestine* (Oxford: One World, 2006).

7. Ben Smoke, 'Exist, Resist, Return: Photos from Britain's largest Palestine Demo In History', *Huck*, 24 May 2021, huckmag.com.

8. 'Former Tory chair James Cleverly Appointed New Middle East Minister', *Jewish News*, 17 February 2020, jewishnews.com.

9. 'Boris Johnson Urges Both Sides in Israel-Gaza Violence to "step Back"', *BBC News*, 12 May 2021, bbc.co.uk.

10. Laurence Cox and Alf Gunvald Nilsen, *We Make Our Own History: Marxism and Social Movements in the Twilight of Neoliberalism* (London: Pluto Press, 2014), 60, 72.

11. Ibid., 58, 64.

12. Ibid., 60, 70, 68.

13. Ibid., xi.

14. Inderjeet Parmar, *Foundations of the American Century: The Ford, Carnegie, and Rockefeller Foundations in the Rise of American Power* (Chichester: Columbia University Press, 2012), 16.

15. Janine Wedel, *Shadow Elite: How the World's New Power Brokers Undermine Democracy, Government, and the Free Market* (New York: Basic Books, 2009), 15, 19–20.

16. Inderjeet Parmar, 'Conceptualising the State-Private Network in American Foreign Policy', in *The US Government, Citizen Groups and the Cold War: The State-Private Network*, Helen Laville and Hugh Wilford, eds (London: Routledge), 13.

17. Wedel, *Shadow Elite*, 16, 5.

18. Jan Melissen, 'Wielding Soft Power: The New Public Diplomacy' (Wassenaar: Netherlands Institute of International Relations Clingendael, 2005), 4.

19. Ibid., 12.

20. Shaun Riordan, 'Dialogue-Based Public Diplomacy: A New Foreign Policy Paradigm?', in *The New Public Diplomacy: Soft Power in International Relations*, Jan Melissen, ed. (Basingstoke: Palgrave Macmillan, 2005), 190.

21. Melissen, 'Wielding Soft Power', 12.

22. Ibid., 26, 30, 9.

23. Riordan, 'Dialogue-Based Public Diplomacy', 191, 193.

24. Ibid., 191.

25. Lesley Hodgson, 'Manufactured Civil Society: Counting the Cost', *Critical Social Policy* 24, no. 2 (2004): 145, 159.

26. See Charles Cho et al., 'Astroturfing Global Warming: It Isn't Always Greener on the Other Side of the Fence', *Journal of Business Ethics* 104, no. 4 (2011).

27. Ian Cobain et al., 'Revealed: UK's Covert Propaganda Bid to Stop Muslims Joining Isis', *Guardian*, 2 May 2016, theguardian.com.

28. 'Quilliam Circle', Quilliam Foundation, quilliaminternational.com.

29. Ian Cobain et al., 'Inside Ricu, the Shadowy Propaganda Unit Inspired by the Cold War', *Guardian*, 2 May 2016, theguardian.com.

30. Jessica Doyle, 'Civil Society as Ideology in the Middle East: A Critical Perspective', *British Journal of Middle Eastern Studies* 43, no. 3 (2016): 417.

31. Ron Nixon, *Selling Apartheid: South Africa's Global Propaganda War* (London: Pluto Press, 2016), xi; William Hachten and Anthony Giffard, *The Press and Apartheid: Repression and Propaganda in South Africa* (Basingstoke: Palgrave Macmillan, 1984), 254.

32. Cited in James Sanders, *South Africa and the International Media, 1972–1979: A Struggle for Representation* (Abingdon: Routledge, 2011), 57.

33. Ibid.

34. Ibid., 55.

35. Nixon, *Selling Apartheid*, 81.

36. Ibid., 65.

37. Parmar, 'Conceptualising the State-Private Network', 6, 15, 23, 24.

38. Hugh Wilford, *The Mighty Wurlitzer: How the CIA Played America* (Cambridge, MA: Harvard University Press, 2009), 117, 107.

39. Giles Scott-Smith, *The Politics of Apolitical Culture: The Congress for Cultural Freedom, the CIA and Post-war American Hegemony* (London: Routledge, 2002), 10.

40. Sean McMeekin, *The Red Millionaire: A Political Biography of Willi Münzenberg, Moscow's Secret Propaganda Tsar in the West* (London: Yale University Press, 2005), 1.

41. David Cronin, *Balfour's Shadow: A Century of British Support for Zionism and Israel* (London: Pluto, 2017).

42. Paul Kelemen, *The British Left and Zionism: History of a Divorce* (Manchester: Manchester University Press, 2012), 3.

43. John Newsinger, 'The Labour Party, Anti-Semitism and Zionism', *International Socialism* 153 (Winter 2017).

44. Gilbert Achcar, 'Zionism, Anti-Semitism and the Balfour Declaration', *OpenDemocracy*, 2 November 2017, opendemocracy.net.

45. Arun Kundnani, 'The Way Out of the Labour Party's "Anti-Semitism Crisis" Requires a Politics of Solidarity', *OpenDemocracy*, 11 May 2016, opendemocracy.net.

46. Paul Kelemen, 'Looking the Other Way: The British Labour Party, Zionism and the Palestinians', in *Jews, Labour and the Left, 1918–1948*, Christine Collette and Stephen Bird, eds (Farnham: Ashgate, 2000)

47. Newsinger, 'The Labour Party'.

48. Ibid.

49. Joseph Massad, 'Blaming the Israel Lobby', *Counterpunch*, 25 March 2006, counterpunch.org.

50. Mark Lacy, 'A History of Violence: Mearsheimer and Walt's Writings from "An Unnecessary War" to the "Israel Lobby" Controversy', *Geopolitics* 13, no. 1 (2008): 110.

51. John Mearsheimer and Stephen Walt, *The Israel Lobby and US Foreign Policy* (New York: Farrar, Straus & Giroux, 2007), 14.

52. James Petras, 'Why Condemning Israel and the Zionist Lobby Is so Important', *Journal of Contemporary Asia* 37, no. 3 (2007): 385.

53. 'Minnesota Congresswoman Ignites Debate on Israel And Anti-Semitism', *NPR*, 7 March 2019, npr.org.

54. Lacy, 'A History of Violence', 109.

55. Ian Cobain and Ewen MacAskill, 'Israeli Diplomat Caught on Camera Plotting to "Take Down" UK MPs', *Guardian*, 7 January 2017, theguardian.com.

56. David Wearing, 'AIPAC Is Not the Reason for US-Israeli Ties', *Novara*, 14 February 2019, novaramedia.com.

57. Ministry of Defence, *Defence in a Competitive Age* (London: Ministry of Defence, 2021), 31.

58. Asa Winstanley, 'Professor David Miller Fired after Israel Lobby Smear Campaign', *Electronic Intifada*, 1 October 2021, electronicintifada.net.

59. Jamie Doward, 'British Arms Exports to Israel Reach Record Level', *Guardian*, 27 May 2018, theguardian.com.

60. George Allison, 'UK and Israel Sign Military Cooperation Agreement', *UK Defence Journal*, 7 December 2020, ukdefencejournal.org.uk.

61. Peter Frankental, 'Britain Is Funding Apartheid', *Tribune*, 10 June 2022, tribunemag.co.uk.

62. Cox and Nilsen, *We Make Our Own History*, 63.

63. Ibid., 61.

64. Wearing, 'AIPAC Is Not the Reason'.

65. Eric Hobsbawm, *The Age of Extremes: The Short Twentieth Century, 1914–1991* (London: Abacus, 2009), 116.

66. Mazen Masri, *The Dynamics of Exclusionary Constitutionalism: Israel as a Jewish and Democratic State* (London: Bloomsbury, 2017).

67. Yasmeen Abu-Laban and Abigail Bakan, 'The Racial Contract: Israel/Palestine and Canada', *Social Identities: Journal for the Study of Race, Nation and Culture* 14, no. 5 (2008), 644.

68. Fiona Adamson, 'Constructing the Diaspora: Diaspora Identity Politics and Transnational Social Movements' (paper prepared for the Forty-Ninth Annual Conference of the International Studies Association, San Francisco, March 26–29, 2008), 17, 18.

69. Walter Lehn, 'The Jewish National Fund', *Journal of Palestine Studies* 3, no. 4 (1974), 77–8. As scholar Joseph Massad points out, pioneering thinkers like Herzl themselves defined Zionism as a settler-colonial movement, and early Zionist organisations included the unambiguously named 'Jewish Colonisation Association'.

70. Mansour Nasasra, 'The Ongoing Judaisation of the Naqab and the Struggle for Recognising the Indigenous Rights of the Arab Bedouin People', *Settler Colonial Studies* 2, no. 1 (2012), 81–107.

71. Mazin Qumsiyeh, *Sharing the Land of Canaan: Human Rights and the Israeli-Palestinian Struggle* (London: Pluto, 2004), 149.

72. William Mallison Jr., 'The Legal Problems Concerning the Juridical Status and Political Activities of the Zionist Organization / Jewish Agency: A Study in International and United States Law', *William and Mary Law Review* 9, no. 3 (1968), 571.

73. Rashid Khalidi, *The Iron Cage: The Story of the Palestinian Struggle for Statehood* (Oxford: One World, 2006): xviii.

74. 'Aliyah, Absorption and Development', Jewish Agency for Israel, 21 July 2005, jewishagency.org.

75. Natan Aridan, *Britain, Israel and Anglo-Jewry: 1949–57* (London: Routledge, 2004), 195.

76. Evyatar Friesel, cited in Stephan Wendehorst, *British Jewry, Zionism, and the Jewish State, 1936–1956* (Oxford: Oxford University Press, 2012), 5.

77. Narzanin Massoumi, Tom Mills and David Miller, *What Is Islamophobia? Racism, Social Movements and the State* (London: Pluto, 2017), 23.

78. Cited in Mallison, 'Legal Problems', 585.

2. Selling Apartheid

1. Josh Harkinson, 'Why Are US Taxpayers Subsidizing Right-Wing Israeli Settlers?', *Mother Jones,* 11 March 2015, motherjones.com.

2. Martin Bright, 'Government in Chaos over "Land Grab" Video', *Jewish Chronicle*, 25 August 2011, thejc.com.

3. Alan Duncan, 'Sir Alan Duncan MP: It's Time to Take on Israel's Settlements – and Those Who Endorse Them', *Conservative Home*, 14 October 2014, conservativehome.com.

4. Ian Cobain and Ewen MacAskill, 'Israeli Diplomat Caught on Camera Plotting to "Take Down" UK MPs', *Guardian*, 7 January 2017, theguardian.com.

5. Yehuda Ben Meir and Owen Alterman, *The Delegitimization Threat: Roots, Manifestations, and Containment* (Tel Aviv: Institute for National Security Studies, 2011), 123.

6. Miriyam Aouragh, 'Hasbara 2.0: Israel's Public Diplomacy in the Digital Age', *Middle East Critique* 25, no. 3 (2016): 283.

7. Abigail Bakan and Yasmeen Abu-Laban, 'Palestinian resistance and international solidarity: the BDS campaign', *Race and Class* 51, no. 1 (2009): 29.

8. See, for example, Dean Obeidallah, 'In the Middle East, the Two-State Solution Is Dead', *Daily Beast*, 2 January 2015, thedailybeast.com; Michelle Goldberg, 'Liberal Zionism Is dying: The Two State Solution Should Go with It', *Nation*, 26 August 2014, thenation.com; Michael Cohen, 'Think Again: The Two-State Solution', *Foreign Policy*, 14 September 2011, foreignpolicy.com.

9. Reut Institute, *San Francisco as a Delegitimization Hub: Initial Report on the 1st Study Visit* (Tel Aviv: Reut Institute, 2011), 5.

10. Grace Augustine and David Vannette 'Branding Israel A', unpublished documents from the William Davidson Institute of the University of Michigan, 8 April 2009, 10.

11. Amanda Borschel-Dan, '"Devastating" Survey Shows Huge Loss of Israel Support among Jewish College Students', *Times of Israel*, 21 June 2017, timesofisrael.com.

12. 'Views of Israel and Palestinians', Pew Research Center, 5 May 2016, pewresearch.org.

13. Lahav Harkov, 'Brainstorming BDS Battle Strategies', *Jerusalem Post*, 6 January 2016.

14. Reut Institute, *Building a Political Firewall*, 11.

15. Mazin Qumsiyeh, *Popular Resistance in Palestine: A History of Hope and Empowerment* (London: Pluto Press, 2011), 208.

16. Yoel Goldman, 'Abbas: Don't Boycott Israel', *Times of Israel*, 13 December 2013, http://timesofisrael.com.

17. Nathan Thrall, 'BDS: how a controversial non-violent movement has transformed the Israeli-Palestinian debate', *Guardian*, 14 August 2018, the guardian.com.

18. 'Palestinian Civil Society Call for BDS', BDS Movement, 9 July 2005, bdsmovement.net.

19. Reut Institute, 'Contending with BDS and the Assault on Israel's Legitimacy', Reut Institute, 25 June 2015, reut-institute.org.

20. Michael Schaeffer Omer-Man, 'Israel's President Calls BDS a "Strategic Threat"', +972 *Magazine*, 28 May 2015, 972mag.com.

21. Richard Gold, 'Contemporary Left Antisemitism – David Hirsh's Manchester Book Launch', 23 August 2017, engageonline.word press.com.

22. Charlotte Silver, 'Zionism Neoliberal Style', *Al Jazeera*, 11 February 2013, aljazeera.com.

23. Horit Herman-Peled, 'Unchosen Borderlines', in *Remapping the Region: Culture and Politics in Israel/Palestine* (Vienna: O.K. Books, 2004), 48.

24. Paul Kelemen, *The British Left and Zionism: History of a Divorce* (Manchester: Manchester University Press, 2012).

25. Neve Gordon and Erez Tzfadia, 'Privatising Zionism', *Guardian*, 14 December 2007, theguardian.com; Tariq Dana, 'The Symbiosis between Palestinian "Fayyadism" and Israeli "Economic Peace": The Political Economy of Capitalist Peace in the Context of Colonisation', *Conflict, Security and Development* 15, no. 5 (2015): 456.

26. Gil Feiler, *From Boycott to Cooperation: The Political Economy of the Arab Boycott of Israel* (London: Frank Cass, 1998), 146.

27. Keith Dinnie, *Nation Branding: Concepts, Issues, Practice* (Oxford: Elsevier, 2008), 18, 17.

28. Ido Aharoni, 'Nation Branding: Some Lessons from Israel', Know ledge@Wharton, University of Pennsylvania, 1 March 2012, knowledge.wharton.upenn.edu.

29. Yuval Ben-Ami, 'About Face', *Haaretz*, 20 September 2005, haaretz.com.

30. Dan Senor and Saul Singer, *Start-Up Nation: The Story of Israel's Economic Miracle* (Toronto: McClelland & Stewart, 2011).

31. Vera Michlin, 'Winning the Battle of Narrative' (working paper presented at Herzliya conference, Interdisciplinary Centre Herzliya, Herzliya, Israel, 31 January–3 February 2010), 3.

32. John Brown, 'Should the Piper Be Paid? Three Schools of Thought on Culture and Foreign Policy during the Cold War', *Place Branding* 1, no. 4 (2005): 422.

33. Ethan Bronner, 'After Gaza, Israel Grapples with Crisis of Isolation', *New York Times*, 18 March 2009, nytimes.com.

34. Ben-Ami, 'About Face'.

35. Yitzhak Laor, 'Putting Out a Contract on Art', *Haaretz*, 25 July 2008, haaretz.com.

36. Ben-Ami, 'About Face'.

37. Itamar Eichner, 'Foreign Ministry Finds Itself Battling Israel Boycott Alone', *Ynet*, 6 April 2015, ynetnews.com.

38. Ahiva Raved, 'Ya'alon: Breaking the Silence Being Investigated for Treason', *Ynet*, 21 March 2016, ynetnews.com.

39. Sharmila Devi, 'Palestinian Health NGO Leader Detained', *Lancet*, 7 August 2021, thelancet.com.

40. United Nations Office of the High Commissioner for Human Rights, 'Israel's "Terrorism" Designation an Unjustified Attack on Palestinian Civil Society – Bachelet', 26 October 2021, ohchr.org.

41. Yossi Melman, 'The Terrorist Kills, and the Bank Pays', *Haaretz*, 14 February 2007, haaretz.com.

42. Interview with Elliot Matthias, 29 April 2013, cited in Hil Aked, 'Israeli State Power and the Zionist Movement in the UK: The Case of the Counter-Campaign against the Boycott, Divestment and Sanctions (BDS) Movement for Palestinian Rights', doctoral thesis, University of Bath, 2019.

43. Nathan Guttman, 'StandWithUs Draws the Line on Israel', *Forward*, 27 November 2011, forward.com; 'Prime Minister's Office Hires Rightist Israel Advocacy Group for 1 Million Shekels', *Haaretz*, 13 January 2015, haaretz.com.

44. Dov Shinar et al., *The Neaman Document: A Study on Israeli Public Diplomacy* (Haifa: Neaman Institute, Technion and the Israeli Ministry of Foreign Affairs, 2009), neaman.org.il.

45. Reut Institute, *Building a Political Firewall*, 17.

46. Shmuel Bachar, Shmuel Bar and Rachel Machtiger, 'The "Soft Warfare" against Israel: Motives and Solution Levers' (working paper presented at Herzliya conference, Interdisciplinary Centre Herzliya, Herzliya, Israel, 31 January–3 February 2010).

47. World Jewish Congress, 'World Jewish Congress 2012–13 Global Review', 12 November 2015, 11, worldjewishcongress.org; Eliahu Elath, *Zionism at the UN: A Diary of the First Days* (Skokie, IL: Varda Books), 27.

48. Dan Diker, *BDS Unmasked: Radical Roots, Extremist Ends* (Jerusalem: Jerusalem Center for Public Affairs, 2016).

49. Maram Stern, 'Strategic Consultation: "Building Partnerships and Synergies in Countering the Assault on Israel's Legitimacy"', World Jewish Congress, 19 December 2010.

50. Ibid.

51. Lahav Harkov, 'We Have a Broad Government Program to Fight Boycotts', *Jerusalem Post*, 5 May 2016, jpost.com.

52. Alexander Apfel, 'Strategic Affairs Minister: Fight Against BDS about to Become a "Whole New Ball Game"', *Jewish Press*, 21 February 2016, jewishpress.com.

53. Harkov, 'We Have a Broad Government Program'.

54. Ofer Neiman, 'Most US Jewish Students Don't See Israel as "Civilized" or a "Democracy", Luntz Tells Secret Anti-BDS Conference', *Mondoweiss*, 22 February 2016, mondoweiss.net.

55. David Daoud, 'Jewish Leaders Attend "Global Coalition for Israel" Conference in Jerusalem', *Algemeiner*, 22 February 2016, algemeiner.com.

56. Marcus Dysch, 'Secret London Meeting to Plan Battle against Israel Boycott', *Jewish Chronicle*, 9 April 2014, thejc.com.

57. Bachar, Bar and Machtiger, 'Soft Warfare'.

58. Ibid., 34.

59. Shivi Greenfield, *Israeli Hasbara: Myths and Facts* (Jerusalem: Molad, 2012), 29.

60. Reut Institute, *2011: The Year We Punched Back on the Assault on Israel's Legitimacy* (Tel Aviv: Reut Institute, 2011), 3.

61. Barak Ravid, 'Ministers Split on Strategic Plan over How to Counter Boycott Threats', *Haaretz*, 31 January 2014, haaretz. com.

62. Barak Ravid, 'Netanyahu Convenes Ministers to Discuss Growing Israel Economic Boycott Threats', *Haaretz*, 9 February 2014, haaretz.com.

63. Alex Kane, 'Israel's Scheme to Defund the BDS Movement', *In These Times*, 11 November 2019, inthesetimes.com.

64. Charles Tripp, *The Power and the People: Paths of Resistance in the Middle East* (Cambridge, UK: Cambridge University Press, 2013), 227.

65. Barak Ravid, 'Military Intelligence Monitoring Foreign Left-Wing Organizations', *Haaretz*, 21 March 2011, haaretz.com.

66. Noa Landau, 'Mossad Involved in Anti-boycott Activity, Israeli Minister's Datebooks Reveal', *Haaretz*, 12 June 2019, haaretz.com.

67. Ali Abunimah, 'Leaked Report Highlights Israel Lobby's Failures', *Electronic Intifada*, 28 April 2017, electronicintifada.net.

68. Ali Abunimah, 'Israel's New Strategy: "Sabotage" and "Attack" the Global Justice Movement', *Electronic Intifada*, 16 February 2010, electronicintifada.net.

69. Noa Landau, 'Israel Publishes BDS Blacklist: These Are the 20 Groups Whose Members Will Be Denied Entry', *Haaretz*, 16 January 2018, haaretz.com.

70. Itamar Benzaquen, 'Israeli Ministry Paying for Anti-BDS Propaganda in Major News Outlets', +972 *Magazine*, 14 January 2020, 972mag.com.

71. Ali Abunimah, 'Israel Using "Black Ops" against BDS, Says Veteran Analyst', *Electronic Intifada*, 5 September 2016, electronicintifada.net.

72. Ibid.

73. Ali Abunimah, 'Who Is Lying about Israeli Embassy Agent Shai Masot?', *Electronic Intifada*, 12 January 2017, electronicintifada.net.

74. 'Devices of Palestinian Human Rights Defenders Hacked with NSO Group's Pegasus Spyware', CitizenLab, 8 November 2021, citizenlab.ca.

75. Uri Blau, 'Inside the Clandestine World of Israel's 'BDS-Busting' Ministry', *Haaretz*, 26 March 2017, haaretz.com.

76. Ibid.

77. 'Bill Calling to Keep Strategic Affairs Ministry's Efforts to Combat Delegitimization Secret Passes First Reading', Knesset press release, 18 July 2017, knesset.gov.il.

78. Micah Lakin Avni, 'How Will We Combat Israel's Delegitimization? In Concert', *Times of Israel*, 1 November 2018, timesofisrael. com.

79. Aiden Pink, 'U.S. Pro-Israel groups Failed to Disclose Grants from Israeli Government', *Forward*, 31 August 2020, forward.com.

80. Refaella Goichman, 'This Anti-BDS Initiative Failed. So Israel Throws Another $30 Million at It', *Haaretz*, 26 January 2022, haaretz.com.

81. 'About Us', Birthright Israel, birthrightisrael.com.

82. Daniel Lark, 'Call of Duty', *Jewish Currents*, 10 August 2020, jewishcurrents.org.

83. John Reed, 'Israel: A New Kind of War', *Financial Times*, 12 June 2015, ft.com.

84. Aiden Pink, 'US Pro-Israel Groups'.

85. Itamar Benzaquen, 'Lapid Brings Back to Life Netanyahu and Arden's "Mass Consciousness" Project', *Seventh Eye*, 20 January 2022, the7eye.org.il.

86. Lahav Harkov, 'Has the Strategic Affairs Ministry Achieved Its Goals?', *Jerusalem Post*, 24 June 2021, jpost.com; Itamar Benzaquen, 'The New Hasbara Campaign Israel Doesn't Want You to Know About', *+972 Magazine*, 25 January 2022, 972mag.com.

87. Bachar, Bar and Machtiger, 'Soft Warfare', 1.

88. Meir and Alterman, 'The Delegitimization Threat'.

89. Dysch, 'Secret London Meeting to Plan Battle against Israel Boycott'.

90. Eitan Arom, 'As BDS Opponents Move from Campuses to state Capitols, California Is Up Next', *Jewish News Service*, 13 April 2016, jns.org.

91. Apfel, 'Whole New Ball Game'.

92. Ben White, 'A Multiple Front War', *Newsweek Middle East*, 27 April 2016, newsweekme.com.

93. Aiden Pink, 'Israel Approved Grant to Tennessee Anti-Muslim "Hate Group"', *Forward*, 31 August 2020, forward.com.

94. '10 Things to Know about Anti-BDS Legislation', Palestine Legal, updated 23 October 2017, palestinelegal.org.

95. 'Missouri Becomes 30th US State to Punish Boycotts for Palestinian Freedom', Palestine Legal, 14 July 2020, palestinelegal.org; Philip

Weiss, 'Israeli Government Minister Takes Credit for 27 U.S. States Passing Anti-BDS laws', *Mondoweiss*, 2 July 2019, mondoweiss. net.

96. Melman, 'The Terrorist Kills'.

97. Orde Kittrie, *Lawfare: Law as a Weapon of War* (Oxford: Oxford University Press, 2016), 325–6, 311.

98. Kane, 'Israel's Scheme'.

99. Noam Rotem, 'Israeli Government "Lawfare Contractor" Sues Facebook for $1b', +972 *Magazine*, 15 July 2016, 972mag.com; 'Israeli NGO Sues Terrorists, Ties Up PA Money', US Embassy Tel Aviv, 20 August 2007, published by Wikileaks, 1 September 2011, wikileaks.org.

100. Asa Winstanley, 'Israeli Lawyers Group Shurat HaDin Unmasked as Mossad proxy', *Electronic Intifada*, 24 October 2013, electron icintifada.net.

101. 'Harpoon: How The Mossad and an Israeli NGO Destroyed Terrorist Money Networks', email from Shurat HaDin mailing list, 9 November 2017.

102. Yossi Gurvitz, 'The Israeli Government's Official "Lawfare" Contractor', +972 *Magazine*, 19 October 2013, 972mag.com.

103. Alan Goodman, 'Meet the Legal Wonks Who Brought Down the Flotilla', *Commentary*, 22 August 2011, commentarymagazine. com.

104. Alex Kane, 'Israel's Scheme to Defund the BDS Movement', *In These Times*, 11 November 2019, inthesetimes.com.

105. Ibid.

106. Mayaan Jaffe-Hoffman, '30 Financial Accounts Associated with BDS-Promoting NGOs Shut Down', *Jerusalem Post,* 11 June 2019, jpost.com.

107. Prime Minister's Office, 'Special Report: The Ties between NGOs Promoting BDS and Terror Organizations', 5 March 2019, gov.il.

108. Phan Nyugen, 'StandWithUs Invests Nearly Half a Million Dollars in Ongoing Anti-BDS Lawsuit against Olympia Food Co-Op', *Mondoweiss*, 29 May 2015, mondoweiss.net.

109. 'Israeli Civil Rights Center Launches Legal Task Force to Combat BDS', *Jewish Business News*, jewishbusinessnews.com.

110. Kane, 'Israel's Scheme'.

111. Mayaan Jaffe-Hoffman, 'Strategic Affairs Ministry to Form anti-BDS legal network', *Jerusalem Post*, 20 December 2018, jpost.com.

112. Chaim Levinson and Barak Ravid, 'Israel Secretly Using U.S. Law Firm to Fight BDS Activists in Europe, North America', *Haaretz*, 26 October 2017, haaretz.com.

113. Cited in Alexis De Greiff, 'The Politics of Noncooperation: The Boycott of the International Centre for Theoretical Physics', *Osiris* 21, no. 1 (2006): 91.

114. Feiler, *From Boycott to Cooperation*, 135.

115. Ravid, 'Netanyahu Convenes Ministers'.

116. Lenny Ben-David, 'Turkey and Armenia: What Jews Should Do', *Jerusalem Post*, 4 September 2007.

117. Josh Nathan-Kazis and Justin Elliott, 'Pro-Israel Group Secretly Ran Misleading Facebook Ads to Target Palestinian-American Poet', *Forward*, 12 September 2018, forward.com.

118. Josh Nathan-Kazis, 'Campus Pro-Israel Group Monitored Progressive Jewish Students', *Forward*, 25 September 2018, forward.com; Josh Nathan-Kazis, 'A New Wave of Hardline Anti-BDS Tactics Are Targeting Students and No-one Knows Who's behind It', *Forward*, 2 August 2018, forward.com.

119. Asa Winstanley and Ali Abunimah, 'Censored Film Names Adam Milstein as Canary Mission Funder', *Electronic Intifada*, 27 August 2018, electronicintifada.net.

120. Canary Mission, 'Students', canarymission.org, accessed 23 October 2022.

121. Natan Aridan, 'Israel's Refusal to Endorse the American Friends of Israel (1956)', *Israel Studies* 15, no. 3 (2010): 189, 192.

122. Michael Weiss, 'Israel's D.C. Embassy Slaps Down J Street', *Tablet*, 12 October 2009, tabletmag.com.

123. Tom Perkins, 'Pro-Israel Donors Spent over $22m on Lobbying and Contributions in 2018', *Guardian*, 15 February 2019, theguardian.com.

124. Kane, 'Israel's Scheme'.

125. Jessica Elgot, 'Jewish Students Cancel "Controversial" Lawyer's Invite', *Jewish Chronicle*, 15 March 2012, thejc.com.

126. Noa Landau, 'Israel Set Up a Front Company to Boost Image and Fight BDS. This Is How It Failed', *Haaretz*, 29 July 2020, haaretz.com.

127. Pink, 'Israel Approved Grant'.

128. Aiden Pink, 'Think-Tank Failed to Disclose Six-Figure Grant from Israeli Government', *Forward*, 31 August 2020, forward.com.

129. Stern, 'Strategic Consultation'.

130. 'JVP's Approach to Zionism', Jewish Voice for Peace, jewishvoiceforpeace.org.

131. Marc Lamont Hill and Mitchell Plitnick, *Except for Palestine: The limits of Progressive Politics* (New York: The New Press, 2021).

132. Robert J. Brulle, 'Institutionalizing Delay: Foundation Funding and the Creation of U.S. Climate Change Counter-movement Organizations', *Climatic Change* 122, no. 4 (2014), 681–94; International Jewish Anti-Zionist Network, *The Business of Backlash: The Attack on the Palestinian Movement and Other Movements for Justice*, 2015, ijan.org.

133. JTA, 'Black Lives Matter Endorses BDS: Israel Is "Apartheid State"', *Haaretz*, 4 August 2016, haaretz.com; Noura Erekat and Marc Lamont Hill, eds, 'Black Palestinian Transnational Solidarity', special issue, *Journal of Palestine Studies* 48, no. 4 (Summer 2019).

3. Evolution of the British Zionist Movement

1. Jonathan Cook, Dylan Collins and Ezz Zanoun, 'Nakba Survivors Share Their Stories of Loss and Hope', *Al Jazeera*, 19 May 2016, aljazeera.com.

2. Ilan Pappé, *The Ethnic Cleansing of Palestine* (Oxford: One World, 2006).

3. 'FAQs – The Roots of the Current Israeli-Palestinian Conflict – What Caused the Palestinian Refugee Problem?', BICOM, bicom.org.uk.

4. 'FAQs – The Israeli Palestinian Arena Today: What Is the Status of the West Bank?', BICOM, bicom.org.uk.

5. 'FAQs – Life in Israel: How Are Rights and Freedoms Respected in Israel?', BICOM, bicom.org.uk.

6. Orna Almog, *Britain, Israel and the United States, 1955–1958: Beyond Suez* (London: Frank Cass, 2003), 18.

7. Gil Feiler, *From Boycott to Cooperation: The Political Economy of the Arab Boycott of Israel* (London: Frank Cass, 1998), 144.

8. Natan Aridan, *Britain, Israel and Anglo-Jewry: 1949–57* (London: Routledge, 2004), 191.

9. 'Who We Are: Our Structure', Board of Deputies, bod.org.uk.

10. Vivian Wineman, interview by the author, 3 August 2016, cited in Hil Aked, 'Israeli State Power and the Zionist Movement in the UK: The Case of the Counter-Campaign against the Boycott, Divestment and Sanctions (BDS) Movement for Palestinian Rights', PhD diss., University of Bath, 2019, 152.

11. David Blackburn et al., *A Community of Communities* (London: Institute of Jewish Policy Research, 2000), 31.

12. Board of Deputies, *Board of Deputies Charitable Foundation Trustees' Report for the Year Ended 31 December 2020*, 2021, available at register-of-charities.charitycommission.gov.uk.

13. Board of Deputies, 'Constitution', 21 September 2008, available at web.archive.org/web/20130227081459/http://www.bod.org.uk/content/Constitution2008-09-21.pdf; Jonathan Arkush, 'British Jewry – Loud and Proud', *Jewish News*, 5 November 2013, timesofisrael.com.

14. Keith Kahn-Harris, *Uncivil War: The Israel Conflict in the Jewish Community* (London: David Paul Books, 2014), 74.

15. Aridan, *Britain, Israel and Anglo-Jewry*, 191–2.

16. David Cronin, *Balfour's Shadow: A Century of British Support for Zionism and Israel* (London: Pluto Press, 2017), 12.

17. Aridan, *Britain, Israel and Anglo-Jewry*, 191–2.

18. Keith Kahn-Harris, *Turbulent Times: The British Jewish Community Today* (London: Continuum, 2010), 25.

19. Barry Kosmin, Antony Lerman and Jacqueline Goldberg, *The Attachment of British Jews to Israel* (London: Institute for Jewish Policy Research, 1997), 3.

20. Aridan, *Britain, Israel and Anglo-Jewry*, 193.

21. Ibid., 194.

22. Hilary Rose and Steven Rose, 'Israel, Europe and the Academic Boycott', *Race and Class* 50, no. 1 (2008), 2.

23. Amy Spiro, 'A Taste of Tel Aviv in London', *Jerusalem Post*, 18 July 2017, jpost.com.

24. 'Maurice Orbach Dead at 76', *Jewish Telegraphic Agency*, 27 April 1979, jta.org.

25. Special Purpose Committee meeting minutes, 12 February 1959, Wiener Library, Board of Deputies Defence Committee papers, 1658/7/9/1/25; Special Purpose Committee meeting minutes, 12 February 1959, Wiener Library, Board of Deputies Defence Committee papers, 1658/7/9/1/26.

26. Feiler, *From Boycott to Cooperation*, 131.

27. 'The Arab Boycott – Notes of a Meeting with Mr A. Livernan', Wiener Library, Board of Deputies Defence Committee papers, 1658/7/9/1/30.

28. Feiler, *From Boycott to Cooperation*, 130

29. Ibid., 133.

30. Dan Chill, *The Arab Boycott of Israel: Economic Aggression and World Reaction* (New York: Praeger, 1976), 47.

31. Feiler, *From Boycott to Cooperation*, 134.

32. Alexis De Greiff, 'The Politics of Noncooperation: The Boycott of the International Centre for Theoretical Physics', *Osiris* 21, no. 1 (2006): 91.

33. Chill, *Arab Boycott of Israel*, 75.

34. Feiler, *From Boycott to Cooperation*, 132.

35. 'Arabs Dictating to British Firms, Trade Secretary Is Told', press release by Board of Deputies, 23 April 1975, London Metropolitan Archives, Board of Deputies collection, ACC/3121/E/04/0946.

36. 'Britain and the Arab Boycott', paper by M. Savitt and J. Gewirtz, n.d., London Metropolitan Archives, Board of Deputies collection, ACC/3121/E/04/0946, 2.

37. 'About Us', B'nai B'rith, bnaibrith.org.

38. 'Anti-boycott Coordination', meeting minutes, 11 September 1975, London Metropolitan Archives, Board of Deputies collection, ACC/3121/E/04/0946.

39. 'Anti-boycott Coordination', meeting minutes, 12 June 1975, London Metropolitan Archives, Board of Deputies collection, ACC/3121/E/04/0946.

40. Terence Prittie and Walter Henry Nelson, *The Economic War against the Jews* (New York: Random House, 1977), sleeve note: 'About the Authors'.

41. 'Anti-boycott Coordination', meeting minutes, 12 June 1975.

42. 'Arab Boycott Campaign (ABC) – Draft Programme', by Terence Prittie, n.d., London Metropolitan Archives, Board of Deputies collection, ACC/3121/E/04/0946, 18.

43. 'Anti-boycott Coordination', meeting minutes, 11 September 1975.

44. Ibid.

45. 'Anti-boycott Coordination', meeting minutes, 12 June 1975.

46. 'Anti-boycott Coordination', meeting minutes, 11 September 1975.

47. 'BIPAC Made Impact', *Jewish Chronicle*, 8 October 1976, 6.

48. Tom Mills et al., *The Britain Israel Communications and Research Centre: Giving Peace a Chance?* (Glasgow: Public Interest Investigations, 2013), 17.

49. Feiler, *From Boycott to Cooperation*, 287.

50. 'We Cannot Sell Arms to Israel and Pretend to Be Shocked if They Are Used', *Independent*, 8 July 2002, independent.co.uk.

51. Feiler, *From Boycott to Cooperation*, 218–19.

52. Mills et al., *Giving Peace a Chance*, 17.

53. Jenni Frazer, 'BIPAC – Boldly Speaking Out in Defence of Israel', *Jewish Chronicle*, 28 October 1982, 6.

54. Bashir Abu-Manneh, 'Israel's Leaders Are Trying to Cancel the Debate Because They Know They're Losing', *Jacobin*, 1 November 2021, jacobinmag.com.

55. Arun Kundnani, 'The Way Out of the Labour Party's "Anti-Semitism Crisis" Requires a Politics of Solidarity', *OpenDemocracy*, 11 May 2016, opendemocracy.net.

56. Lahav Harkov, 'Israel's Strategic Affairs Minister Heads to London on BDS-Fighting Mission', *Jerusalem Post*, 4 September 2016, jpost.com; Reut Institute, *Building a Political Firewall against the Assault on Israel's Legitimacy: London as a Case Study* (Tel Aviv: Reut Institute, 2010), 49, 1–2.

57. Marc Greendorfer, 'The BDS Movement: That Which We Call a Foreign Boycott, by Any Other Name, Is Still Illegal', *Roger Williams Law Review* 22, no. 1 (Winter 2017), 17.

58. Shir Hever, 'Private Funding of Right-Wing Ideology in Israel', *The Economy of the Occupation: A Socio-economic Bulletin* 29–30 (May 2013), 31; Omar Barghouti, *Boycott, Divestment, Sanctions: The Global Struggle for Palestinian Rights* (Chicago: Haymarket Books, 2011), 6.

59. Yoni Kempinski and Tova Dvorin, 'Experts: Combat BDS with Emotions and Values', *Arutz Sheva*, 18 February 2014.

60. Maia Carter Hallward, *Transnational Activism and the Israeli-Palestinian Conflict* (Basingstoke: Palgrave Macmillan, 2013), 24.

61. Mitchell Bard and Gil Troy, 'Delegitimization of Israel: "Boycotts, Divestment and Sanctions"' (notes from working group at the Global Forum for Combatting Anti-Semitism, 16–17 December 2009, Jerusalem), 7.

62. Reut Institute, 'Policy Paper: Reut's Broad Tent and Red-Lines Approach', Reut Institute, 28 July 2011, reut-institute.org.

63. Eran Shayson, 'Our "Egyptian" Revolution against the Assault on Israel', *Jerusalem Post*, 25 April 2011, jpost.com.

64. Hil Aked, 'Big Tent for Israel', *Powerbase*, 20 November 2012, powerbase.info.

65. Leslie Bunder, 'Fair Play for Israel', *Something Jewish*, 10 January 2007, somethingjewish.co.uk.

66. 'Kudos . . . and caution', *Jewish Chronicle*, 24 October 2003, thejc.com.

67. Anonymous interviewee cited in Aked, 'Israeli State Power', 148.

68. Anonymous interviewee, cited in Aked, 'Israeli State Power', 148.

69. Jewish Leadership Council, 'Annual Report and Financial Statements for the Year Ended 31 December 2015', 2, available at register-of-charities.charitycommission.gov.uk; Simon Johnson, 'Simon Johnson: The JLC and Israel', Jewish Leadership Council, 1 May 2014, thejlc.org.

70. 'Facilitating Appropriate Community Response and Action when Israel Related Issues Impact upon the UK Jewish Community', Jewish Leadership Council, available at web.archive.org/web/20160320143654/thejlc.org/what-we-do/facilitating-appropriate-community-response-action-when-israel-related-issues-impact-upon-the-uk-jewish-community.

71. 'Facilitating Appropriate Community Response'.

72. 'The JLC's Strategic Priorities for 2014–2016', Jewish Leadership Council, 27 February 2014, available at web.archive.org/web/20140905174850/thejlc.org/2014/02/the-jlcs-strategic-priorities-for-2014–2016.

73. Tom Mills et al., *Giving Peace a Chance?* 37.

74. Jewish Leadership Council, 'Annual Report and Financial Statements for the Year Ended 31 December 2014', 19, available at register-of-charities.charitycommission.gov.uk.

75. Jewish Leadership Council, 'Annual Report 2015', 11.

76. Jewish Leadership Council, 'Annual Report 2014'; Jewish Leadership Council, 'Annual Report 2015'; Jewish Leadership Council, 'Annual Report and Financial Statements for the Year Ended 31 December 2017', available at register-of-charities.charitycommission.gov.uk; and Jewish Leadership Council, 'Annual Report and Financial Statements for the Year Ended 31 December 2018', available at register-of-charities.charitycommission.gov.uk.

77. 'Home', Fair Play Campaign Group, fairplaycg.org.uk.

78. Bunder, 'Fair Play for Israel'.

79. Henry Grunwald, 'So What Is the Board of Deputies Doing to Fight Israel's Corner?', *Jewish Chronicle*, 8 June 2007, 6.

80. Justin Cohen, 'Vicious War of Words after JNF UK Dramatically Quits Jewish Leadership Council', *TotallyJewish*, 3 March 2011, available at web.archive.org/web/20110306091819/totallyjewish.com/news/national/c-15864/vicious-war-of-words-after-jnf-uk-dramatically-quits-jewish-leadership-council.

81. Henry Grunwald and Brian Kerner, 'Fair Play a Priority', *Jewish Chronicle*, 29 May 2009, 32.

82. Jennifer Lipman, 'London Protest against Israel Hosting Under-21s', *Jewish Chronicle*, 24 May 2013, 6.

83. Grunwald and Kerner, 'Fair Play a Priority', 32.

84. Daniella Peled, 'Boycott and Divestment Battle Not Over for Britain's Jews', *Jerusalem Post*, 27 June 2005.

85. Wineman, interview.

86. 'Fair Play Leaders Plan Their Strategy', *Jewish Chronicle*, 16 February 2007, 10; 'We Believe in Israel Conference Sessions 2015', We Believe in Israel, available at web.archive.org/web/20160405132648/webelieveinisrael.org.uk/believe-israel-conference-sessions-2015.

87. Shaun Riordan, 'Dialogue-Based Public Diplomacy: A New Foreign Policy Paradigm?', in *The New Public Diplomacy: Soft Power in International Relations*, Jan Melissen, ed. (Basingstoke: Palgrave Macmillan, 2005), 191–3.

88. Barak Ravid, 'Israeli Ministries Feud over Anti-BDS Warfare in UK', *Haaretz*, 29 September 2016, haaretz.com.

89. 'Fair Play Campaign Group Breakfast', Jewish Leadership Council, 1 May 2014, thejlc.org.

90. 'Hilda Worth', Jewish Leadership Council, 21 February 2018, available at web.archive.org/web/20180221223525/thejlc.org/hilda _worth1; Lee Harpin, 'Sole Nomination for Next Jewish Leadership Council Chair Is Keith Black', *Jewish News*, 5 January 2010, jewishnews.co.uk; Simon Rocker, 'New Jewish Leadership Council Chair: "Merger with the Board of Deputies Would Be a Colossal Waste of Time"', *Jewish Chronicle*, 20 January 2022, thejc.com.

91. Sources: data for year ending 2020, from organisational websites, Charity Commission and Companies House, except where indicated.

92. 'About', JNF UK, jnf.co.uk.

93. Simon Rocker, 'Calls for JNF UK Chair Samuel Hayek to Quit Over "Islamophobic comments"', *Jewish Chronicle*, 4 January 2022, thejc.com.

94. Lee Harpin, '"I've been cancelled": Board VP Quits after Jewish News Exposé into Far-Right Posts', *Jewish News*, 13 January 2022, jewishnews.co.uk.

95. 'Our People', JNF UK, jnf.co.uk.

96. 'What We Do', UJIA, ujia.org.

97. 'Birthright Israel', UJIA, ujia.org.

98. Dan Sabbagh, 'Theresa May: I Do Not Underestimate Antisemitism Threat', *Guardian*, 17 September 2018, theguardian. com.

99. Justin Cohen, 'Gerald Ronson: "Corbyn More Likely to Join Anti -Semitic Anti-Zionism" than Oppose It', *Jewish News*, 2 March 2017, jewishnews.co.uk.

100. Matthew Hancock, 'Take Action against Discrimination', *Jewish Chronicle*, 17 February 2016, thejc.com.

101. Community Security Trust, 'CST Annual Dinner', Community Security Trust, 19 March 2015, cst.org.uk.

102. Kahn-Harris, *Turbulent Times*, 160.

103. 'Our Founding Statement of Core Principles: An Idea Whose Time Has Come', Yachad, yachad.org.uk.

104. 'The Board of Deputies Must Speak Out against Racism in Jerusalem', Yachad, 10 May 2021, yachad.org.uk.

105. 'FAQs: Does Yachad Support the Boycott Divestment Sanctions Movement (BDS)?', Yachad, yachad.org.uk.

106. Barak Ravid, 'Netanyahu, Lapid Play Politics over BDS, Stand in Way of Real Fighters', *Haaretz*, 8 March 2016, haaretz.com.

107. Mills et al., *Giving Peace a Chance*, 29.

108. David Graham and Jonathan Boyd, *Committed, Concerned, Conciliatory: The Attitudes of Jews in Britain towards Israel* (London: Institute for Jewish Policy Research, 2010), 9; Stephen Miller, Margaret Harris and Colin Shindler, *The Attitudes of British Jews towards Israel* (London: City University, 2015), 9.

109. Aked, 'Israeli State Power', 73.

110. 'About', Christians United for Israel, updated 29 July 2017, available at web.archive.org/web/20170720162734/cufi.org/site/PageServer?pagename=about_AboutCUFI; Jenni Frazer, 'Grassroots Pro-Israel Group Celebrates 20,000th Activist Sign Up', *Jewish News*, 28 May 2019, jewishnews.co.uk.

4. Insulating Parliament

1. Human Rights Watch, *Precisely Wrong: Gaza Civilians Killed by Israeli Drone-Launched Missiles*, Human Rights Watch, 30 June 2009, hrw.org.

2. Amnesty International, 'Amnesty Urges Suspension of UK Arms Sales to Israel as Evidence Revealed That Israel Military Drones May Use British-Built Engines', Amnesty International, 9 January 2009, amnesty.org.uk.

3. 'Elbit Protest: Pro-Palestine Activists "Shut Down" Drone Factory', *Al Jazeera*, 21 May 2021, aljazeera.com.

4. Neil Tweedie, Robert Winnett, Rachel Sylvester and Richard Edwards, 'Gordon Brown in the Eye of the Storm', *Daily Telegraph*, 1 December 2007, telegraph.co.uk.

5. 'Double Role of a Top Tory Lobbyist', *Sunday Times*, 21 October 2012, thetimes.co.uk.

6. Cedarsoak Ltd company profile, Companies House, available at find-and-update.company-information.service.gov.uk; Rajeev Syal and Caelainn Barr, 'Are APPGs a "Dark Space" for Covert Lobbying?', *Guardian*, 6 January 2017, theguardian.com.

7. David Cronin, *Balfour's Shadow: A Century of British Support for Zionism and Israel* (London: Pluto Press, 2017), 7.

8. Vera Michlin, 'Winning the Battle of Narrative' (working paper presented at Herzliya conference, Interdisciplinary Centre Herzliya, Herzliya, Israel, 31 January – 3 February 2010).

9. Quoted in Robert Fisk, 'Israel Feels under Siege. Like a Victim. An Underdog', *Independent*, 2 February 2010; Jonathan Cummings, 'Briitsh-Israel Relations Seen through Visiting Elite Opinionmaker Delegations', *MERIA Journal*, 5 June 2010.

10. Paul Kelemen, *The British Left and Zionism: History of a Divorce* (Manchester: Manchester University Press, 2012), 7.

11. John Newsinger, 'The Labour Party, Anti-Semitism and Zionism', *International Socialism* 153 (Winter 2017).

12. Kelemen, *The British Left*, 168.

13. June Edmunds, 'Labour, Suez and Israel: The End of a "Special Relationship"?', in *The Left and Israel: Party-Policy Change and Internal Democracy* (London: Palgrave Macmillan, 2014).

14. James Vaughan, '"Keep Left for Israel": Tribune, Zionism and the Middle East, 1937–1967', *Contemporary British History* 27, no. 1 (2012), 8.

15. This was the opinion of Christopher Mayhew, cited in James Vaughan, '"Mayhew's Outcasts": Anti-Zionism and the Arab Lobby in Harold Wilson's Labour Party', *Israel Affairs* 21, no. 1 (2015), 3.

16. Asa Winstanley, 'When Israel's Friends in Labour Advocated Genocide', *Electronic Intifada*, 25 July 2017, electronicintifada.net.

17. Newsinger, 'The Labour Party'.

18. Kelemen, *The British Left*, 203.

19. Christopher Mayhew and Michael Adams, *Publish It Not: The Middle East Cover-Up* (London: Longman, 1975), 49.

20. Jessica Elgot, 'Michael Foot: "I Owe a Great Debt to Jews"', *Jewish Chronicle*, 3 March 2010, thejc.com.

21. For LFI figures, see June Edmunds, 'The Evolution of British Labour Party Policy on Israel from 1967 to the Intifada', *Twentieth Century British History* 11, no. 1 (2000), 26; For LMEC figures, see Vaughan, 'Mayhew's Outcasts', 5.

22. Vaughan, 'Mayhew's Outcasts', 5.

23. 'The British Anti-apartheid Movement', *South African History Online*, 13 November 2012, sahistory.org.za.

24. Robert Philpot, 'The Yom Kippur War and British Politics', *Fathom*, June 2020.

25. Benad Avital, letter to *Jerusalem Post Weekly*, 29 January 1974, cited in Mayhew and Adams, *Publish It Not*, 243n51.

26. Philpot, 'Yom Kippur War'.

27. Newsinger, 'The Labour Party'.

28. Joseph Finklestone, 'Election '79', *Jewish Chronicle*, 27 April 1979, 8.

29. Richard Seymour, 'Labour's Antisemitism Affair', *Jacobin*, 6 April 2018, jacobinmag.com.

30. Tom Mills et al., 'The UK's Pro-Israel Lobby in Context', *Open-Democracy*, 2 December 2013, opendemocracy.net.

31. Bill Williams, *Michael Fidler (1916–1989): A Study in Leadership* (Stockport: R&D Graphics, 1997), 315.

32. *American Jewish Yearbook, 1980*, 199, cited in Mills et al., 'The UK's Pro-Israel Lobby in Context'.

33. Kelemen, *The British Left*, 169.

34. Steve Bell (former head of policy, Communication Workers Union), interview, 25 July 2016, cited in Aked, 'Israeli State Power'; see also Kelemen, *The British Left*, 171.

35. June Edmunds, 'The British Labour Party in the 1980s: The Battle over the Palestinian/Israeli Conflict', *Politics* 18, no. 2 (1998), 112–17.

36. Edmunds, 'Evolution of British Labour, 33–5.

37. June Edmunds, 'The Left's Views on Israel: From the Establishment of the Jewish State to the Intifada', PhD diss., London School of Economics and Political Science, 1997, 210–11.

38. Vaughan, 'Keep Left for Israel', 15.

39. Azriel Bermant, 'When Thatcher Turned against Israel', *Jewish Chronicle*, 5 October 2012, thejc.com.

40. Robert Philpot, 'Thatcher and Israel', *Jerusalem Post*, 21 August 2017, jpost.com.

41. Thomas Friedman, 'Thatcher Is First British Premier in Israel', *New York Times*, 25 May 1986, nytimes.com.

42. Edmunds, 'Evolution of British Labour', 36.

43. Toby Greene, *Blair, Labour and Palestine: Conflicting Views on Middle East Peace after 9/11* (London: Bloomsbury, 2014).

44. Paul Nuki, Nick Rufford and Gareth Walsh, 'The Man Called Mr Cashpoint', *Sunday Times*, 2 July 2000.

45. Mills et al., 'The UK's Pro-Israel Lobby in Context'.

46. Andrew Pierce 'Blair's Chance to Raise Cash for Pounds 1m Refund', *Times*, 18 November 1997.

47. Anonymous interviewee, cited in Hil Aked, 'Israeli State Power and the Zionist Movement in the UK: The Case of the Counter-Campaign against the Boycott, Divestment and Sanctions (BDS) Movement for Palestinian Rights', PhD diss., University of Bath, 2019, 148.

48. Pierce, 'Blair's chance'.

49. Peter Oborne and James Jones, 'The Pro-Israel Lobby in Britain: Full Text', *OpenDemocracy*, 13 November 2009, opendemocracy. net.

50. Andrew Porter, *The Business*, 30 June 2002.

51. Greene, *Blair, Labour and Palestine*, 8.

52. Richard Allen Greene, 'Jewish Vote Evenly Split in Britain', *Jewish Telegraphic Agency*, 8 May 2001, available at web.archive.org/web /20141118150310/jta.org/2001/05/08/life-religion/features/jewish-vote-evenly-split-in-britain.

53. Yasmin Alibhai-Brown, 'The Shadowy Role of Labour Friends of Israel', *Independent*, 3 December 2007; Chris Hastings and Andrew Alderson, 'David Abrahams' Glory Days as Blair Ally', *Daily Telegraph*, 3 December 2007, telegraph.co.uk.

54. Mary Dejevsky, 'Police to Interview Hain as a Suspect "within Days" over Gifts to Deputy Leadership Campaign', *Independent*, 20 April 2008, independent.co.uk.

55. Greg Palast, 'Brown's Fixer Spills the Beans', *Morning Star*, 1 December 2007.

56. Jim Pickard and Robert Wright, 'Priti Patel Scandal Turns Spotlight on Stuart Polak', *Financial* Times, 8 November 2017, ft.com.

57. James Landale, 'Priti Patel Held Undisclosed Meetings in Israel', *BBC News*, 3 November 2017, bbc.co.uk.

58. Areeb Ullah, 'Meet Stuart Polak, the Israel Lobbyist at Centre of Priti Patel Scandal', *Middle East Eye*, 8 November 2017, middle easteye.net.

59. Oborne and Jones, 'Pro-Israel Lobby'.

60. Peter Geoghegan, Seth Thévoz and Jenna Corderoy, 'Revealed: The Elite Dining Club behind £130m+ Donations to the Tories', *OpenDemocracy*, 22 November 2019, opendemocracy.net.

61. Oborne and Jones, 'Pro-Israel Lobby'.

62. Jonathan Oliver, 'Developer Gave Secret Donation to Ken Livingstone', *Sunday Times*, 16 March 2008, thetimes.co.uk.

63. Geoghegan, Thévoz and Corderoy, 'Elite Dining Club'.

64. Gabriel Pogrund and Henry Zeffman, 'The Tory Donors with Access to Boris Johnson's Top Team', *The Times*, 19 February 2022, thetimes.co.uk.

65. Pickard and Wright, 'Priti Patel Scandal'.

66. Aiden Pink, 'U.S. Pro-Israel Groups Failed to Disclose Grants from Israeli Government', *Forward*, 31 August 2020, forward.com; 'Pritchard, Mark (The Wrekin)', Register of Members' Financial Interests as on 1st August 2016, available at publications.parliament.uk.

67. Arnon Regular, 'British Lawmakers Say IDF Shot at Them', *Haaretz*, 20 June 2004, haaretz.com; Oborne and Jones, 'Pro-Israel Lobby'.

68. Conservative Home, 'William Hague & George Osborne at the CFI', YouTube video, 25 June 2008, youtube.com.

69. Pickard and Wright, 'Priti Patel Scandal'.

70. 'Double Role of a Top Tory Lobbyist'.

71. Pargav was also registered to the address of CQS, the hedge fund of CFI's Michael Hintze, though there is no evidence he donated.

72. Tom Mills et al., *The Britain Israel Communications and Research Centre: Giving Peace a Chance?* (Glasgow: Public Interest Investigations, 2013), 65–7.

73. Marcus Dysch, 'Priti Patel: The Ambitious Politician Whose Reach Exceeded Her Grasp', *Jewish Chronicle*, 8 November 2017, thejc.com.

74. Adam Ramsay, 'We Can't Ignore Priti Patel's Background in Lobbying', *OpenDemocracy*, 8 November 2017, opendemocracy.net.

75. Tom Griffin et al., *The Henry Jackson Society and the Degeneration of British Neoconservatism: Liberal Interventionism, Islamophobia and the 'War on Terror'* (Glasgow: Public Interest Investigations, 2015).

76. 'Our People', JNF UK, jnf.co.uk.

77. Conservative Friends of Israel, 'Alan Dershowitz Addresses Supporters in Parliament at CFI-HJS-Gatestone Institute Event', 23 September 2016, cfoi.co.uk.

78. James Landale, 'Priti Patel Held Undisclosed Meetings in Israel', *BBC News*, 3 November 2017, bbc.co.uk.

79. James Ball and Harry Davies, 'There Are New Conflict-of-Interest Questions over One of Priti Patel's Israel Meetings', *Buzzfeed*, 8 November 2017, buzzfeed.com.

80. Joe Watts, 'Priti Patel Discussed Giving British Foreign Aid Money to Israeli Army, Downing Street Confirms', *Independent*, 7 November 2017, independent.co.uk.

81. Ian Cobain and Ewen MacAskill, 'Israeli Diplomat Caught on Camera Plotting to "Take Down" UK MPs', *Guardian*, 7 January 2017, theguardian.com.

82. Ewen MacAskill and Ian Cobain, 'Israeli Diplomat Who Plotted against MPs Also Set Up Political Groups', *Guardian*, 8 January 2017, theguardian.com.

83. Asa Winstanley, 'Disgraced Israeli Agent Shai Masot Attended Minister's Secret London Meeting', *Electronic Intifada*, 8 December 2017, electronicintifada.net.

84. Ali Abunimah, 'Who Is Lying about Israeli Embassy Agent Shai Masot?', *Electronic Intifada*, 12 January 2017, electronicintifada. net.

85. MacAskill and Cobain, 'Israeli Diplomat Who Plotted'.

86. Conservative Friends of Israel, 'Israeli Public Security Minister Gilad Erdan Briefs Conservative MPs and Peers in Parliament', Conservative Friends of Israel, 9 September 2016, cfoi.co.uk.

87. Ali Abunimah, 'AIPAC's Secretive Strategy to Transform UK Politics', *Electronic Intifada*, 14 January 2017, electronicintifada. net.

88. 'Joint LFI, CFI and Israeli Embassy Event on Jewish Refugees from Arab Countries and Iran', Labour Friends of Israel, 3 December 2018, lfi.org.uk.

89. '"Poisonous Conduct Is a Disgrace": Minister Who Served in David Cameron's Government Says It Is Time to End the Problem of Israel Buying UK Policy', *Daily Mail*, 7 January 2017, dailymail. co.uk.

90. Denis MacShane, interview by the author, 17 March 2014 and 29 April 2013, cited in Aked, 'Israeli State Power', 154.

91. MacAskill and Cobain, 'Israeli Diplomat Who Plotted'.

92. Asa Winstanley, 'Is Labour Friends of Israel an Israeli Embassy Front?', *Electronic Intifada*, 12 January 2017, electronicintifada.net.

93. Asa Winstanley, 'Labour Friends of Israel Denies Funding from Israeli Spy', *Electronic Intifada*, 17 July 2019, electronicintifada. net.

94. Labour Friends of Israel, Twitter post, 16 July 2019, twitter.com/_ LFI/status/1151099311666728961.

95. Freddy Mayhew, 'Ofcom Clears Al Jazeera of Anti-Semitism over Probe into Israeli Lobbying of Parliament', *Press Gazette*, 9 October 2017, pressgazette.co.uk.

96. David Cronin, 'Game over for Labour Friends of Israel?', *Electronic Intifada*, 5 August 2015, electronicintifada.net.

97. Jenni Frazer, 'Israeli MK Stav Shaffir Stars at LFI, but Disappointment at Corbyn No-Show', *Jewish News*, 27 September 2017, jewishnews.co.uk.

98. Simon Rocker, 'Corbyn Says No to Balfour Dinner', *Jewish Chronicle*, 20 October 2017, thejc.com.

99. Anoosh Chakelian, 'From Kes to Benefit Sanctions: Ken Loach on Why He Is Still Making Films about Inequality in Britain', *New Statesman*, 20 October 2016, newstatesman.com.

100. Arieh Kochavi, 'The Struggle against Jewish Immigration to Palestine', *Middle Eastern Studies* 34, no. 3 (1998): 146–67.

101. David Feldman, Ben Gidley and Brendan McGeever, 'The EHRC Report Shows How Difficult Building Real Anti-Racist Politics Will Be', *Guardian*, 3 November 2020, theguardian.com.

102. Asa Winstanley, 'Labour's "Anti-Semitism crisis" Is a Manufactured Scare Campaign', *New Arab*, 22 November 2019, english. alaraby.co.uk.

103. Asa Winstanley, 'UK Labour MP Ruth Smeeth Was Funded by Israel Lobby', *Electronic Intifada*, 6 December 2016, electronicintifada. net.

104. Asa Winstanley, 'Jewish Labour Movement was Refounded to Fight Corbyn', *Electronic Intifada*, 7 March 2019, electronicintifada.net; 'What Is the Jewish Labour Movement?', Jewish Labour Movement, jewishlabour.uk.

105. Asa Winstanley, 'New Jewish Labour Movement Director Was Israeli Embassy Officer', *Electronic Intifada,* 21 September 2016, electronicintifada.net.

106. Asa Winstanley, 'Joan Ryan, MP Who Fabricated Anti-Semitism, Quits Labour', *Electronic Initifada,* 20 February 2019, electronicintifada.net.

107. L. Daniel Staetsky, *Antisemitism in Contemporary Great Britain: A Study of Attitudes towards Jews and Israel,* Institute for Jewish Policy Research and Community Security Trust, 2017, cst.org.uk.

108. Rajeev Syal, 'Labour Suspends NEC Member over Antisemitism Claims', *Guardian,* 31 May 2019, theguardian.com.

109. 'Labour's Shame', *Jewish Chronicle,* 17 March 2016, thejc.com.

110. Jessica Elgot and Peter Walker, 'Antisemitism Issue Used as "Factional Weapon" in Labour, Report Finds', *Guardian,* 19 July 2022, theguardian.com.

111. Richard Seymour, 'Labour's Antisemitism Affair', *Jacobin,* 6 April 2018, jacobinmag.com.

112. Jamie Stern-Weiner, 'Jeremy Corbyn Hasn't Got an "Antisemitism Problem". His Opponents Do', *OpenDemocracy,* 27 April 2016, opendemocracy.net; Frances Perraudin, 'Labour Suspends Donor over Corbyn "Nazi Stormtroopers" Article', *Guardian,* 11 September 2016, theguardian.com; Benjamin Kentish, 'Labour Says Margaret Hodge Comments "Disconnected from Reality" after She Calls Corbyn Antisemitic and Compares Party to Nazi Germany', *Independent,* 16 August 2018, independent.co.uk; David Graeber, 'For the First Time in My Life, I'm Frightened to Be Jewish', *OpenDemocracy,* 6 September 2019, opendemocracy.net.
Richard Seymour, 'Once More on Labour and Antisemitism', Patreon, 31 July 2018, patreon.com; Graeber, 'For the First Time'; Richard Seymour, 'The "Antisemitism" Panic', *Lenin's Tomb,* 28 April 2016, leninology.co.uk.

113. Toby Helm, 'Labour MPs and Peers Plan to Defy Corbyn on Antisemitism Definition', *Guardian,* 21 July 2018, theguardian.com.

114. Ben Gidley, Brendan McGeever and David Feldman. 'Labour and Antisemitism: A Crisis Misunderstood', *Political Quarterly* 91, no. 2 (2020): 413–21.

115. 'Letters: Palestinian Rights and the IHRA Definition of Antisemitism', *Guardian,* 29 November 2020, theguardian.com.

116. Yair Wallach, 'The EHRC Report Shows That Anti-racist Solidarity, Not Special Protection, Is the Way Forward', *JewThink*, 6 November 2020, jewthink.org.

117. 'How Does the Left Defeat Antisemitism?' (in conversation with Tania Shew, Aviah Sarah Day, and Lev Taylor), *Owen Jones Show*, YouTube video, December 13, 2020, youtube.com/watch?v=C_eWRtAp8_s.

118. Simon Hooper, '"Hostile environment" Supporter Appointed to EHRC Equality Watchdog', *Middle East Eye*, 12 November 2020, middleeasteye.net.

119. Nasar Meer, 'A Damning Parliamentary Report on Racism Makes It Clear: The System Isn't Working', *Guardian*, 12 November 2020, theguardian.com.

120. Kate Proctor, 'Equalities Watchdog Drops Plan for Tory Islamophobia Inquiry', *Guardian*, 12 May 2020, theguardian.com.

121. Meer, 'A Damning Parliamentary Report'.

122. Barnaby Raine, interviewed on *Politics, Theory, Other*, '#100 Corbyn, Labour, and the EHRC report w/ Barnaby Raine', available at soundcloud.com.

123. John Pring, 'EHRC Failed to Consult Its Own Disabled Advisers before Snubbing DWP Deaths Probe', *Disability News Service*, 2 July 2020, disabilitynewsservice.com; Meg Hill, 'LGBT organisations ask UN to Revoke Status of British Rights Watchdog', *Independent*, 11 February 2022, independent.co.uk.

124. Damien Gayle, '"Hierarchy of Racism" Fears Threaten Starmer's Hopes of Labour Unity', *Guardian*, 13 August 2020, theguardian.com.

125. 'Letters: As BAME Communities, We Stand United against Attempts to Suppress Our Voices', *Independent*, 18 August 2018, independent.co.uk.

126. Liz Fekete, 'Fault Lines in the Fight against Racism and Antisemitism', *Transnational Institute*, 12 February 2020, tni.org.

127. Liz Fekete, 'Reclaiming the Fight against Racism in the UK', *Race and Class* 61, no. 4 (2020): 87–95.

128. Fekete, 'Fault Lines'.

129. 'Race Report: "UK Not Deliberately Rigged against Ethnic Minorities"', *BBC News*, 31 March 2021, bbc.co.uk.

130. Amanda Parker, 'UK Report on Race Is a Masterclass in Gaslighting', *Financial Times*, 1 April 2021, ft.com.

131. Fekete, 'Fault Lines'.

132. Amanda Holpuch and Matthew Weaver, 'Gaza: Nakba Day Protests as Palestinians bury those killed in Embassy Unrest – as It Happened', *Guardian*, 15 May 2018, theguardian.com.

133. Asa Winstanley, 'Another MP Dumps Labour Friends of Israel', *Electronic Intifada*, 24 April 2019, electronicintifada.net.

134. Jessica Elgot, 'Antisemitism: Israeli Labor Leader Cuts Ties with Jeremy Corbyn', *Guardian*, 10 April 2018, theguardian.com.

135. Asa Winstanley, 'Defying Israel lobby, Labour Votes for Arms Freeze', *Electronic Intifada*, 26 September 2018, electronicintifada. net; and 'Labour's Foreign Spokesperson Emily Thornberry Endorses Israeli Racism', *Electronic Intifada*, 14 December 2017, electronicintifada.net.

136. Justin Cohen, 'Labour Friends of Israel Stand Missing from Annual Conference', *Jewish News*, 23 September 2018, jewishnews.co.uk.

137. 'After Corbyn, UK Labour Elects Keir Starmer, Zionist with Jewish Wife, as Leader', *Times of Israel*, 4 April 2020, timesofisrael.com.

138. 'Donation Summary: Sir Keir Starmer (Great Britain), Cash (C0495835)', Electoral Commission, electoralcommission.org.uk; Henry Dyer, 'Labour Group with Links to Keir Starmer Fined £14,250 for Failing to Declare Donations', *Business Insider*, 21 September 2021, businessinsider.com.

139. Damien Gayle, 'Keir Starmer Urged to Return Donations from "Islamophobic" Property Developer', *Guardian*, 1 December 2020, theguardian.com.

140. James Morris, 'Labour MP Tells Michael Gove to "Do One" over Keir Starmer Criticism', *Yahoo News*, 30 October 2020, uk.news. yahoo.com.

141. Rayhan Uddin, 'Exclusive: Keir Starmer Ignores Palestinian Letter amid Iftar Cancellation Controversy', *Middle East Eye*, 23 April 2021, middleeasteye.net.

142. Alan George, '"Making the Desert Bloom": A Myth Examined', *Journal of Palestine Studies* 8, no. 2 (1979): 88–100

143. Jake Wallis Simons, 'Israel Is Not an Apartheid State, Says Keir Starmer as He Apologises for the Corbyn Years', *Jewish Chronicle*, 7 April 2022.

144. Rachel Shabi, '"They Don't Value Us" – Labour's Problem with Anti -Black Racism', *Independent*, 1 March 2021, independent.co.uk.

145. Labour Friends of Israel, email, 5 October 2021.

146. Ali Abunimah, 'Spectacular Defeat for Israel Lobby at Labour Party Conference', *Electronic Intifada*, 27 September 2021, electronicintifada.net.

147. Luke Akehurst, 'The Fightback for Israel in the UK Starts on Sunday 22nd March', *Jewish News*, 11 March 2015, blogs.timesofisrael.com; Abunimah, 'Spectacular Defeat for Israel Lobby'.

148. Martin Bright, 'Community Needs to Re-think How to Make Israel's Case', *Jewish Chronicle*, 14 September 2012, 7.

149. Neville Teller, 'A "passionate Zionist"', *Jerusalem Post*, 25 July 2019, jpost.com.

150. Oborne and Jones, 'Pro-Israel Lobby'.

151. Jim Pickard and Robert Wright, 'Priti Patel Scandal Turns Spotlight on Stuart Polak', *Financial Times*, 8 November 2017, ft.com.

152. Oborne and Jones, 'Pro-Israel Lobby'.

5. Manufacturing Consent

1. Mouin Rabbani, 'Israel Mows the Lawn', *London Review of Books* 36, no. 15 (31 July 2014).

2. Dina Rickman, 'Everything David Cameron Said about Gaza before Baroness Warsi Resigned', *Independent*, 6 August 2014, indy100.com.

3. Mark Leftly, 'Israel-Gaza Conflict: David Cameron Is "in the Wrong" over Gaza, says Ed Miliband', *Independent*, 4 August 2014, independent.co.uk.

4. 'Baroness Warsi Quits as Foreign Office Minister over Gaza', *BBC News*, 5 August 2015, bbc.co.uk.

5. Shivi Greenfield, *Israeli Hasbara: Myths and Facts* (Jerusalem: Molad, 2012), 29; Reut Institute, *2011: The Year We Punched Back on the Assault on Israel's Legitimacy* (Tel Aviv: Reut Institute, 2011), 3.

6. The JC, 'Interview: Ron Prosor', *Jewish Chronicle*, 26 May 2011, thejc.com.

7. Jan Melissen, 'Wielding Soft Power: The New Public Diplomacy' (Wassenaar: Netherlands Institute of International Relations Clingendael, 2005), 30.

8. Keith Kahn-Harris, 'How High Can Grass Roots Grow?', *Jewish Chronicle*, 11 September 2014, thejc.com; Lesley Hodgson,

'Manufactured Civil Society: Counting the Cost', *Critical Social Policy* 24, no. 2 (2004): 145.

9. Barak Ravid, 'Netanyahu, Lapid Play Politics Over BDS, Stand in Way of Real Fighters', *Haaretz*, 8 March 2016, haaretz.com.

10. Ewen MacAskill and Ian Cobain, 'Israeli Diplomat Who Plotted against MPs Also Set Up Political Groups', *Guardian*, 8 January 2017, theguardian.com.

11. Ben White, 'Israeli Embassy Embraces Extremists to Save Flagging Brand', *Middle East Monitor*, 11 October 2016, middleeastmonitor. com.

12. Campaign4Truth, 'Debunking the Libels Series 1: Human Rights as a Weapon of Delegitimisation – Amir Ohana MK', YouTube video, 1 October 2016, youtube.com

13. Stephen Jaffe, 'There's a Growing Army of Grassroots Groups Working to Defend Israel', Board of Deputies of British Jews, 21 October 2014, bod.org.uk.

14. Jewish Leadership Council, 'Annual Report for the Year Ended 31 December 2015', 27, available at register-of-charities.charitycommission.gov.uk. North West Friends of Israel self-identifies as 'grassroots' on its website: nwfoi.org.uk.

15. North West Friends of Israel, 'Gilad Erdan Sends Greetings to North West Friends of Israel', video, 14 March 2016, available at facebook.com/watch/?v=1752104055025544; Josh Jackman, 'Manchester Israel Rally Set to Attract 2,000 People, Say Organisers', *Jewish Chronicle*, 11 March 2016, thejc.com.

16. Hil Aked, 'Is New UK Zionist Group Funding Settlements?', *Electronic Intifada*, 9 December 2015, electronicintifada.net.

17. 'Investigation Reveals Israel Embassy's Murky Role in UK Politics', *Wire*, 12 January 2017, thewire.in.

18. Marcus Dysch, 'BICOM Aims to Win Back Israel in UK', *Jewish Chronicle*, 11 March 2011, 14.

19. We Believe In Israel, 'Zionism Month', We Believe In Israel, 4 May 2016, webelieveinisrael.org.uk.

20. Luke Akehurst, 'Luke Akehurst's Personal Response to McCluskey Email', We Believe in Israel, webelieveinisrael.org.uk.

21. Doreen Wachmann, 'Why Non-Jewish Luke's Family Has Always Given Support to Israel', *Jewish Telegraph*, n.d., jewishtelegraph. com.

22. Luke Akehurst, emails, 22 June 2016, 18 July 2016, cited in Hil Aked, 'Israeli State Power and the Zionist Movement in the UK: The Case of the Counter-Campaign against the Boycott, Divestment and Sanctions (BDS) Movement for Palestinian Rights', PhD diss., University of Bath, 2019, 152.

23. Ibid.

24. See, for instance, Edinburgh Friends of Israel: 'Friends Groups Will Work to Resist Boycott Efforts', *Jewish Chronicle*, 2 April 2015 thejc.com; 'Events', Northern Ireland Friends of Israel, nifriendsofisrael.wordpress.com/nifi-events; West of England Friends of Israel, 'Acting Ambassador Eitan Na'eh speaks at several locations in the south west', web.archive.org/web/20170423235604/https://wefriendsofisrael.org/2015/11/29/acting-ambassador-eitan-naeh-speaks-at-several-locations-in-the-south-west/.

25. Jenni Frazer, 'Grassroots Pro-Israel Group Celebrates 20,000th Activist Sign Up', *Jewish News*, 28 May 2019, jewishnews.timesofisrael.com.

26. 'Scottish Christians and Jews Unite to Combat Antisemitism', *Jewish Chronicle*, 25 November 2016, thejc.com.

27. Jenni Frazer, 'Grassroots Pro-Israel Group Celebrates'.

28. Ben White, 'Israeli Embassy Embraces Extremists'.

29. Ethan Bronner, 'After Gaza, Israel Grapples with Crisis of Isolation', *New York Times*, 18 March 2009, nytimes.com; Ido Aharoni, 'Nation Branding: Some Lessons from Israel', Knowledge@Wharton, University of Pennsylvania, 1 March 2012, knowledge.wharton.upenn.edu; Yuval Ben-Ami, 'About Face', *Haaretz*, 20 September 2005.

30. Ben White, 'Behind Brand Israel: Israel's Recent Propaganda Efforts', *Electronic Intifada*, 23 February 2010, electronicintifada.net.

31. 'Letters: Dismay at Globe Invitation to Israeli Theatre', *Guardian*, 29 March 2012, theguardian.com; 'Habima at the Globe', Jewish Leadership Council, 1 June 2012, thejlc.org.

32. Leon Symons, 'Israeli Heckled at Edinburgh Festival', *Jewish Chronicle*, 5 September 2008, 10.

33. StandWithUs UK, standwithus.com/uk.

34. Michael Dickson, 'Shalom Festival', StandWithUs, 2 August 2016, standwithus.co.uk.

35. Ruth Maclean and Ben Goldstein, 'Israelis Denounce Israel Society', *Oxford Student*, 6 February 2014, oxfordstudent.com.

36. Gurpreet Narwan, 'Show Will Go On, Israeli Shalom Festival Vows amid Protest Threat', *Times*, 8 August 2017, thetimes.co.uk.

37. 'Exhibition', Shalom Festival, available at web.archive.org/web/20201125044301/shalomfestival.org/exhibition.html; 'Films', Shalom Festival, available at web.archive.org/web/20201125051434/shalomfestival.org/films.html.

38. 'Letters: The Shrill Screams of Anti-Israel Activists Keep People Apart', 29 August 2016, *Herald Scotland*, heraldscotland.com; Ben Wray, 'Exclusive: Scottish Pro-Israel Group Distances Itself from Former Convener over Racist Facebook Page', *Source News*, 15 March 2019, sourcenews.scot.

39. Francine Wolfisz, 'Meet the Man Bringing Tel Aviv to London', *Jewish News*, 18 August 2017, jewishnews.com.

40. 'New Festival Brings Taste of London to Tel Aviv', *Ynet*, 25 November 2019, ynetnews.com.

41. Andy Levy-Alzenkopf, 'Brand Israel Set to Launch in GTA', *Canadian Jewish News*, 28 August 2008, available at web.archive.org/web/20091102045657/cjnews.com/index2.php?option=com_content&task=view&id=15198&pop=1&page=0&Itemid=86.

42. Email from [REDACTED], British Council in Israel, to [REDACTED], 'Hi', 29 October 2015, obtained via freedom of information request.

43. Candice Krieger, 'Interview: Stanley Fink', *Jewish Chronicle*, 18 September 2009, thejc.com.

44. Letter from [REDACTED] to Ed Vaizey, 1 October 2015; signed off 'A' and with the name of Andrew Feldman's company, Jayroma, in email footer.

45. Arifa Akbar, 'Barbican's Tribute to 1948 Accused of Demonising Israel', *Independent*, 30 April 2008.

46. Damien Gayle, 'Manchester University Puts Palestinian Solidarity Statement Back in Gallery', *Guardian*, 18 August 2021, theguardian.com; Maya Wolfe-Robinson, 'Whitworth Gallery Director Alistair Hudson Forced Out over Palestinian Statement', *Guardian*, 22 February 2022, theguardian.com.

47. Sarah Cascone, 'A Manchester Museum Director Has Been Forced Out After a Group of Pro-Israel Attorneys Objected to His Forensic Architecture Show', *Artnet News*, 23 February 2022, news.artnet.com.

48. Itamar Eichner, 'Foreign Ministry Finds Itself Battling Israel Boycott Alone', *Ynet*, 6 April 2015, ynetnews.com.

49. Leo Barraclough, 'Jewish Film Fest Pulls Screenings from London Theater in Israeli Funding Clash', *Variety*, 6 August 2014, variety.com.

50. Caroline Davies, 'Tricycle Theatre Does U-turn and Lifts Ban on Jewish Film Festival', *Guardian*, 15 August 2014, theguardian.com; 'About UK Jewish Film', UK Jewish Film, ukjewishfilm.org.

51. Simon Round, 'Interview: Judy Ironside', *Jewish Chronicle*, 11 October 2011, thejc.com.

52. Tracy McVeigh and Harriet Sherwood, 'Theatre's Decision to Ban Jewish Film Festival Is 'Thin End of Wedge'', *Guardian*, 9 August 2014, theguardian.com.

53. Stephen Margolis, email to Philippe Sands (cc: Indhu Rubasingham, Jonathan Levy, Peter Bazalgette, Alan Davey, Daniel Taub and Simon Johnson), 10 August 2014, obtained via freedom of information request

54. Nick Curtis, 'Theatre Director Indhu Rubasingham: I Just Didn't Want to Take Sides in a Very Emotional, Passionate Situation', *Evening Standard*, 6 August 2014, standard.co.uk.

55. Stephen Margolis, email to Philippe Sands.

56. Curtis, 'Theatre Director'.

57. Tricycle Theatre, 'The Tricycle Theatre and the UK Jewish Film Festival', *Tricycle Theatre Backstage Blog*, 5 August 2014, available at web.archive.org/web/20140808133513/tricycle.co.uk/16748/the-tricycle-theatre-and-the-uk-jewish-film-festival.

58. Hadley Freeman, 'Please Don't Tell Me What I Should Think about Israel', *Guardian*, 8 August 2014, theguardian.com.

59. Curtis, 'Theatre Director'.

60. Kahn-Harris, 'How High Can Grass Roots Grow?'

61. 'Patrons', Campaign Against Antisemitism, available at web.archive.org/web/20180314040949/antisemitism.uk/about/patrons.

62. 'Campaign Against Antisemitism Meets with Home Secretary, Police and CPS Chiefs to Address Antisemitism', Campaign Against AntiSemitism, 19 January 2015, antisemitism.uk.

63. Jenni Frazer, 'More than 70 Attend Re-launch of UK Zionist Group', *Jewish News*, 19 February 2018, jewishnews.timesofisrael.com.

64. Jenni Frazer, 'Pro-Israel "Lone Warrior" Stares Down Weekly Anti-Israel Protests in London', *Times of Israel*, 3 August 2015, timesofisrael.com.

65. Rosa Doherty, ' Israel Advocacy Movement Insists It Held Debate with Neo-Nazi "to Show How Evil" Far-Right Is', *Jewish Chronicle*, 19 June 2019, thejc.com.

66. 'Why Doesn't Israel Let the Palestinian Refugees Return?', Israel Advocacy Movement, israeladvocacy.net.

67. Richard Silverstein, Facebook post, 4 July 2020, facebook.com/photo?fbid=10158253526057850&set=a.402873517849.

68. Kahn-Harris, 'How High Can Grass Roots Grow?'

69. Board of Deputies, 'Community Briefing 5 March 2014', 5 March 2014, available at us5.campaign-archive.com/?u=005d3cc2d6e-6144d71149ef84&id=d0eed29b21&e=a47403c891.

70. 'About Us', Campaign Against Antisemitism.

71. Anna Dubuis, Louise Jury and Alexandra Rucki, 'Huge Protest Calling on Boycott of Tricycle Theatre over Jewish Film Festival Ban', *Evening Standard*, 7 August 2014, standard.co.uk.

72. 'Action Campaign', Campaign Against Anti-Semitism Facebook post, 5 August 2014, facebook.com/campaignagainstantisemitism/posts/1448836702061934.

73. Philippe Sands, letter to Stephen Margolis, 8 August 2014, obtained via freedom of information request.

74. 'About', The PR Office, theproffice.co.uk.

75. Joe Lepper, 'Campaign: Jewish Film Festival Enjoys Media Success', *PR Week*, 7 February 2008, prweek.com. The PR Office, 'Volunteers from across London Help JNF UK Celebrate Its First Blue Box Sunday', The PR Office, 18 September 2014, theproffice.co.uk; Sandy Rashty, 'Shimon Cohen, the Sultan of Spin', *Jewish Chronicle*, 15 August 2015, thejc.com. The PR Office's managing director Marc Cohen previously worked for Kreab Gavin Anderson, a lobbying firm whose Brussels office was hired by the Israeli government in 2011 to work in the European Union (David Cronin, 'Revealed: Israel Hires Lobby Firm to Win Euro-MPs' Backing for Trade Deal', *Electronic Intifada*, 14 March 2012). The PR Office had also worked for law firm Mishcon de Reya, which represented pro-Israel lecturer Ronnie Fraser in his case against the UCU, as

well as the British Technion Society and a range of Israeli businesses.

76. 'Deputy Debut for PR Boss', *Jewish Chronicle*, 18 May 2012, 25. UK Israel Business was formerly known as the British Israel Chamber of Commerce.

77. Daniella Peled, 'Enough with Polite', *Jerusalem Report*, 3 October 2005; Shimon Cohen, 'Brand Israel', *Jewish Chronicle*, 8 December 2006, 38.

78. 'UK Jewish Film Festival', The PR Office.

79. Curtis, 'Theatre Director'.

80. 'Tal Ofer', author bio, *Jewish News*, blogs.timesofisrael.com.

81. Sandy Rashty, 'Tricycle Theatre "on Thin Ice" over Jewish Film Festival Boycott', *Jewish Chronicle*, 14 August 2014, thejc.com. However, by January 2017, Chinn was listed as a supporter once more.

82. Harry Phibbs, 'Why Is Brent Council Funding Anti-Semitism?', *Conservative Home*, 8 August 2014, conservativehome.com.

83. Alan Davey, letter to Mike Freer, 15 August 2014.

84. Vivian Wineman and Mick Davis, letter to Sajid Javid, 12 August 2014.

85. Sandy Rashty, 'Culture Secretary Says Tricycle "Misguided" over Jewish Film Festival Boycott', *Jewish Chronicle*, 12 August 2014, thejc.com.

86. Marcus Dysch, '"Sack Tricycle Directors" Call Despite Deal', *Jewish Chronicle*, 21 August 2014, thejc.com.

87. Kate [REDACTED] (Tricycle Theatre), email to Jenny Killick, 6 August 2014.

88. Indhu Rubasingham, letter to Sajid Javid, 12 August 2014.

89. April De Angelis, interview, 10 August 2016, cited in Aked, 'Israeli State Power'.

90. Vivian Wineman, interview, 3 August 2016, cited in Aked, 'Israeli State Power'.

91. Sajid Javid, letter to chair of the UK Jewish Film Festival, 11 August 2014, obtained via freedom of information request.

92. 'Culture Secretary Sajid Javid Speaks at UJS Conference', *Jewish Chronicle*, 17 December 2014, thejc.com.

93. Conservative Friends of Israel, 'Culture Secretary Sajid Javid: "No Tolerance" for Israel Boycotts', Conservative Friends of Israel, 16

March 2015, available at web.archive.org/web/20170819234246/
cfoi.co.uk/culture-secretary-sajid-david-has-no-tolerance-for-
israel-boycotts.

94. Daniel Taub, letter to Sajid Javid, 18 August 2014, obtained via freedom of information request.

95. Philippe Sands, letter to Stephen Margolis, 8 August 2014.

96. Conservative Friends of Israel, 'Culture Secretary Sajid Javid: "No tolerance"'.

97. Conservative Party, 'Government to Stop "Divisive" Town Hall Boycotts and Sanctions', 3 August 2015, *Medium*, medium. com.

98. Melissen, 'Wielding Soft Power', 10.

99. Janine Wedel, *Shadow Elite: How the World's New Power Brokers Undermine Democracy, Government, and the Free Market* (New York: Basic Books, 2009), 9–20, 5.

100. Ibid., 1, 3, 17–18.

101. Robert Booth, 'Tory Intrusion "Chilling" Independence of National Bodies, Critics', *Guardian*, 7 November 2021, theguardian. com.

102. James Landale, 'Priti Patel Held Undisclosed Meetings in Israel', *BBC News*, 3 November 2017, bbc.co.uk.

103. Yael Khan, interview, 21 July 2016, cited in Aked, 'Israeli State Power'.

104. Alison Flood, 'Authors Back Sally Rooney's Boycott of an Israeli Publisher', *Guardian*, 22 November 2021, theguardian.com.

6. Waging Lawfare

1. Ilan Pappé, 'Jenin Won't Forget', *Electronic Intifada*, 18 April 2017, electronicintifada.net.

2. Human Rights Watch, 'Israel, the Occupied West Bank and Gaza Strip, and Palestinian Authority Territories', *Human Rights Watch World Report 2003*, hrw.org.

3. Ian Black, 'UK to Review War Crimes Warrants after Tzipi Livni Arrest Row', *Guardian*, 15 December 2009, theguardian.com.

4. Vivian Wineman, interview, 3 August 2016, cited in Hil Aked, 'Israeli State Power and the Zionist Movement in the UK: The

Case of the Counter-Campaign against the Boycott, Divestment and Sanctions (BDS) Movement for Palestinian Rights', PhD diss., University of Bath, 2019.

5. Conservative Friends of Israel, *Informed*, Conservative Friends of Israel, 2015/2016, 19, cfoi.co.uk.

6. Barak Ravid, 'British Prosecutor Blocks Arrest Warrant for Livni on U.K. Visit', *Haaretz*, 6 October 2011, haaretz.com.

7. Hil Aked, 'War Crimes Suspect Shaul Mofaz Evades Arrest at UK Parliament', *Electronic Intifada*, 23 June 2015, electronicintifada. net. Karake was released after fifty days on bail, on the basis that 'the relevant laws on the conduct alleged in this case do not cover the acts of non-UK nationals or residents abroad' (Agencies, 'UK Court Drops Extradition Case against Rwandan Spy Chief', *Guardian*, 10 August 2015).

8. Jeff Handmaker, 'Lawfare against Academics and the Potential of Legal Mobilization as Counterpower', in *Enforcing Silence: Academic Freedom, Palestine and the Criticism of Israel*, David Landy, Ronit Lentin and Conor McCarthy, eds (London: Zed Books, 2020).

9. Shmuel Bachar, Shmuel Bar and Rachel Machtiger, 'The "Soft Warfare" against Israel: Motives and Solution Levers' (working paper presented at Herzliya conference, Interdisciplinary Centre Herzliya, Herzliya, Israel, 31 January – 3 February 2010), 6.

10. Ant Katz, 'Israel's Top Anti-BDS Man', *MyShtetl*, 6 February 2013, available at web-beta.archive.org/web/20130426082929/myshtetl. co.za/community/israel/israelnews/israel%E2%80%99s-top-anti-bds-man.

11. 'Israel', Mishcon de Reya, n.d., mishcon.com/services/israel; Jessica Elgot, 'Ahava finally Closes Its Doors in London', *Jewish Chronicle*, 27 September 2011, thejc.com. Mishcon de Reya, solicitors on behalf of the Embassy of Israel and Ariel Sharon, Press Complaints Commission, Repot 62, 2003, available at pcc.org.uk.

12. Asa Winstanley, 'How Israel's Supporters Are Attempting to Shut Down Boycott Debate in UK Unions', *Electronic Intifada*, 27 December 2012, electronicintifada.net.

13. Anonymous interviewee, cited in Aked, 'Israeli State Power'.

14. *Mr R Fraser v. University & College Union*, Case Number: 2203290 /2011 (London Central Employment Tribunal, 2013), 44, available at judiciary.gov.uk.

15. Marcus Dysch, 'Trial Scheduled over Disinvited Israeli Academic', *Jewish Chronicle*, 30 August 2013, thejc.com.

16. Anonymous interviewee, cited in Aked, 'Israeli State Power'; Anshel Pfeffer, 'Jewish Leaders Hope to Delegitimize Britain's Israel Boycott', *Haaretz*, 24 August 2012, haaretz.com.

17. 'A Statement by Professor Moty Cristal', Jewish Leadership Council, 29 May 2014, thejlc.org.

18. 'LGPS Investments', Palestine Solidarity Campaign, lgpsdivest.org.

19. 'Boycott Movement Claims Victory as Veolia Ends All Investment In Israel', *Newsweek*, 1 September 2015, newsweek.com.

20. Julie Regan (Merton FOI officer), email, 16 December 2015.

21. 'Jewish Leadership Council Annual Reports and Financial Statements for the Year Ended 31 December 2015', available at apps.charitycommission.gov.uk.

22. Jenni Frazer, 'Grassroots Pro-Israel Group Celebrates 20,000th Activist Sign Up', *Jewish News*, 28 May 2019, jewishnews.com.

23. Luke Akehurst, email, 18 July 2016.

24. Doreen Wachman, 'Why Non-Jewish Luke's Family Has Always Given Support to Israel', *Jewish Telegraph*, jewishtelegraph.com.

25. Jenni Frazer, 'Grassroots Pro-Israel Group Celebrates'.

26. Luke Akehurst, email to Hackney councillors, 25 June 2015.

27. 'Leader – Anti-Veolia Deputation Fails the "Spirit Test"', *Hackney Citizen*, 13 December 2012, hackneycitizen.co.uk; Adam Barnett, 'Hackney Mayor Backs Conservative Bid to Block Anti-Veolia Deputation', *Hackney Citizen*, 29 November 2012, hackneycitizen.co.uk.

28. Ibid.

29. Adam Barnett, 'Veolia Dumps Bid for Hackney Waste Contract', *Hackney Citizen*, 21 December 2012, hackneycitizen.co.uk.

30. Ibid.

31. Wedel, *Shadow Elite*, 3.

32. Emma Bartholomew, 'Veolia Revelations: Pro-Israel Group Steps in Claiming Victory for Blocking Campaigner's Five-Minute Speech', *Hackney Gazette*, 24 December 2012, hackneygazette.co.uk.

33. Daniel Sugarman, 'Taking the Lead, the Legal Experts Who Are Showing the Way to Defend against Hatred', *Jewish Chronicle*, 2 December 2016.

34. Hil Aked, 'What Is UK Lawyers for Israel's Relationship to the Israeli Government?', *Mondoweiss*, 12 March 2019, mondoweiss. net.

35. Jenni Frazer, 'More than 70 Attend Re-launch of UK Zionist Group', *Jewish News*, 19 February 2018, jewishnews.com.

36. 'UK Lawyers for Israel', Ministry of Foreign Affairs, 17 May 2011, available at webcache.googleusercontent.com/search?q=cache:mfa. gov.il/MFA/internationalLaw/Pages/UK_Lawyers_for_Israel. aspx.

37. 'Our Activities – Invoking Laws to Support Israel', UK Lawyers for Israel, uklfi.com; Aked, 'UK Lawyers for Israel'.

38. Jonathan Turner and Fiona Sharpe, 'Are Street Protests the Right Way to Fight Back?', *Jewish Chronicle*, 15 October 2015, thejc. com.

39. 'An Upcoming Event for UK Readers', BBC Watch, 15 January 2017, bbcwatch.org. In May 2016, UKLFI also held a joint event with NGO Monitor, a body close to the Israeli government (NGO Monitor, 'Anti-Israel Activity and the UK: BDS, Lawfare, and Demonization of Israel', NGO Monitor, 15 May 2016, ngo-monitor. org); 'Ensuring Fair Treatment of Israel in International Tribunals – Daniel Taub', UKLFI Charitable Trust, 19 October 2020, eventbrite.co.uk.

40. 'Meet our Team', International Legal Forum, 18 May 2021, available at web.archive.org/web/20210518123601/ilfngo.org/meet-our -staff.

41. Jessica Elgot, 'The Lawyers Who Stopped the Gaza Flotilla', *Jewish Chronicle*, 15 December 2011, thejc.com.

42. Aked, 'UK Lawyers for Israel'.

43. Aron Keller, 'How British Pro-Israel Groups Are Rewriting Middle East History Textbooks', +972 *Magazine*, 16 July 2021, 972mag.com.

44. Barnett, 'Veolia Dumps Bid'; Barnett, 'Hackney Mayor Backs Conservative Bid'.

45. Anonymous, 'How We Helped Justice to Prevail in Hackney', *Jewish Chronicle*, 29 November 2012, thejc.com.

46. Bartholomew, 'Veolia Revelations'.

47. Malaka Mohammed, 'Veolia Withdraws Bid for North London Waste Contract under Boycott Pressure', *Mondoweiss*, 23 December 2012, mondoweiss.net.

48. Michael Deas, interview, 8 August 2016.

49. Reut Institute, *Building a Political Firewall against the Assault on Israel's Legitimacy: London as a Case Study* (Tel Aviv: Reut Institute, 2010), 74.

50. Stuart Winer, 'Justice Minister Said Gearing Up to Sue Israel Boycotters', *Times of Israel*, 17 June 2015, timesofisrael.com.

51. Ben White, 'Israel and Friends Battle the Boycott', *Middle East Monitor*, 1 March 2016, middleeastmonitor.com.

52. Levi Winchester, 'Legal Action Launched against "Anti-Semitic" Council over Israeli Goods Boycott', *Daily Express*, 25 August 2015, express.co.uk.

53. Ryvka Barnard, interview, cited in Aked, 'Israeli State Power'.

54. Patrick Kitterick, interview, cited in Aked, 'Israeli State Power'.

55. Judith Butler, 'Is the Show Finally Over for Donald Trump?', *Guardian*, 5 November 2020, theguardian.com.

56. 'Anti-Semitic Claim against Swansea and Gwynedd Councils Dismissed', *BBC News*, 28 June 2016, bbc.co.uk.

57. 'Leicester City Council "Anti-Semitism" Claims Dismissed', *BBC News*, 4 July 2018, bbc.co.uk.

58. 'Leicester Council to Boycott Israeli Settlement Goods', *Jewish Chronicle*, 25 November 2016, thejc.com.

59. *Jewish Human Rights Watch v. Leicester City Council*, Gwynedd Council and City and County of Swansea, Case Nos: CO/4008/2015, CO/5026/2015 and CO/5027/2015 (High Court of Justice. 2016), 5.

60. Keith Kahn-Harris, 'How High Can Grass Roots Grow?', *Jewish Chronicle*, 11 September 2014, thejc.com.

61. 'About', Jewish Human Rights Watch, jhrw.com. Companies House lists its incorporation date as December 2014.

62. Eliezer Sherman, 'Jewish Human Rights Group Ad in Guardian Compares Boycott of Israel to Nazi Boycott of Jews', *Algemeiner*, 30 October 2015, algemeiner.com; Daniel Sugarman, 'Meet the Group Dedicated to Bringing Down BDS in the UK', *Jewish Chronicle*, 6 April 2017, thejc.com.

63. Josh Jackman, 'Poverty Charity's Boycott Is Like Nazi Germany, Says New Group', *Jewish Chronicle*, 19 February 2015, thejc.com.

64. Tom Griffin et al., *The Henry Jackson Society and the Degeneration of British Neoconservatism: Liberal Interventionism,*

Islamophobia and the 'War on Terror' (Glasgow: Public Interest Investigations, 2015).

65. Marko Attila Hoare, interview, cited in Aked, 'Israeli State Power'.

66. Henry Jackson Society, 'HJS Summer Reception', Henry Jackson Society, 9 July 2012, available at web.archive.org/web/20150401161025 /henryjacksonsociety.org/2012/07/09/announcing-hjs-academic-political-policy-councils.

67. Holly Watt and Heidi Blacke, 'City Financiers Fund Michael Gove's Private Office', *Telegraph*, 21 October 2011, telegraph.co.uk; 'Netanyahu's "List of Millionaires"', *Ynet*, 22 October 2010, ynet-news.com.

68. Jonathan Rosenblum, 'Think Again: For the Sake Of "Klal Yisrael"', *Jerusalem Post*, 12 November 2010, jpost.com.

69. Lee Harpin, '"Robinson Is Not My Client," says Jewish lawyer', *Jewish Chronicle*, 5 July 2017, thejc.com.

70. 'Staff', North West Friends of Israel, available at web.archive.org/ web/20150812010237/http:/nwfoi.org.uk/staff.

71. Lee Harpin, '"Far-Right" Row ahead of Vote for New Board of Deputies President', *Jewish News*, 15 April 2021, jewishnews. co.uk.

72. David Collier, 'It Is as if Amnesty Has Declared War on Israel', *Jewish Chronicle*, 20 December 2019, thejc.com.

73. Asa Winstanley, 'Scottish College Censors Israel's Critics', *Electronic Intifada*, 4 November 2021, electronicintifada.net.

74. Orde Kittrie, *Lawfare: Law as a Weapon of War* (Oxford: Oxford University Press, 2016), 326.

75. 'Bill Calling to Keep Strategic Affairs Ministry's Efforts to Combat Delegitimization Secret Passes First Reading', Knesset press release, 18 July 2017, knesset.gov.il.

76. Ewen MacAskill and Ian Cobain, 'Israeli Diplomat Who Plotted against MPs Also Set Up Political Groups', *Guardian*, 8 January 2017, theguardian.com; Ali Abunimah, 'Israel "Quietly" Pushed for Anti-BDS Legislation in US, UK', *Electronic Intifada*, 24 February 2016, electronicintifada.net.

77. Jewish Leadership Council, 'The Jewish Leadership Council Meets with Prime Minister David Cameron', Jewish Leadership Council, 13 January 2016, thejlc.org.

78. Cabinet Office, 'Ministerial Meetings Jan – March 2016', gov.uk.

79. Matthew Hancock, 'Take Action against Discrimination', *Jewish Chronicle*, 17 February 2016, thejc.com.

80. Michel Gove, 'Michael Gove – 2016 Speech on Anti-Semitism', Political Speech Archive, 17 March 2016, ukpol.co.uk.

81. Cabinet Office, 'Putting a Stop to Public Procurement Boycotts', Cabinet Office, 17 February 2016, gov.uk.

82. Barnard, interview.

83. Robert Cusack, 'UK Court Case on Boycotting Israeli Investments Draws Apartheid Comparisons', *Al Araby*, 14 June 2017.

84. Conservative Party, 'Government to Stop "Divisive" Town Hall Boycotts and Sanctions', 3 August 2015, *Medium*, medium.com.

85. Chris McGreal, 'Rightwing Lobby Group Alec Driving Laws to Blacklist Companies That Boycott the Oil Industry', *Guardian*, 8 February 2022, theguardian.com.

86. Kitterick, interview.

87. Ryvka Barnard, 'Britain's Anti-BDS Law Is an Attack on Democracy', *Jacobin*, 2 February 2022, jacobin.com.

88. David Harvey, *A Brief History of Neoliberalism* (New York: Oxford University Press), 23.

89. Barnard, interview; Ryvka Barnard, 'Thatcherism Returns: UK Councils Banned from Divesting from Occupation', *Middle East Eye*, 4 October 2016, middleeasteye.net.

90. Davina Cooper and Didi Herman, 'Doing Activism Like a State: Progressive Municipal Government, Israel/Palestine and BDS', *Environment and Planning C: Politics and Space* 38, no. 1 (2020): 40–59.

91. Rowena Mason, 'Councils and NHS Trusts to Be Blocked from Boycotting Israeli Products', *Guardian*, 15 February 2016, the guardian.com; Conservative Friends of Israel, 'Local Government Minister Reaffirms UK Government Commitment to Outlawing Israel Boycotts', 2 October 2020, cfoi.co.uk.

92. John Aston, 'Israel Boycott Ban: Local Councils Face Legal Action at High Court over Boycott on Israeli Goods Made in West Bank', *Independent*, 4 May 2016, independent.co.uk.

93. Barnard, interview.

94. Ben Jamal, 'This Ruling Allows Councils to Boycott Israel. It's a Crucial Victory', *Guardian*, 26 June 2017, theguardian.com.

95. 'Israel's Anti-BDS Lawfare Dealt Major Blow by UK Supreme Court', BDS Movement, 30 April 2020, bdsmovement.net.

96. Asa Winstanley, 'Major UK Pension Fund Body Demanding Answers on Israeli Settlements', *Electronic Intifada*, 8 October 2020, electronicintifada.net.

97. Lee Harpin, 'Queen's Speech Includes Measures to Stop Council Boycotts', *Jewish News*, 11 May 2021, jewishnews.co.uk; 'UK to Outlaw BDS in the "Following Months", Conservative MP Says', *Jerusalem Post*, 14 December 2021, jpost.com.

98. See 'Civil Society Statement', Right to Boycott, righttoboycott.org.uk.

99. Handmaker, 'Lawfare against Academics'.

100. Dan Goldberg, 'Australian Court Case Fires Up BDS Campaign against Israel', *Haaretz*, 30 April 2012, haaretz.com.

7. Battling Academic Boycott

1. Yorum Kaniuk, *Commander of the Exodus* (New York: Grove Press, 2000), 32.

2. Ibid., 30–4.

3. Ibid., 45–6

4. Anita Shapira, *Yigal Allon, Native Son: A Biography* (Philadelphia: University of Pennsylvania Press, 2015), 173.

5. Ibid., 174.

6. Walid Khalidi, *All That Remains: The Palestinian Villages Occupied and Depopulated by Israel in 1948* (Washington, DC: Institute for Palestine Studies, 1992), 527.

7. Lawrence Joffe, 'Yossi Harel', *Guardian*, 29 April 2008, the guardian.com.

8. 'Yossi Harel Chair of Israel Studies', University of Sussex, sussex.ac.uk.

9. The David Project, *A Burning Campus? Rethinking Israel Advocacy at America's Universities and Colleges* (Boston, MA: The David Project, 2012), 15.

10. BRICUP, *Why Boycott Israeli Universities?* (London: British Committee for the Universities of Palestine, 2007), 22.

11. Josef Federman and Collin Binkley, 'Israeli Academics Face Growing Boycott Pressures', *Sun Sentinel*, 1 February 2017, sunsentinel.com.

12. Corey Robin, 'A Very Elite Backlash', *CoreyRobin.com*, 2 January 2014, coreyrobin.com.

13. StandWithUs, 'Important Announcement: University of Bath Rejects BDS, Distances School from Promoting BDS', StandWithUs, 10 April 2017, standwithus.co.uk.

14. The David Project, *A Burning Campus?*, 15.

15. Elsa Buchanan, 'Israel: Boris Johnson Not Welcome at Palestinian Charity after "Lefty Academics" Boycott Comments', *International Business Times*, 12 November 2015, ibtimes.co.uk.

16. Community Security Trust, *Antisemitic Discourse in Britain in 2010* (London: Community Security Trust, 2010), 40.

17. Lesley Klaff, 'Antisemitism on Campus: A New Look at Legal Interventions', *Journal for the Study of Antisemitism* 2, no. 2 (2010): 303; Harold Brackman, *Boycott Divestment Sanctions against Israel: An Anti-Semitic, Anti-Peace Poison Pill* (Los Angeles: Simon Wiesenthal Center, 2013).

18. Hilary Rose and Steven Rose, 'Israel, Europe and the Academic Boycott', *Race and Class* 50, no. 1 (2008): 2.

19. Labor for Palestine, 'UCU Boycott Resolutions: Full Text and Results (PCACBI)', Labor for Palestine, 31 May 2007, laborforpalestine.net.

20. 'The British Fghtback', *Jewish Chronicle*, 15 June 2007.

21. Bernard Josephs, 'Boycott Battle to Cost £1m a Year', *Jewish Chronicle*, 20 July 2007.

22. Anthea Lipsett and Alison Benjamin, 'Storm of Student Protest over Gaza Gathers Force', *Guardian*, 23 January 2009, theguardian.com.

23. Robert Tait, 'Netanyahu Condemns UK Students over Pro-boycott Vote', *Daily Telegraph*, 3 June 2015, telegraph.co.uk.

24. Ilan Pappé, *The Idea of Israel: A History of Power and Knowledge* (London: Verso, 2014), 249.

25. Uri Ram, 'The Colonization Perspective in Israeli Sociology', in *The Israel/Palestine Question*, Ilan Pappé, ed. (London: Routledge, 1999) 52–3.

26. 'About Us', Association for Israel Studies, reg.co.il.

27. Hil Aked, 'Whose University? Academic Freedom, Neoliberalism and the Rise of "Israel Studies"', in *Enforcing Silence: Academic Freedom, Palestine and the Criticism of Israel*, David Landy, Ronit Lentin and Conor McCarthy, eds (London: Zed Books, 2020).

28. Ido Aharoni, 'Nation Branding: Some Lessons from Israel', Knowledge@Wharton, University of Pennsylvania, 1 March 2012, knowledge.wharton.upenn.edu.

29. Mitchell Bard, 'Introducing Israel Studies in US Universities', Jerusalem Center for Public Affairs, 23 December 2008, jcpa.org.

30. Hil Aked, 'Israeli State Power and the Zionist Movement in the UK: The Case of the Counter-Campaign against the Boycott, Divestment and Sanctions (BDS) Movement for Palestinian Rights', PhD diss., University of Bath, 2019; Annette Koren and Emily Einhorn, *Searching for the Study of Israel: A Report on the Teaching of Israel on U.S. College Campuses, 2008–09* (Waltham, MA: Cohen Center for Modern Jewish Studies, 2010), 19.

31. Mitchell Bard and Gil Troy, 'Delegitimization of Israel: "Boycotts, Divestment and Sanctions"', notes from working group at the Global Forum for Combatting Anti-Semitism, 16–17 December 2009, Jerusalem, 11.

32. Calev Ben Dor, 'Fighting Delegitimacy: Israel Studies Departments', *Vision to Reality: The Reut blog*, 22 November 2009, available at web.archive.org/web/20100103022230/http:/reut-blog.org/2009/11/22/fighting-delegitimacy-reut-israel-studies-david-newma.

33. Annette Koren and Shira Fishman, *Israel Studies Directory: 2013–14 Report Update* (Waltham, MA: Cohen Center for Modern Jewish Studies), 10.

34. Miriam Shenkar, 'The Politics of Normalization: Israel Studies in the Academy', PhD diss., Ohio State University, 2010, 15.

35. John Mearsheimer and Stephen Walt, *The Israel Lobby and U.S. Foreign Policy* (New York: Farrar, Straus & Giroux, 2007), 181.

36. Israel on Campus Coalition, *In Search of Israel Studies: A Survey of Israel Studies on American College Campuses* (Washington, DC: Israel on Campus Coalition, 2006), 22.

37. Hil Aked, 'Charles and Lynn Schusterman Family Foundation', Powerbase, 19 July 2012, powerbase.info.

38. Scott Jaschik, 'Return of $5 Million Gift Spurs Academic Freedom Debate', *Inside Higher Ed*, 28 February 2022, insidehighered.com.

39. Chris Cook, 'Saudis Donate Most to UK Universities', *Financial Times*, 27 September 2012, ft.com.

40. Inderjeet Parmar, 'Conceptualising the State-Private Network in American Foreign Policy', in *The US Government, Citizen Groups*

and the Cold War: The State-Private Network, Helen Laville and Hugh Wilford, eds (London: Routledge), 24.

41. Peter Oborne and James Jones, 'The Pro-Israel Lobby in Britain: Full Text', *OpenDemocracy*, 13 November 2009, opendemocracy. net

42. 'Sir Trevor Pears CMG', Pears Foundation, pearsfoundation.org.uk.

43. Based on university gift agreements obtained under freedom of information legislation and powerbase.info profiles.

44. Marcus Dysch, 'Lord Weidenfeld Dies Aged 96', *Jewish Chronicle*, 20 January 2016, thejc.com.

45. 'Music Boss Len Blavatnik Named as Britain's Richest Man', *BBC News*, 26 April 2015, bbc.co.uk.

46. Shuki Sadeh, 'Benjamin Netanyahu's Billionaires Club', *Haaretz*, 18 June 2016, haaretz.com.

47. 'Oxford's First Israel Chair', *Jewish Chronicle*, 14 April 2011, thejc.com.

48. '"Vital" New Chair for Students', *Jewish Chronicle*, 2 March 2012, thejc.com.

49. 'The Pears Family Charitable Foundation and School of Oriental and African Studies Deed of Gift' (EAIS), 3, obtained via freedom of information request.

50. Emanuele Ottolenghi, 'The Isaiah Berlin Public Lectures in Middle East Dialogue: An Introductory Note', *Israel Studies* 10, no. 2 (2005): v.

51. Aked, 'Whose University?'.

52. Helen Davis and Douglas Davis, *Israel in the World: Changing Lives through Innovation* (London: Weidenfeld & Nicolson, 2005); Reut Institute, *Building a Political Firewall against Israel's Delegitimization* (Tel Aviv: Reut Institute, 2010), 73.

53. Harold Laski, 'Foundations, Universities and Research', in *The Dangers of Obedience and Other Essays* (New York: Harper & Bros, 1930), 171.

54. Hil Aked, 'Did Publishing Giant Influence Israel Studies Post in British University?', *Electronic Intifada*, 22 April 2019, electronicintifada.net.

55. Christian Wiese, email to Chris Martin, Marina Pedreira Villarino and Matthew Cragoe, 9 March 2011; 'Yossi Harel Chair of Israel Studies', University of Sussex, sussex.ac.uk.

56. Michael Arthur, email to Roger Gair, Michelle Calvert and Jeremy Higham, 'Fwd: POLIS and the Pears Foundation', 23 June 2011, obtained via freedom of information request.

57. Laski, 'Foundations, Universities and Research', 170–1.

58. Colin Shindler, email to Paul Webley, 6 January 2011.

59. Christian Weiss, email to Michael Farthing, 22 September 2010.

60. Inderjeet Parmar, *Foundations of the American Century: The Ford, Carnegie, and Rockefeller Foundations in the Rise of American Power* (Chichester: Columbia University Press, 2012), 9.

61. 'Charter', European Association of Israel Studies, israelstudies.eu.

62. Susan Frith, 'Radical Threats, Studied Solutions', *Pennsylvania Gazette*, 26 June 2014, thepenngazette.com.

63. Ehud Zion Waldoks, 'PM, Brown Launch New Academic Exchange Program', *Jerusalem Post*, 20 July 2008, jpost.com.

64. British Council Israel, email, 'Draft letter DQ to [REDACTED]', 26 August 2015.

65. The David Project, *A Burning Campus?*, 8.

66. British Council Israel / FCO, email, 'Israel: Danny Danon, Minister of Science, Technology and Space', 10 June 2015.

67. British Council, 'Enhancing Academic Cooperation between the UK and Israel. Britain-Israel Research and Academic Exchange Scheme (BIRAX) Technical Proposal', May 2008, 4.

68. Judy Siegel-Itzkovich, 'UK-Israel Biology Research Gets Boost by Envoy's Project', *Jerusalem Post*, 26 January 2011, jpost.com.

69. Victoria Ward, 'Rich List 2015: Super rich's wealth soars as new money floods in from abroad', *The Telegraph*, 26 April 2015, telegraph.co.uk; Anna Brosnan (head of media, British Council), email, 4 March 2016.

70. Sarah Gordon, 'EU Remain Donor Connected to West Bank Security Barrier', *Financial Times*, 12 May 2016.

71. Charles Wolfson Charitable Trust, 'Financial Statements 5 April 2012', 20, available at apps.charitycommission.gov.uk.

72. Anthony Lerman, *The Making and Unmaking of a Zionist: A Personal and Political Journey* (London: Pluto Press, 2012), 104.

73. 'Former Ambassador to the UK Daniel Taub Joins Yad Hanadiv as Director of Strategy and Planning', Yad Hanadiv, yadhanadiv.org.il.

74. Jennifer Lipman, 'British Council: No Support for Boycott Aims of Palestinian Festival', *Jewish Chronicle*, 3 May 2012, available at

web.archive.org/web/20120508221638/thejc.com/news/uk-news/
67145/british-council-no-support-boycott-aims-palestinian-
festival.

75. Natan Aridan, *Britain, Israel and Anglo-Jewry: 1949–57* (London:
Routledge, 2004), 52.

76. Tom Mills, *The BBC: Myth of a Public Service* (London: Verso,
2016), 56.

77. British Council Israel / FCO, email, 'Bio/photo request', 24 Jan 2014.

78. British Council, 'Enhancing Academic Co-operation', 3.

79. The UK-Israel Science Council was itself established in November
2010. 'UK-Israel Science Council', British Council, britishcouncil.
org.il.

80. Grant confirmation letter from [REDACTED] (Atkin Foundation)
to [REDACTED] (British Council in Israel), April 2013.

81. British Council Israel, email, '[REDACTED] Letter of May 5,
2015', 26 May 2015.

82. Email from [REDACTED] to [REDACTED] (British Council in
Israel), 17 June 2015.

83. Email from [REDACTED] (British Council in Israel) to [REDACTED],
'Bio/photo request', 28 February 2014.

84. Lipman, 'British Council'.

85. Email from [REDACTED] (British Council in Israel) to [REDACTED],
'BDS', 3 June 2015.

86. Email from [REDACTED] (British Council in Israel) to [REDACTED],
'Hi', 29 October 2015.

87. Kahn-Harris, *Turbulent Times*, 139.

88. Asa Winstanley, 'Israeli Government Cash to UK's Union of Jewish
Students Exposed', *Electronic Intifada*, 12 January 2017, elec-
tronicintifada.net.

89. Union of Jewish Students of the United Kingdom and Ireland, 'Articles of Governance', as of December 2013.

90. Toby Greene, *Blair, Labour and Palestine: Conflicting Views on
Middle East Peace after 9/11* (London: Bloomsbury, 2014), 50.

91. Union of Jewish Students, 'Be Proud, Be Passionate, and Maybe a
little More Patient and Pragmatic', Union of Jewish Students, 29
March 2019, ujs.org.uk.

92. Shira Hanau, 'U.K. Professor Who Called Jewish Students "Pawns" of
Israel Fired over Comments', *Haaretz*, 3 October 2021, haaretz.com.

93. Joseph Findlay, 'These BDS-Supporting Jewish Students Are Changing Their Community', *Forward*, 7 December 2017, forward. com.

94. Daniel Sugarman, 'UJS Presidential Candidate Abused for Pro-BDS Stance', *Jewish Chronicle*, 1 December 2016, thejc.com.

95. Union of Jewish Students, 'Bridges Not Boycotts Conference', Union of Jewish Students, ujs.org.uk.

96. Colin Leys, 'Still a Question of Hegemony', *New Left Review* 181 (1990): 127.

97. Udi Shaham, 'Bennett Advances New Ethics Code Banning Professors from Expressing Political Views', *Jerusalem Post*, 10 June 2017, jpost.com.

98. MEE Staff, 'US: CUNY's Law Faculty Becomes Latest University Department to Endorse BDS', *Middle East Eye*, 19 May 2022, middleeasteye.net.

99. Terence Karran and Lucy Mallinson, *Academic Freedom in the UK: Legal and Normative Protection in a Comparative Context: Report for the University and College Union* (May 2017).

100. Palestine Legal and Center for Constitutional Rights, *The Palestine Exception to Free Speech: A Movement Under Attack in the US*, 2015.

101. Lee Harpin, 'UJS Survey Shows 80 Per Cent of Universities Have Not Adopted IHRA Definition', *Jewish Chronicle*, 30 September 2020, thejc.com.

102. Eleanor Busby, 'Universities May Face Cuts if They Reject Definition of Antisemitism, Says Education Minister', *Independent*, 9 October 2020, independent.co.uk.

103. Jewish News, 'Nearly 100 universities Have Now Adopted the IHRA Definition of Antisemitism', *Jewish News,* 10 November 2021, jewishnews.co.uk.

104. Sai Englert, 'With This Flawed Antisemitism Definition, Britain Is Closing Down Academic Freedom', *Middle East Eye*, 9 December 2020, middleeasteye.net.

105. UCL Academic Board Working Group on Racism and Prejudice, *Report of the Academic Board Working Group on Racism and Prejudice*, 16 December 2020, ucl.ac.uk.

106. Asa Winstanley, 'Israel-Funded "infiltrators" behind London Campus "Provocation"', *Electronic Intifada*, 21 March 2017, electronicintifada.net; Winstanley, 'Israeli Government Cash'.

107. 'New Israel Forum on Campus Seeks to "Transform" Debate', *Jewish News*, 22 March 2016, jewishnews.co.uk.

108. Hil Aked, 'Revealed: Pro-Israel Students Plot "Smear Campaigns" to "Attack BDS"', *Electronic Intifada*, 16 January 2015, electronic intifada.net.

109. Hil Aked, 'Violence, Abuse by Israel Supporters Caught on Video at London College', *Electronic Intifada*, 28 October 2016, electronic intifada.net.

110. Don Nutbeam, letter to Matthew Gould, 24 November 2014; Jerry Lewis, 'Southampton University Defends Anti-Israel Conference Set for Next Month', *Jerusalem Post*, 11 March 2015, jpost.com.

111. Justin Cohen, 'Pickles Warns Southampton over "One-sided Diatribe"' *Jewish News,* 13 March 2015; Patrick Sawer and Jonny Paul, 'University's "Anti-Semitic" Israel Conference Condemned', *Telegraph*, 21 Mar 2015, telegraph.co.uk; 'International Israel "Delegitimising" Conference Organised by UK University', *Jewish News*, 13 February 2015, jewishnews.com.

112. Sawer and Paul, 'University's "Anti-Semitic" Israel Conference'.

113. Douglas Murray, 'This Is No Debate but a Rally of Hate Directed at Israel', *Express*, 13 March 2015, express.co.uk.

114. Lewis, 'Southampton University'.

115. Francesco Amoruso, Ilan Pappé and Sophie Richter-Devroe, introduction to 'Knowledge, Power, and the "Settler Colonial Turn" in Palestine Studies', special issue, *Interventions: International Journal of Postcolonial Studies* 21, no. 4 (2019), 451–63.

116. 'Campaign to Counter Israel Apartheid Week Will Focus on Anti-Semitism Definition', *Jewish News*, 13 February 2018, jewishnews. co.uk.

117. Sally Weale and Steven Morris, 'Universities Spark Free Speech Row after Halting Pro-Palestinian Events', *Guardian*, 27 February 2017, theguardian.com.

118. Marcus Dysch, 'Envoy Attack Sparks Fear for Israelis' Safety', *Jewish Chronicle*, 6 May 2010, thejc.com.

119. Arun Kundnani, *The Muslims Are Coming! Islamophobia, Extremism, and the Domestic War on Terror* (London: Verso, 2014), 153–6.

120. Hannah Abrey, 'UCL Students Face Disciplinary Measures after October's Anti-Israel Protest', *Tab*, 1 February 2017, thetab.com.

121. Daniel Finn, 'In British Politics, Pro-Palestinian Activism Is Now Considered Criminal', *Jacobin*, 14 November 2021, jacobinmag.com.

122. Malaka Mohammed Shwaikh and Rebecca Ruth Gould, *The Palestine Exception to Academic Freedom: Intertwined Stories from the Frontlines of UK-Based Palestine Activism Biography* 42, no. 4 (2020).

123. Murtaza Hussain, 'Israeli Diplomat Pressured UNC to Remove Teacher Who Criticized Israel', *Intercept*, 28 September 2021, theintercept.com.

124. Nora Barrows-Friedman, 'UK Israel Lobby Takes Aim at Palestinian University Lecturer', *Electronic Intifada,* 22 January 2022, electronicintifada.net.

125. European Legal Support Center, 'The Case of Shahd Abusalama – A Palestinian Scholar Successfully Defeated Attempts to Silence Her', European Legal Support Center, 17 February 2022, elsc.support.

126. Alison Campsie, 'Glasgow University Accused of Undermining Academic Freedom in "Antisemitic" Ruling', *Scotsman*, 25 October 2021, scotsman.com.

127. David Collier, 'Glasgow University Publishes Antisemitic Conspiracy Theory', *David-Collier.com*, 11 December 2020, david-collier.com.

128. Jane Jackman, 'Advocating Occupation: Outsourcing Zionist Propaganda in the UK', *eSharp* 25, no. 1 (2021); Damien Gayle, 'Glasgow University Retreats over "Antisemitic" Label for Journal Article', *Guardian*, 19 November 2021, theguardian.com.

129. BRISMES, letter to Professor Anton Muscatelli, 27 October 2021, available at brismes.ac.uk; Alison Campsie, 'Scholar Pulls Out of University Talk amid Fresh Row over Academic Freedom', *Scotsman*, 7 November 2021, scotsman.com.

130. Shwaikh and Gould, *The Palestine Exception*, 15.

131. Rachel Hall, 'Bristol University Sacks Professor Accused of Antisemitic Comments', *Guardian*, 1 October 2021, theguardian.com.

132. Damien Gayle, 'UK University Censors Title of Holocaust Survivor's Speech Criticising Israel', *Guardian*, 29 September 2017, theguardian.com.

133. Maya Wolfe-Robinson, 'Whitworth Gallery Director Alistair Hudson Forced Out over Palestinian Statement', *Guardian*, 22 February 2022, theguardian.com.

134. Lara Deeb and Jessica Winegar, *Anthropology's Politics: Disciplining the Middle East* (Stanford, CA: Stanford University Press, 2016).

8. Influencing the Media

1. Amnesty International, *Israel/Gaza: Operation 'Cast Lead': 22 Days of Death and Destruction*, Amnesty International, 2 July 2009, 17, amnesty.org.
2. Mark Thompson, 'BBC and the Gaza Appeal', *BBC News: The Editors*, 24 January 2009, bbc.co.uk.
3. 'Tony Benn attacks the BBC for Refusing to Air Gaza Appeal – Video', *Mirror*, 27 January 2009, mirror.co.uk.
4. Peter Oborne and James Jones, 'The Pro-Israel Lobby in Britain: Full Text', *OpenDemocracy*, 13 November 2009, opendemocracy.net.
5. Brian Klug, 'The Collective Jew: Israel and the New Antisemitism', *Patterns of Prejudice* 37, no. 2 (2003), 124.
6. Jessica Hodgson, 'Editor Apologises for "Kosher Conspiracy" Furore', *Guardian*, 7 February 2002, theguardian.com.
7. Vera Michlin, 'Winning the Battle of Narrative' (working paper presented at Herzliya conference, Interdisciplinary Centre Herzliya, Herzliya, Israel, 31 January–3 February 2010).
8. Bob Franklin, *Packaging Politics: Political Communications in Britain's Media Democracy* (London: Bloomsbury, 2004), 3.
9. John Plunkett, 'Current Affairs Shows Face PR Attacks, Says Channel 4 News Boss', *Guardian*, 19 October 2011, theguardian.com.
10. Phil Reeves, 'BBC Denies Israel Influenced Coverage of conflict', *Independent*, 21 September 2001, independent.co.uk.
11. John Mearsheimer and Stephen Walt, *The Israel Lobby and US Foreign Policy* (New York: Farrar, Straus & Giroux, 2007), 169.
12. Judith Butler, *Frames of War: When Is Life Grievable?* (London: Verso Books, 2016).
13. Greg Philo and Mike Berry, *More Bad News from Israel* (London: Pluto Press, 2011), 332, 312, 313.
14. Ben Quinn, 'Mod Study Sets Out How to Sell Wars to the Public', *Guardian*, 26 September 2013, theguardian.com.

15. Itamar Benzaquen and The Seventh Eye, 'Jerusalem Post Took Government Money to Publish Anti-BDS Special', *+972 Magazine*, 4 October 2020, 972mag.com.

16. Philo and Berry, *More Bad News*, 322.

17. Sanya Burgess, 'Shireen Abu Akleh: How Two Videos Represent Two Versions of a Journalist's Death', *Sky News*, 11 May 2022, news.sky.com.

18. Nick Davies, *Flat Earth News* (London: Vintage, 2009), 16.

19. Philo and Berry, *More Bad News*, 322.

20. Tom Mills, *The BBC: Myth of a Public Service* (London: Verso, 2016), 208, 137–9.

21. Edward Herman and Noam Chomsky, *Manufacturing Consent* (London: Bodley Head, 2008).

22. Anthony Lerman, *The Making and Unmaking of a Zionist: A Personal and Political Journey* (London: Pluto Press, 2012), 87.

23. Tim Llewelyn, 'A Public Ignored: The BBC's False Portrayal of the Israel-Palestine Struggle', in *The Battle for Public Opinion in Europe: Changing Perceptions of the Palestine-Israel Conflict*, Duad Abdullah and Ibrahim Hewitt, eds (London: MEMO, 2012), 39.

24. *Observer*, 17 June 2001, cited in Philo and Berry, *More Bad News*, 323.

25. 'Israkit Manual', *Jewish Chronicle*, 16 December 1977.

26. Rachel Shabi and Jemima Kiss, 'Wikipedia Editing Courses Launched by Zionist Groups', *Guardian*, 18 August 2010, the guardian.com.

27. Karl Sabagh, 'Perils of Criticising Israel', *British Medical Journal*, 25 February 2009, bmj.com.

28. George Conger, 'Jewish Leaders Praise Report on BBC', *Jerusalem Post*, 8 May 2006, jpost.com.

29. Tom Griffin et al., *The Henry Jackson Society and the Degeneration of British Neoconservatism: Liberal Interventionism, Islamophobia and the 'War on Terror'* (Glasgow: Public Interest Investigations, 2015), 28–30.

30. Simon Rocker, 'Just Journalism Forced to Close', *Jewish Chronicle*, 22 September 2011, thejc.com.

31. Keith Kahn-Harris, *Turbulent Times: The British Jewish Community Today* (London: Continuum, 2010), 49.

32. Bernard Josephs, 'Leaders Seeking Top Media Team to Defend Israel', *Jewish Chronicle*, 15 December 2000.

33. Simon Rocker, 'So They Say They're in Charge', *Jewish Chronicle*, 17 May 2006.

34. Tom Mills et al., *The Britain Israel Communications and Research Centre: Giving Peace a Chance?* (Glasgow: Public Interest Investigations, 2013), 13.

35. Michael Levy, *A Question of Honour* (London: Simon & Schuster, 2008), 90–1, cited in Mills et al., *Giving Peace a Chance?*, 18.

36. Daniella Peled, 'Research into Bias Gave Me a One-Side View', *Jewish Chronicle*, 27 November 2008.

37. Quoted in Robert Fisk, 'Israel Feels under Siege. Like a Victim. An Underdog', *Independent*, 2 February 2010.

38. Jonathan Cummings, 'British-Israel Relations seen through Visiting Elite Opinionmaker Delegations', *MERIA Journal*, 5 June 2010, gloria-center.org.

39. 'UK News in Brief: Prize for Article in *Guardian* / Lynne Reid Banks', *Guardian*, 18 June 1986.

40. Cummings, 'British-Israel Relations'.

41. 'BICOM: The Highs and Lows', *Jewish Chronicle*, 23 June 2006, 4.

42. Simon Childs, 'The Weird History and Dire Present of Britain's Role in Israel and Palestine', *Vice*, 3 November 2017, vice.com.

43. Lorna Fitzsimons, email, 12 September 2011, cited in Mills et al., *Giving Peace a Chance*, 45.

44. Mills, *The BBC*, 24, 45, 18.

45. Ibid., 110, 113–15.

46. Jim Waterson, 'BBC Journalists Told Not to "Virtue Signal" in Social Media Crackdown', *Guardian*, 29 October 2020, theguardian.com.

47. 'BBC Pulls Out of Stonewall Diversity Scheme', *BBC News*, 10 November 2021, bbc.co.uk.

48. Oborne and Jones, 'The Pro-Israel Lobby in Britain'.

49. Philo and Berry, *More Bad News*, 2.

50. Davies, *Flat Earth News*, 125.

51. Herb Keinon, 'BBC Barred from Sharon Briefing', *Jerusalem Post*, 15 July 2003.

52. Oborne and Jones, 'The Pro-Israel Lobby in Britain'.

53. Anthony Lerman, 'What Did Jeremy Bowen Do Wrong?', *Guardian*, 16 April 2009, theguardian.com.

54. Keith Dovkants, 'The Secret Report at Heart of BBC's Gaza Paranoia', *Evening Standard*, 13 April 2012, standard.co.uk.

55. Oborne and Jones, 'The Pro-Israel Lobby in Britain'.

56. 'BBC Removes Kids' Educational Videos about Palestine after Pressure from Pro-Israel Lobbyists', *Bywire*, 1 June 2021, bywire.news.

57. Oborne and Jones, 'The Pro-Israel Lobby in Britain'.

58. Quentin Thomas, 'Report of the Independent Panel for the BBC Governors on Impartiality of BBC Coverage of the Israeli-Palestinian Conflict', 11 April 2006, 7, available at downloads.bbc.co.uk /bbctrust/assets/files/pdf/our_work/govs/panel_report_final.pdf.

59. Tim Llewellyn, 'The Story TV News Won't Tell', *Observer*, 20 June 2004, theguardian.com.

60. *The BBC's Reporting of the Israeli-Palestinian Conflict August 1 2005 – January 31 2006*, Loughborough University Communications Research Centre, April 2006, available at downloads.bbc. co.uk/bbctrust/assets/files/pdf/our_work/govs/loughborough_ final.pdf; Ivor Gaber and Lisa Thomas 'Is the BBC Biased? The Corporation and the Coverage of the 2006 Israeli-Hezbollah War', in *Media, Religion and Conflict Farnham*, Lee Marsden and Heather Savigny, eds (Surrey: Ashgate, 2009).

61. Philo and Berry, *More Bad News*, 189, 215, 222.

62. Ibid., 228–31, 207, 196.

63. 'Row Breaks Out over University Meeting', *BBC News*, 18 December 2009, news.bbc.co.uk.

64. Raheem Kassam, 'How Do You Convince the BBC That Jerusalem Is the Capital of Israel?', *Times of Israel*, 20 November 2012, blogs. timesofisrael.com.

65. 'Israel Solidarity Campaign', Institute for Middle East Democracy, available at web.archive.org/web/20091215055047/http:/instmed. org/isc.

66. Hil Aked, 'Who Is Jonathan Sacerdoti, the BBC's Go-To Man on Gaza?', *New Left Project*, 16 November 2012, available at web.archive.org/web /20160617025649/newleftproject.org/index.php/site/article_comments /who_is_jonathan_sacerdoti_the_bbcs_go_to_man_on_gaza.

67. Hil Aked, 'Former Zionist Federation Official on the Run', *New Left Project*, 17 November 2012, available at web.archive.org/web /20160309102658/newleftproject.org/index.php/site/article_ comments/former_zionist_federation_official_on_the_run.

68. Hil Aked, 'BBC Finally Admits Bias over Pro-Israel Commentator', *Electronic Intifada*, 5 February 2014, electronicintifada.net.

69. Helen Pidd, 'BBC Says Interview with Epstein Lawyer Did Not Meet Its Standards', *Guardian*, 30 December 2021, theguardian.com.

70. Oborne and Jones, 'The Pro-Israel Lobby in Britain'.

71. Letter to CAABU, 23 January 1974, cited in Christopher Mayhew and Michael Adams, *Publish It Not: The Middle East Cover-Up* (London: Longman, 1975), 115.

72. Jasper Jackson, 'BBC Says It Was "Inadvisable" for TV Chief to Sign Letter Opposing Israel Boycott', *Guardian*, 27 January 2016, theguardian.com.

73. 'Leading Journalist John Ware Wins Wizo Media Award', *Jewish Chronicle*, 7 July 2015, thejc.com.

74. Lee Harpin, 'Panorama Journalist John Ware Reflects on Visiting Israel Welfare Projects', *Jewish News*, 12 May 2021, jewishnews. timesofisrael.com.

75. Jane Corbin, 'The Balfour Declaration: My Ancestor's Hand in History', *BBC News*, 31 October 2017, bbc.co.uk.

76. Mills et al., *Giving Peace a Chance*, 47.

77. Julian Lewis, 'Monitoring Works', *Daily Telegraph*, 3 July 1999, cited in Mills, *The BBC*, 118.

78. Mills, *The BBC*, 177.

79. Mills et al., *Giving Peace a Chance*, 64.

80. Natan Aridan, *Britain, Israel and Anglo-Jewry: 1949–57* (London: Routledge, 2004), 40.

81. Daphna Baram, *Disenchantment: The Guardian and Israel* (London: Guardian Books, 2008).

82. Geoffrey Gelberg, 'Europe and the Palestinians', *Guardian Weekly*, 31 May 1981.

83. Oborne and Jones, 'The Pro-Israel Lobby in Britain'.

84. Ibid.

85. Hadley Freeman, 'Please Don't Tell Me What I Should Think about Israel', *Guardian*, 8 August 2014, theguardian.com.

86. Ben White, 'Excusing Ethnic Cleansing: Liberal Zionists, Israel and the Nakba', *Middle East Monitor*, 16 May 2014, middleeast-monitor.com.

87. 'We Believe in Israel', BICOM, 15 May 2011, available at web. archive.org/web/20110726070411/webelieveinisrael.org.

88. Bart Cammaerts, Brooks DeCillia, João Magalhães and César Jimenez -Martínez, '*Journalistic Representations of Jeremy Corbyn in the British Press: From Watchdog to Attack Dog*, Media@LSE, 1 July 2016, lse.ac.uk; David Deacon et al., *General Election 2019: Report 5, 7 November – 11 December 2019*, Loughborough University Centre for Research in Communication and Culture, lboro.ac.uk.

89. Asa Winstanley, 'Guardian Censors Jeremy Corbyn Cartoon', *Electronic Intifada*, 26 November 2020, electronicintifada.net.

90. David Cesarani, *The Jewish Chronicle and Anglo-Jewry, 1841–1991* (Cambridge, UK: Cambridge University Press, 2009), 87, 192.

91. Ben Weich, 'Jewish Group "Says Kaddish" for Palestinians Killed in Gaza', *Jewish Chronicle*, 18 May 2018, thejc.com.

92. Kevin Rawlingson and Pippa Crerar, 'Jewish Newspapers Claim Corbyn Poses "Existential Threat"', *Guardian*, 26 July 2018, theguardian.com.

93. Editorial, 'Where Next for the Jewish Left?', *Vashti*, 24 October 2020, vashtimedia.com.

94. David Wolfson, 'JC Trust Approves Sale to Consortium', *Jewish Chronicle*, 23 April 2020, thejc.com.

95. 'Values', Axel Springer, axelspringer.com; 'New Politico Owner Says Will Enforce pro-Israel Policy', *Haaretz*, 17 October 2021, haaretz.com.

96. Matt Wells, 'The Black Arts Leave Writers Riled', *Guardian*, 16 March 2001, guardian.co.uk.

97. William Dalrymple, 'Bullied into Silence on Israel', *Guardian*, 16 March 2001, theguardian.com.

98. Peter Oborne, 'Why I Have Resigned from the *Telegraph*', *OpenDemocracy*, 17 February 2015, opendemocracy.net.

99. Helen Davis and Douglas Davis, *Israel in the World: Changing Lives through Innovation* (London: Weidenfeld & Nicolson, 2005); Reut Institute, *Building a Political Firewall against Israel's Delegitimization* (Tel Aviv: Reut Institute, 2010), 73.

100. Davies, *Flat Earth News*, 17.

101. Cited in ibid., 22.

102. Ibid., 19.

103. Cited in Mayhew and Adams, *Publish It Not*, 98–9.

104. 'Israeli Ambassador Criticizes Times', *Associated Press*, 24 December 1980.

105. Robert Fisk, 'Why I Had to Leave the *Times*', *Independent*, 11 July 2011, independent.co.uk.

106. 'Jerusalem Prize Awarded at Annual Zionist Federation Dinner', World Zionist Organization Department for Zionist Activities, 17 February 2008, doingzionism.org.il.

107. Danny Finkelstein, Twitter post, 15 August 2018, twitter.com/Dannythefink/status/1029680947862687744.

108. 'Mordechai Vanunu: The *Sunday Times* Articles', *Sunday Times*, 21 April 2004, thetimes.co.uk.

109. Sam Kiley, 'The Middle-East's War of Words', *Evening Standard*, 25 September 2001.

110. Associated Press, 'Murdoch Apologizes for *Sunday Times*' Netanyahu Cartoon', *Ynet*, 28 January 2013, ynetnews.com.

111. Oborne and Jones, 'The Pro-Israel Lobby', n24.

112. Roy Greenslade, '*Sunday Times* Apology for Netanyahu Cartoon', *Guardian*, 4 February 2013, theguardian.com.

113. Associated Press, 'Murdoch Apologizes'.

114. Alistair Dawber, 'The Killing of 12-Year-Old Mohammed al-Durrah in Gaza Became the Defining Image of the Second Intifada. Only Israel Claims It Was All a Fake', *Independent*, 21 May 2013, independent.co.uk.

115. Adi Kuntsman and Rebecca Stein, *Digital Militarism: Israel's Occupation in the Social Media Age* (Stanford, CA: Stanford University Press, 2015), 55–71.

116. Sarah Kendzior, 'The Telegenically Dead', *Al Jazeera*, 14 August 2014, aljazeera.com.

117. Andrew Roth, 'Kremlin Reverts to Type in Denial of Alleged War Crimes in Ukraine's Bucha', *Guardian*, 4 April 2022, theguardian.com.

Conclusion

1. Fintan Smith, 'EuroTrack: Israel's Favourability Falls Following Gaza Strikes', *YouGov*, 4 June 2021, yougov.co.uk.

2. Ron Kampeas, 'Poll Finds a Quarter of US Jews Think Israel Is "Apartheid State"', *Times of Israel*, 13 July 2021, timesofisrael.com.

3. Michael Arria, 'Support for Israel Is Even Dropping among Evangelical Christians', *Mondoweiss*, 3 June 2021, mondoweiss.net.

4. Omar Barghouti, *Boycott, Divestment and Sanctions: Globalized Palestinian Resistance to Israeli's Settler Colonialism and Apartheid*, Institute for Palestine Studies, 2020, 14, available at palestine-studies.org.

5. Ben Gidley, Brendan McGeever and David Feldman. 'Labour and Antisemitism: A Crisis Misunderstood', *Political Quarterly* 91, no. 2 (2020): 413–21.

6. Vivian Wineman, 'If Black Lives Matter to Us, Palestinian Lives Should Too', *Vashti,* 17 July 2020, vashtimedia.com.

7. Mick Davis, 'Opinion – Sir Mick Davis: Israeli Politics Violates Values of the Diaspora', *Jewish News*, 30 April 2020, jewishnews.co.uk.

8. Luke Akehurst, 'The Fightback for Israel in the UK Starts on Sunday 22nd March', *Jewish News*, 11 March 2015, blogs.timesofisrael.com.

9. Alex Kane, 'Israel's Scheme to Defund the BDS Movement', *In These Times*, 11 November 2019, inthesetimes.com.

10. Intelligence and Security Committee of Parliament, *Russia*, 21 July 2020, 15, available at upload.wikimedia.org.

11. Andrew Roth, 'Vladimir Putin Urged to End Crackdown on Russian Journalists', *Guardian*, 27 August 2021, theguardian.com.

12. Robert Seely, 'Foreign Interference Unchecked: Models for a UK Foreign Lobbying Act', Henry Jackson Society, 10 February 2021, henryjacksonsociety.org; Rebecca Cooney, 'Charity Commission Looking into the Henry Jackson Society', *Third Sector*, 15 February 2017, thirdsector.co.uk.

13. Home Office, 'Consultation Outcome: Legislation to Counter State Threats', 13 May 2021, gov.uk.

14. Ryvka Barnard, 'Boycotting Apartheid Is a Moral Duty', *Tribune*, 29 April 2022, tribunemag.co.uk.

15. Editorial, 'The Guardian View on Tory Party Funding: Shine the Light', *Guardian*, 5 Aug 2021, theguardian.com.

16. Jim Waterson and Felicity Lawrence, 'Tory MP Needing "to Pay School Fees" Pleaded for Lucrative Middle East Work', *Guardian*, 15 December 2021, theguardian.com.

17. James Dowsett and Thomas Rowley, 'Revealed: Tory MP Was "Fed" Propaganda by Azerbaijani Embassy for Parliamentary Debates', *OpenDemocracy*, 4 February 2022, opendemocracy.net.

18. Amrit Wilson, 'Why Is the UK Government Wheeling Back on Legislation against Caste Discrimination?', *Open Democracy*, 24 May 2017, opendemocracy.net.

19. Sean McGoey, 'UK Must Radically Reform to Cease Being Haven for Kleptocrats, Report Says', International Consortium of Investigative Journalists, 10 December 2021, icij.org; Media Reform Coalition, *Who Owns the Media?*, Media Reform Coalition, 14 March 2021, mediareform.org.uk.

20. Charity and Security Network, 'The Alarming Rise of Lawfare to Suppress Civil Society: The Case of Palestine and Israel', 28 September 2021, charityandsecurity.org.

21. 'Civic Space', Civicus, monitor.civicus.org.

22. Alys Samson Estapé, 'Israel: The Model Coercive State', *Transnational Institute*, May 2021; Stephanie Kirchgaessner et al., 'Revealed: Leak Uncovers Global Abuse of Cyber-surveillance Weapon', *Guardian*, 18 July 2021, theguardian.com.

23. Amira Mattar, 'At Risk in Israel's Backlash against Ben and Jerry's? The Right to Protest', *Nation*, 11 August 2021, thenation.com.

24. Narzanin Massoumi, 'The Role of Civil Society in Political Repression: The UK Prevent Counter-Terrorism Programme', *Sociology* 55, no. 5 (2021), 959–77.

25. Ben White, Bina Ahmad and Phyllis Bennis, *Shrinking Space and the BDS Movement*, Transnational Institute, 2018, tni.org.

26. Barghouti, *Boycott, Divestment and Sanctions*, 14.

27. Josh Nathan-Kazis, 'Report: Pro-Israel Effort Is Failing – Can Harsh Targeting of BDS "Instigators" Save It?', *Forward*, 10 February 2017, forward.com.

28. Yara Hawari, 'Criminalizing Palestine Solidarity Activism in the UK', *Al Shabaka*, 9 June 2022, al-shabaka.org.

29. Ron Nixon, *Selling Apartheid: South Africa's Global Propaganda War* (London: Pluto Press, 2016).

30. Ryvka Barnard, 'Britain's Anti-BDS Law Is an Attack on Democracy', *Jacobin*, 2 February 2022, jacobin.com.

Index

Index

Index